Guided by the Mountains

D1518927

GUIDED BY THE MOUNTAINS

Navajo Political Philosophy and Governance

Michael Lerma

Foreword by Avery Denny

   and

Afterword by Robert Yazzie

OXFORD
UNIVERSITY PRESS

OXFORD
UNIVERSITY PRESS

Oxford University Press is a department of the University of Oxford. It furthers
the University's objective of excellence in research, scholarship, and education
by publishing worldwide. Oxford is a registered trade mark of Oxford University
Press in the UK and certain other countries.

Published in the United States of America by Oxford University Press
198 Madison Avenue, New York, NY 10016, United States of America.

Names: Lerma, Michael, author.
Title: Guided by the mountains : Navajo political philosophy and governance /
Michael Lerma, with foreword by Avery Denny and afterword by Robert Yazzie.
Description: New York, NY : Oxford University Press, 2017. | Includes
bibliographical references and index.
Identifiers: LCCN 2016024894 (print) | LCCN 2016042536 (ebook) |
ISBN 9780190639853 (hardcover : alk. paper) | ISBN 9780190915773 (paperback : alk. paper) |
ISBN 9780190639860 (Updf) | ISBN 9780190639877 (Epub)
Subjects: LCSH: Navajo Indians—Politics and government. | Navajo philosophy.
Classification: LCC E99.N3 L58 2017 (print) | LCC E99.N3 (ebook) |
DDC 979.1004/9726—dc23
LC record available at https://lccn.loc.gov/2016024894

For my mother Linda

CONTENTS

FIGURES

TABLES

FOREWORD

Is There a Navajo Good Governance?

HATAAŁII AVERY DENNY

This book will answer the question, "Is there a Navajo good governance?" There are many questions among non-Navajos and Navajos alike. There are many doubts among nonbelievers that Navajos have their own way of thinking that predates contact. These ideas seem to go hand in hand with money and profit. As a medicine man (some might call me a shaman), I have been trained to look at the world in a specific way. I look at a situation, such as good governance, and I ask, *"Ha'at'iish bee anáhóót'i'"* or, What is the problem? I need to identify the situation, whether it is for an individual in their home or a larger issue harming communities. To really appreciate my point of view, you have to go back into our Diné "mystical time," but I call it *Diyin k'ego hoogaal*. I think part of the lesson here is that many Diné need to ask themselves who we are as a people. Are we modern? Who do we, as a people, aspire to be? What is our original self, from before Columbus, Cortez, and Custer started coming around? I think these questions can be answered from many points of view, but I just happened to get involved with Mike Lerma, and he wanted to address these issues from a governance perspective.

I think Mike and I agreed we wanted to demonstrate that there is a form of Navajo government that predates any Navajo council. We Navajos did lead ourselves since the beginning, when we emerged from *Diné Tah*. We have our own ethics. We have our Fundamental Laws of the Diné. We have a process for solving our problems according to our laws and according to our ethics that we received from *Diyin Dine'e*, or the Holy Ones. Today, things have changed but our ethics should not change. We have to enhance ourselves with our government. In other words, even though there might be council delegates today, that does not mean we have outgrown our need for our own laws, ethics, and processes for solving our own problems. I think the problem is simple: people are confused today. People need to be made aware of themselves, their Navajo heritage, their laws, and their ethics. Education will expose Navajo people so that they are no longer confused. I know that I am not confused. This has a great deal to do with how I was raised.

I am a *Nihokaa' Diyin Dine'e*. I am proud to say my mind is still of the Diné framework. I haven't been brainwashed. My mother and my father didn't speak English and didn't know it. We lived the Navajo lifeway, which is our own. I didn't know there was another way of living and another belief system out there. I thought being Navajo was being 100 percent the only way. I never thought one could be easily changed to another way of belief. Maybe the weak ones, the ones who had already sold out, were the ones most susceptible to outsider influence. I don't mean to ridicule those who have a different belief system than my own. I only mean to share my assumptions about others who have a non-Diné worldview now. Navajo leaders today did not have the same opportunities I had, I guess, to grow up with a ceremonial and Diné lifeway. I think it didn't matter at the time when I was growing up because we knew the ceremonial way of life. That was our whole life, with no unclear assumptions. Only a few people will understand what I am writing and know this ceremonial way of life. I see other Navajo people, even the older ones who are past sixty years old, who never saw that way of life, didn't see it or live it. They totally missed it. They don't know what it means and don't know how to speak of it. Many people, rather, were taken away to boarding schools, where they learned the Western ways of doing things, and that included non-Diné religion. I don't ridicule them. I simply acknowledge now that they missed out on something I am privileged to see every day.

I myself heard about this Christian God when I went to the Piñon School. What it was all about didn't make any sense to me. It was a church with a mean old father talking about "God," or some person up there in heaven. I didn't understand this invisible and unknown totally different concept of God. Even today it's still that way for me. I can't apologize for what I'm saying because I can't change things. I'm still coming from an original place of being Diné. I believe the sun deserves the thank you, the earth deserves gratitude, the air deserves a special offering, and water needs an offering every day in return for being here, unlike a person up there in the sky. My perspective tends to be taken as controversial by some of my own people if they are scared by my knowledge. Boarding school teachers have ridiculed my teachings, and the impacts are here today. But my teachings have allowed me to have a good life.

All my life I have been respected or ridiculed for my knowledge, depending on who the people are and how they were raised. The Navajo people who do not respect my knowledge were probably raised in a different way and subjected to boarding school education. As an educator, I run into individuals like this all the time. They hear me discussing Diné philosophy, and they think I made it up. They will challenge me in public by asking what books I got my information from, or they may ask me to cite my sources. Some non-Navajo *bilagaanas* (white people) might do the same thing. This opens up a question about why past *bilagaana* scholars would call my knowledge a myth. If you think of the basis of this book as mythical fantasy, then how can you take it seriously? But if this book had been written based solely on the existing research, you would probably have to call it a mythology of Navajo governance. I'm not sure how you take a study on governance seriously if you assume the foundation is as mythical as a unicorn. My request is that readers here and now go beyond thinking of this book as mythical. Still, I understand that if you are going to take Diné philosophy seriously, you must question the sources and validity of the knowledge represented in this book or my knowledge.

As a *Hataałii*, I carry myself as a diagnostician. I am constantly called upon to diagnose a problem, select from a multitude of possible remedies, apply the remedy, and allow for my patients to regenerate themselves. People might wonder how I decide what solution I employ. All I can say is that all of my knowledge that Mike draws on in this book is based on several songs I know. I was taught that the songs I know have been held by my ancestors since time immemorial, or, as I call it, the Diné emergence. Mike and I once joked that I could probably put out an album of songs as a soundtrack for this book, as if it were a movie. But, joking aside, it is true. I do have several songs that could be applied to each chapter in this book. My morals prevent me from "citing" songs or recording them as evidence of my knowledge. Perhaps I should "cite" Google Maps and point out the Sacred Mountains. In the end, I think the proof that I am not just making things up is that we Diné are still here. We, as Diné, have survived many calamities. The worst of the disasters happened before Europeans came to my homeland. We had men and women fighting and boasting about how one did not need the other. We had monsters roaming around and had to put many into the ground. I think these events really happened, and I think they were worse than anything Kit Carson ever did to us. Today, I think we are our own worst enemy because we don't carry ourselves as we did during the Diné creation. Today, we treat each other worse than Carson treated us.

I was taught that the Diné carried themselves through four worlds. We first came up through the ground from the black world. Then we went into the blue world. Then we went through the yellow world, and now we are in the white world. In each of these journeys, there were bundles we were instructed to carry with us. Sometimes we even carried seeds with us so that we could eat in the next world. But while some of this sounds literal, there is a figurative side too. Within our bundles is *azee'*, or medicine. Even this is too simple. Our medicine can be different seeds or plants that we need and use today, right now. For example, within our bundles is *tadidiin*, or pollen, that we used to grow plant life when we first emerged in the white world. But bundles are also associated with *sin*, or songs, and *nahagha*, or instructions about ceremonies and prayers, and this included our language too. So while my people literally carried bundles for healing and protection, they also carried instructions on ceremonial practice. They carried these instructions in their minds and hearts. I believe the songs I know now were first carried into this world at the time of emergence. So how reliable can my information really be?

Believe it or not, I'm not just a superstitious old man. Sometimes I read a book or a chapter. One of my favorite Indigenous scholars is Vine Deloria. I don't agree with everything he writes, but he has some good things to say. I liked his first book, where he talks about missionaries:

> Indian religion required a personal commitment to act. Holy men relied upon revelations experienced during fasting, sacrifices, and visions. Social in impact, most Indian religious experience was individualistic in origin. Visions defined vocations in this world rather than providing information concerning salvation in the other world. (Deloria 1988, 102)

I like this statement. As a practitioner I *must* act. I can't just talk about my knowledge. I have to sing and carry out the ceremony. I can't just write about it either. My knowledge is about here and now, even though it goes back to creation. And the idea of oral knowledge is also just as reliable as anything historians or anthropologists ever wrote.

Some people might say Mike did a bad job because he did not talk to every knowledge holder in Navajo Nation. I think people who believe that writers should interview everyone still don't understand the point of this book. So, to rely on another book-writing tool, here is Vine Deloria again:

> Tribal elders did not worry if their version of creation was entirely different from the scenario held by a neighboring tribe. People believed that each tribe

had its own special relationship to the superior spiritual forces which governed the universe and that the job of each set of tribal beliefs was to fulfill its own tasks without worrying about what others were doing. Tribal knowledge was therefore not fragmented and was valid within the historical and geographical scope of the people's experience. (Deloria 1997, 51–52)

Remember, Navajo Nation is huge, so we have different stories based on clan! Is this book about my version of things? Yes! Does that mean Robert Yazzie's version is wrong? No way! I think if each clan is trying to "fulfill its own tasks," which probably means keeping the Four Sacred Elements together on a daily basis, then who am I to say another clan is doing it wrong?

What you will see in this book is a set of principles meant to lead a people. In many ways, we Diné have caused our own problems because we stopped going along with the cosmic order. Think of this as *Diné Bibehaz'aani Bitse Siléí*, which in English is called Fundamental Laws of the Diné. What no one has ever called a science many in the past have called a myth. But I'm not talking about myth. I'm talking about the Navajo philosophy of science, of chemistry, of biology, of astronomy, and of healthcare. Believe it or not, Diné people already had all of the benefits that Western scientists claim they have discovered. I recently read an article on Facebook about plants moving around and communicating with one another when animals or humans were picking at them and eating them. But my own teachers gave me and others these lessons when I was a child! In other words, when I was a child, I knew more about plants than what Western scientists are supposedly discovering today. They are merely relearning something they should have learned a long time ago. They are being reminded that if humans follow the cosmic order, life on earth will be great. If only leaders would simply learn to heal themselves with their medicine bundles, they would be witnessing wellness, balance, and purity nationwide in Navajo Nation. When individuals learn that the secret to a good long life is in their hands right now, maybe things will get better. For me, this is the ideal government.

One of the things I always say when I speak on various topics is, "It's already there." If you asked my students about this phrase, I'm not sure if they would really understand what I mean. Some do and others do not. But for those who continue to be confused by my catchphrase, I say the answers to our questions are already in place. It is up to us humans to pay attention, be patient, and learn from plants, animals, and the Four Sacred Elements, which are fire, water, air, and pollen. A long time ago the Holy Ones gave us Natural Law. This is the perfect model for governing ourselves, but no one really understands Natural Law. They still think it might be a myth or maybe it might be some stories to entertain ourselves. I have yet to hear anyone actually say it is a hard science! This perfect model can be used to govern our people again. I say *again* because that is the model our past *Naat'áanii* used to fend off the Spaniards, the Mexicans, and *yes,* the Americans too. They understood a cosmic order based on *Sa'ah Naagháí Bik'eh Hózhóón*, which might be roughly understood in English as healing and protection as necessary for living a long and wisdom-filled life. Let me explain healing and protection a little bit more.

All humans must work to heal themselves and protect themselves. Sometimes you might be in a dark alley, with villains waiting to attack you for your money. If you are attacked, you must protect yourself. You might even have to take a life to protect yourself. If you protect yourself properly, you will need further attention and guidance. People who survive these kinds of attacks must next heal themselves. This is required for your mind as well as your physical wounds. I was taught that if you have a bad state of mind, it will take you longer to heal your physical wounds. If you have a bad state of mind, your mental wounds may never heal. If you constantly monitor your life, you will know when you are drifting into a bad state of being, also known as *anáhóót'i'*. This means that as you mature, you will better understand how you and your family might be drifting too far in one direction or another. The longer you delay protective measures, the further you will drift toward a bad place. The longer you delay your healing, the longer you will suffer from your afflictions. So I define a good and long wisdom-filled life as one where individuals manage a balance between healing and protection. If all you have to worry about in life is a bee sting or missing a breakfast, you are doing okay. I think that a person turning away from the instructions I learned as a child causes most chronic illnesses. Just as it applies to individuals, healing yourself and protecting yourself from afflictions can work on a governmental level. In fact, this is the main idea behind *k'é*, or clan relationship. It's not about a benefit of knowing your uncle, it's about your obligation to your uncle. Does this really work?

It's not surprising that I think the Fundamental Law way of doing things works. What is my proof? I can look back to my own people surviving the Long Walk, or *Hweldí*. Some of our people gave themselves up to lead those on the walk to Bosque Redondo. Others stayed behind and fought to protect the homeland against the Americans. We thought we resolved the issue with the treaty of 1868, when we signed a document believing we would regain the land called *Diné Bikéyah*, or the land within the Sacred Mountains. I can go further and say that Fundamental Law has sustained the Diné people since the emergence, but you might think that's a myth. So I point to the Long Walk, since you can look that one up in the library! Still,

Diné people don't want to do the work to learn my way of doing things. It's probably easier to play video games, play on the computer, or text people all day long. I really don't understand why people would refuse to accept what actually works! Why would you not want to follow the rules water follows to clean itself? Why would you not want to learn from the way water changes from vapor to ice to liquid and everything else there is to learn? Why do we refuse to understand what is obvious? It's already there, and we won't even look to see the truth. Continuing to ignore this way of knowing is scary!

I think that if we continue to ignore our own way of knowing, we risk our very identity. I can't see you as a Diné if you can't begin to respect the Fundamental Laws and the Sacred Elements. What happens to our medicine bundles, also known as the *jish*? I have traveled all over the world, and I hear it all the time: my Indigenous brothers and sisters around the world always talk about how the last elder who had a medicine bundle just passed away. Now they have no one around who can use the medicine bundle. They will need to relearn how to use it, or they will no longer be a people. I see the same thing happening with the elected people of the Navajo Nation government. They often call on me to bless their legislative sessions because they don't know how to do this on their own. Even though they invite me, I think some of them ignore the blessing because they have learned another way of doing things. For whatever reason, these elected officials are scared of my knowledge. Or maybe they are not willing to admit that they don't know how to use my knowledge. Everything I have taught to Mike Lerma is free and for public domain use, but you must be willing to ask.

I will close by saying that I met Mike back in the summer of 2009. We joked around about many things, but when we were not drinking coffee and eating rib-eye steaks, we did get some work done. I have been asked to discuss my knowledge since I was a young man. When I was younger, I would just give the knowledge away without much thought. Most times I would be contacted by *bilagaana* scholars, and they would ask stupid questions. Sometimes they would record me without telling me about it. Then, two or three years later, I would see that they wrote a book based on the knowledge I gave them. I still don't think they got it right, but what does that matter? They got a book deal and they furthered their careers. I don't say this because I'm angry or jealous. I just say this because when people take the knowledge without regard for the protocols, I guarantee that they will get it wrong. Mr. Mike may not have it right either, but I think he is going in the right direction. I also think it telling that he was the first person to ever ask me to contribute to a written work. Everyone else just calls me an informant and lists me in the bibliography, if they even do that. I'm not just a book you check out at the library. I'm a medicine man.

Throughout this book you will see examples of thinking in three dimensions. The drawings are not just art. Sometimes Mike would ask me a question and I would draw as I answered. Mike would take a photo of the drawing, and I thought that would be the end of it. But the next time we saw each other, he would bring the drawing in again with extra information. Sometimes he would infer some other related set of information, and other times he would get it wrong. When he got it wrong, I would steer him in a better direction. We built on this communication over the years, but he still has a great deal to learn. I guess it's good that he keeps coming back, drinking coffee, eating rib eye, and asking questions. In any case I told him one day that we could put this book together and put it on the bookshelf. Then, one hundred years would go by, and some young woman would be in the office wondering about how to solve problems in Navajo Nation. Maybe this book would be on the shelf, all dusty. She'd blow off the dust and open it up. It might take one hundred years, but that's okay. I think everyone involved with this book knows that these are the answers no one wants to hear.

Guided by the Mountains

Introduction

Dził Łeezh—*Enter, Exit, and Return Home*

At the dawn there is a spark in the east. It is the early morning sunlight. This spark can provide simple answers to seemingly complex problems. People can interpret simple answers to complex problems in a few ways. Some may respond with, "Why didn't I think of that?" and take the answer as a gift. Others may dismiss a simple answer as deceptively simple and, therefore, unworthy of attention. Different individuals will respond as they see fit based on their own worldview. Those who have tried out simple answers may come to rely on these answers as they grow more mature. This pattern of simple answers sufficing can create a foundation for a good life. As people find these simple answers providing effective prosperity, they may also begin to apply the simple answers communitywide. Perhaps they will gain a sense of responsibility to their communities as the people undergo tremendous stress. Within the Navajo community are several individuals with varying levels of equity yet uniform equality. All people have talents to contribute to problem solving. What role will the reader play in this global community?

This book is about Diné philosophy of governance. Defining governance may be difficult. Mainstream definitions of governance will vary widely depending on individual taste and proclivities toward various philosophies. There really can't be a single definition, and this book does not intend to offer such a universal definition. With this major challenge in mind, this book is about the five-fingered earth-surface people struggling to come to terms with their relationship with Mother Earth and Father Sky. It can also be about the reader's relationship with Mother Earth and Father Sky. It is a book about a common sense that is no longer common. It is about cycles of logic within nested cycles of logic meant to provide tenets for good leadership and decision making. It is also about learning to work with a creator and learning to work with fellow humans. It will introduce institutional pathways where creator and human can interact with one another. This book endeavors to awaken a dormant path for communication between fellow humans and creators.

The best governance solutions may be so obvious that they are never taken seriously. The solution is so simple it is ignored. A cycle of behavior can be deceptively simple yet impactful. For example, when people enter their home, they should bring with them materials for a good day. When they exit their home, they should be going out in search of missing items to provide for a good day. When they return from the search, they have ideally obtained what they need. Repeated over a lifetime, the cycle of "Enter, Exit, Return Home" could provide a good life. Perhaps contemporary policymakers are not comfortable with solutions that are deceptively simple. Still, a simple solution may in fact be embedded within many complex twists and turns, making it seem impractical. This introduction begins a conversation about simple, yet complex, solutions. The conversation about Navajo (hereafter Diné) philosophy and its potential for positive impact on Diné governance today has, apparently, not taken place. Perhaps this conversation could be started here and now. Let's now *enter* our home in order to gauge and access what is needed for a good day . . . a good life.

First, a common misperception must be mentioned. Some readers might assume that any and all "Indian myths," or Creation Accounts, are not useful for contemporary societal problems. Such an assumption is akin to discounting the role of religious philosophy in Western forms of governance. Perhaps the best way to put this is as follows:

> [O]rthodox traditional Navajos know [Navajo Creation Accounts] to be true and not merely myths or metaphors for western "truths." [The *Hajinéí* Creation Accounts] are a factual recording of a series of events that occurred before recorded time. They represent the sacred history of the Navajo people. As the late Cherokee scholar Robert K. Thomas once stated in a lecture: "Most Indians will tell you they believe these stories, a traditional Indian *knows* they are true." (Pavlik 2014, 35–36)[1]

If European philosophy of governance is, at times, grounded in religious philosophy, it would be prejudicial to assume that contemporary Indigenous or Diné governance cannot be grounded in Indigenous philosophy and religion. Hence, what follows may appear as a Navajo myth, but inherent in the philosophy are the necessary traits for good leadership. In other words, what follows are pre-colonial actor interaction accounts of Diné philosophical discussions about how governing should be carried out.[2]

Some Diné believe that contemporary Diné government officials no longer consider traditional Diné stories a legitimate foundation for leadership or relevant to contemporary issues (Denny 2010). Relevancy and legitimacy questions are an aside. This book will not argue that one point of view should trump another point of view. The role of Diné philosophy does have an important function today and in the future concerning questions of governance and politics. To arrive at conclusions involving traditional Diné governance assumes that Diné philosophy can address contemporary problems. What role can traditional Diné philosophy play in answering the following question: What do traditional Diné institutions of governance offer to our understanding of the contemporary challenges faced by the Navajo Nation today and tomorrow? Before addressing this research question, definitions of traditional Diné philosophy are in order. The leadership characteristics that define Diné philosophy are ones established during the emergence, or *Hajinéí*.

I.1. WE DON'T JUST WRITE ABOUT IT, WE LIVE IT

It is one thing to talk the talk and quite another to walk the walk. Once upon a time *Naat'áanii* would not have been able to get away with simply talking about leadership and governance. While reviewing anthropological literature on Navajo philosophy, it does seem apparent that something is missing or perhaps something has been incorrectly added. When non-Navajo scholars wrote about Navajo "myths," it may have been that a great deal of poetic license was acceptable. It is not possible to know if the authors took the stories seriously or if they thought the stories reflected boredom and creativity among a group of people long ago. The author overtly avoided reading the research of non-Navajo scholars to ensure that Diné philosophy would be from Diné knowledge holders. The intention was to see if key assumptions failed to emerge if the information was learning from the knowledge holders themselves. One key assumption might be that "creation is a myth." Only after some knowledge was disseminated would there be engagement with the existing literature. While it is impossible to know if this strategy improved the final product, perhaps this is the reason why discussions in the literature paint a picture as expressed using concept building. This research is also a response meant to "decolonize" research on Indigenous and Diné studies.

The future of Indian Country is here today. The need for texts on examples of traditional and contemporary approaches to Native nation governance remains largely unmet. There is also a burgeoning need for an Indigenous philosophy of research in Maori Indigenous institutions of higher education. This movement, spearheaded by the work of Linda Tuhiwai Smith, calls for an Indigenous research agenda. This book is the culmination of that inspiring read. The push for Indigenous "decolonization" does not require a hostile stance against any particular philosophy or point of view. Rather, a self-determined focus on maintaining and expanding Indigenous sovereignty can be attained with a systematic analysis of (1) the origin of contemporary governing institutions and (2) the systematic removal of non-Indigenous interests in contemporary governing institutions. On the rare occasion that a Native nation has (1) knowledge holders who are willing to discuss philosophy openly and (2) knowledge holders who wish to either write their philosophy down or collaborate with other writers, it is possible to produce more holistic scholarship. Diné philosophy is still accessible despite overt efforts to destroy it. Consequently, scholars can ask about many areas that have yet to be addressed in the existing literature.

While reading the literature, there must be a mental questioning going on. What about the Sacred Elements? What about the fire? Will the research discuss water, air, and pollen? The questions are endless but ultimately point toward a clear goal of exploring Diné philosophy insofar as it answers contemporary questions about Navajo society here and now. Writing from my own privileged space allows for serious reflection on the purpose of the resulting text.

This book was written for a number of purposes. One purpose involves taking seriously the role of the researcher and contributor to Indigenous communities. This means walking among a community and humbling oneself. This means allowing a community to set the agenda. Once upon a time, non-Indigenous researchers individually attempted to "save Indians" by bringing their own assumptions to address community ills. This book is not meant to "save" anyone. Rather, this book is meant to answer a question posed to those who live their life consistent with Diné philosophy: How can this researcher (Michael Lerma) contribute to Navajo Nation? Again, the assumption does not involve taking a leadership role or otherwise offering solutions from the outside. The assumption, instead, is that the solutions already exist within Diné philosophy and within the knowledge holders. As Denny would say, "It's already there." The process of "humbling oneself" does not require much effort. It is a simple matter of having respect for Indigenous elders who have navigated through acts of genocide for their entire lives. It is a matter of being completely aware and comfortable with the fact that the daily problems members of a privileged class within American society "suffer" are miniscule when compared to the daily struggles of Indigenous knowledge holders. One consequence of this reality is that collaborators may lose "objectivity."

Readers should be aware of the writing style employed in this book. The nature of my relationship with contemporary knowledge holders requires a "unique" approach to the philosophy chapters. I may, on occasion, change tenses. I don't "write" the philosophy. I live it. Knowledge holders, in turn, live the philosophy as well. My original intent in working with knowledge holders was not to write a book. Rather, I wished to find a place where I could contribute to solutions. I never intended to "study" anyone. Rather, I wished to solve problems in concert with others. I found a community to work within, knowledge holders to collaborate with, and problems to focus upon collectively. As I learn more from knowledge holders, I gain their trust and respect. Hence, they have expectations I must live up to, or our mutual collaborations will be put at risk. I, in turn, have also come to respect them. There is a certain respect that should be afforded knowledge holders, but this does not imply uncritical acceptance of all elder statements.

Respect is not admiration. Respect is not unquestioning loyalty. Respect is offered based on an initial observation and continued interaction. The interaction can reinforce the initial instinct to offer respect, or it can lead to reassessment about whether or not the respect offered is misplaced. Professor Tom Holm once said, during a graduation ceremony, that some people are elders and some people are just old. While respect is offered to the "elder," continued interaction will separate the elders from the old. This distinction is what makes an individual a knowledge holder.

There is an intersection between community agendas, knowledge holders, and old people. To be clear, a community agenda is often a "should be" or "ought to be" proposition. All communities suffer a disconnect between how things should be and how they really are. Knowledge holders, those who have survived well into their years and have survived colonial onslaught as individuals, are more likely to possess knowledge about how things should be. (In fact, knowledge holder status can have little to do with chronological age.) Knowledge holders are more likely to have a better idea about the community agenda. Contrary to popular assumptions about Indians, knowledge holders are also likely to be marginalized by their communities. This is because the knowledge holders have criticisms about how things are. Obviously, this "research approach" is highly subjective. Buried in all of this is a potential causal mechanism. Maybe the knowledge holders grow old because they are wise and adhere to a philosophy that demands they carry themselves in a good way. Luckily, some institutional support exists to distinguish between knowledge holders and the old. This book would still be in its infancy had it not been for the Navajo Nation Council having enough courage to admit there are some things they don't know. Maybe the knowledge holders know.

An "oral account" of the history of Diné Policy Institute, or DPI, may help readers better understand how this book was made possible. While a comprehensive history of DPI would be interesting, it is unclear how writing one here advances the needs of Diné people. Still, at least three events occurred to make DPI possible: (1) the Navajo Nation Council codified the Fundamental Laws of the Diné in 2002, (2) Ferlin Clark was hired as president of Diné College in 2003, and (3) Chief Justice Robert Yazzie retired from the Navajo Nation Supreme Court on November 26, 2003. Clark wished to establish an institute tasked with conducting research on Diné philosophy. It is believed he reached out to Justice Yazzie. However the events unfolded, Yazzie became the first director of DPI sometime in 2004. Perhaps it is put best that DPI has worked to identify knowledge holders to carry out research requested by the Navajo Nation Council. The extent to which DPI reached across time and space to link knowledge holders with contemporary issues is obviously debatable. Still, this was the attempt. As a result, this book does not pretend to have played any role in developing this tie. This book does not pretend to give credit to DPI for making this link either. All this book can say for sure is that had it not been for DPI and its institutions attempting to make links across time, space, philosophy, and problems, this book would not have been possible at all.

It is also appropriate to share a brief, yet more official story of DPI:

In 2005, the Navajo Nation Council and the Diné College Board of Regents established Diné Policy Institute (DPI) to articulate, analyze and apply the *Diné Bi Beehaz'áannii* to issues impacting the Navajo people by educating, collaborating and serving as a resource for policy and research. *Są'ah Naagháí Bik'eh Hózhóón* guides the research process of DPI by using Nitsáhákees, Nahatá, Iiná and Siih Hasin. DPI's applied research from Diné knowledge provides innovative solutions that address the social, economic and cultural well-being of the Navajo Nation. Diné Policy Institute is housed at the Tsaile campus of Diné College. (Eldridge et al. 2014, 2, emphasis added)

In many respects, DPI is one of a kind. Yazzie worked to create an institute that would answer the calls for reform from the citizens of Navajo Nation:

Through the principles and values of [Sạ'ah Naagháí Bik'eh Hózhóón], Diné Policy Institute serves as the premiere quality research organization for facilitating, analyzing issues, and educating Bila'ashdlaii, in a way that ensures that beeheezaani are developed to protect the sovereignty and cultural integrity of the Diné. Diné Policy Institute's mission is to articulate, analyze and apply the Diné Bi Beehaz'aannii to issues impacting the Navajo people by educating, collaborating and serving as a resource for policy and research. Through the mission statement, DPI conducts quality law and policy research and provides clarity between Diné research and other paradigms. (Diné College 2008, 32)

This is a complex mission of taking an oral account of Diné philosophy and melding it with contemporary issues faced by Navajo Nation today. Yazzie had previously performed similar work. As Chief Justice of the Navajo Nation Supreme Court, he aimed to take *Diné Bi Beehaz'áannii*, or Fundamental Laws of the Diné, and rely on this canon as a basis or foundation for deciding court case decisions (Austin 2009; Nielsen and Zion 2005).

The first time DPI worked publicly came around 2007, when Navajo Nation Council Speaker Lawrence T. Morgan requested guidance on reforming the current Navajo Nation government (Singer et al. 2007). This would be the first time since treaty making that knowledge holders would work to create commentary on how Navajo Nation government should be built or rebuilt. About a year after this initial report to the Speaker, DPI published its report on the feasibility of writing a Navajo Nation constitution (Yazzie et al. 2008). This is potentially the first example of an Indigenous community attempting to meld its own Indigenous knowledge with contemporary problem solving. Some of the most impressive work involved relearning and reconsidering traditional Diné terms as potentially appropriate for contemporary issues. One term, the *Naach'id,* was discussed as a method of linking contemporary regional committees to more effectively discuss relations with colonial actors[3] (Yazzie et al. 2008, 53). These early DPI documents certainly leave a great deal to be desired, but they are an impressive start toward doing what may seem impossible: making Diné philosophy relevant to the twenty-first century.

All the while, Yazzie and his revolving-door staff continued to work on more projects than they could effectively handle. My impression, in working with Yazzie, has been that he is passionate about his work and rarely has said no to opportunities to contribute to solutions. In addition to official work, DPI also heavily contributed to reteaching faculty and staff at Diné College about Fundamental Law teachings. Diné Educational

Philosophy, or DEP, sessions became required for Diné College staff and faculty. The responsibility to teach these courses often fell to DPI. Yazzie, as director of DPI, was also called upon to perform service to Diné College, requiring meetings and reports internal to the college itself. On top of these responsibilities, Yazzie was often called upon for, or offered of his own accord, DPI services at conferences, including presenting papers, chairing panels, or serving as a discussant. On top of this work, Yazzie always reached out to the youth, offering teenage and young adult students intern opportunities. Many times DPI had an office full of individuals from on or off the reservation, individuals from different reservations, or non-Indigenous students from around the world. DPI, as an institution, was a gateway for me to enter the world of Diné thinking. It was a gateway to write this book. I was fortunate enough to collaborate with DPI on the *Recommendations for Restructuring the Navajo Nation Council* report (Yazzie et al. 2011). I took what I learned from the *Navajo Nation Constitutional Feasibility and Government Reform Project* report (Yazzie et al. 2008) and learned from the knowledge holders all I could about traditional institutions of Diné governance. It seems one of the best traits in a knowledge holder is knowing what you don't know and reaching out when this occurs.

Yazzie is wise to recognize that he does not know everything that there is to know about Diné philosophy. Self-recognition of limits makes one a very respectable knowledge holder. Yazzie uses his wisdom to reach out to others who survived in his home community of *Diné Bikéyah*, or Navajo homeland. He reaches out to knowledge holders hired as faculty at Diné College. Collectively, the knowledge holders create the DPI advisory circle. The advisory circle is a collection of knowledge holders from all areas of life tasked with discussing problems in Navajo society. They attempt to intersect Diné philosophy with contemporary problems to discover and articulate solutions. Advisory circle meetings ideally take place about four times a year. The knowledge holders sit together on the fourth floor of the Ned Hataalii Center of Diné College. They laugh together, drink coffee, have lunch, and generally collaborate for the good of their "young ones." These meetings last all day long and are recorded by DPI staffers with either notes or recording devices.

Relations between the knowledge holders and the youth have also been endearing. The knowledge holders refer to the young as *yazh* or *shiyazh* and strongly inform the youth about misunderstandings concerning topics of import. Many of the young ones (about college age) have varying levels of Navajo language skills. Yet even the most fluent young ones may have only learned conversational Navajo. This type of Navajo language fluency may get people fed and help people discover one another's clan relations but may not be sufficient to fully grasp tenets of Diné philosophy. The young ones who did and do understand their limits, then, have the greatest potential to be knowledge holders. One might say that all young ones have an equal opportunity to become "elders in training." To learn more, all they need to do is listen.

DPI created an access point for young ones to come home and learn from their knowledge holders, contribute to their homeland, and become knowledge holders if they wished to acquire the responsibility. Being a knowledge holder obligates the holder to teach those who ask for assistance. Being a knowledge holder, however, is not solely up to the individual. The knowledge holders say that if someone is meant to carry the knowledge, that person will carry it. If someone forgets, the individual is not meant to carry the knowledge. The knowledge will avoid individuals if they are not in the right place to carry it (Austin 2009, 56). Hence, it was automatically a given that the young ones listening at an advisory circle were already conditioned to accept a community of knowledge holders setting a community agenda. The young ones were humbled by the experience, attentive, respectful, and inquisitive to the degree they could understand the ideas. The "dumb questions" young ones asked were swiftly dismissed, and the correct path was followed again. The intelligent questions were followed as the knowledge holders deliberated. There was no room for distraction or wasted time. Some of the young ones absorbed the knowledge. Others took the paycheck and went home. It was up to the young ones to decide what was important.

From a personal point of view, I was a young one in 2007 when I enrolled in Dr. Manley A. Begay Jr.'s class on American Indian Higher Education. During the first class, Dr. Begay stated that he was involved with DPI. After class, I expressed my interest in working with DPI by allowing them to set the agenda. In exchange, I wished to learn. In 2008, I first attended an advisory circle. Most of the time I was able to "work for food," meaning I rarely asked for a paycheck. I walked into a room full of "old Navajos" wondering what I would get. At first I did not understand a great deal of the conversation. I was surprised to learn that I was learning anyway. I believe this first advisory circle was one that contributed heavily to the constitutional feasibility study (Yazzie et al. 2008). It was as if their thoughts were collecting together in the center of their circle. An example might suffice: DPI wanted to discuss Navajo sovereignty as a condition of the treaty of 1868. The knowledge holders rejected this notion. They elaborated upon a huge topic about how their sovereignty came from creation. As they went on with their discussion, I began to visualize in my mind a tunnel running from slightly above our heads down into the floor. It descended down into the earth. This was the first time I learned about the emergence. I wanted to know more. This meant, in my mind, that I needed to be willing to work longer. This seemed like a no-brainer.

I knew I couldn't just take information. I knew I had to be willing to work for the knowledge I requested. My sincere interest was in allowing the community members to set my agenda. My first teacher was Justice Yazzie. I asked him for information. I asked him for knowledge.

Justice Yazzie and I discussed the first draft of what would become Chapter 3 of this book. It seemed the biggest challenge DPI faced was convincing the world that a bunch of "myths" about leaders was relevant to contemporary issues. Perhaps making Diné philosophy accessible by the community at large could fulfill the community agenda. To learn more, Justice Yazzie's research interests became one focus of this book. Our collaboration was all-encompassing. Some of the work involved this book, but most of the work was learning about many other aspects of Diné philosophy. Our other collaborator and teacher was Avery Denny.

A first complete draft of this book emerged after about a year of working with Justice Yazzie. Dr. Begay and Justice Yazzie would discuss the next steps, as I was a young one, learning and, it was hoped, contributing to the community agenda. They concluded that *Hataałii* Avery Denny, a respected knowledge holder and medicine man, would be an ideal contributor. Working with a knowledge holder requires a student to be a young one contributing to the larger needs identified by the community knowledge holders, such as Denny, and learning along the way. This "research method" was something I was taught as a child.

Perhaps my research methodology was, in fact, gifted to me as a child. I was raised to look for knowledge holders like my grandparents. I was raised to learn all I could, and I learned that I would not have them in my life forever. I learned to watch, to listen, to shut up, and to defer to their better judgment. I learned to give everything I had because it was needed. I didn't need to learn to respect them. Knowledge holders like my grandparents had a home, they had a marriage, and they had kids and grandkids. My grandparents were my leaders. They never steered me wrong. We never starved; it was never cold in our home, and the lights always worked. I learned, maybe too young, that they could not do this for me forever. I learned that I would be next to be the teacher and that the young ones would look to me for guidance all too soon. This book was written because I asked for the responsibility of learning from the knowledge holders again. They never specifically said, "Write this down," just as my grandfather and grandmother never said, "Take care of your mom and brothers." It was common sense. For me, writing this down is common sense. I wrote this book down because it would be foolish not to write this book down.

I.2. CREATION AND RE-CREATION OF FOUR WORLDS

Diné Creation Accounts outline the tenets for contemporary governance and offer moral lessons about proper distance and nearness toward the Four Sacred Elements. The key to a good, well-lived, long life (known as *Sa'ah Naaghái Bik'eh Hózhóón*) is that a human (*bila' 'ashdla'*) must keep a proper distance from each of the Four Sacred Elements. The Four Sacred Elements behave according to a set of deductive outcomes. In this way, we know and understand the Four Sacred Elements in a fashion that is similar to the way Western scientists know them. When certain conditions not conducive to human life are witnessed (or allowed to emerge due to carelessness) the outcome is often a threat to life. In the most extreme encounters life is lost. Humans do not consistently follow the exact same behavior given the exact same conditions. The Four Sacred Elements, on the other hand, are less forgiving. They will always behave as conditions dictate. Regardless of human need, if the temperature is low enough, the water will freeze. If an individual is thirsty and ice is encountered, the ice will not unfreeze for an individual just because of thirst. Once conditions are present (freezing temperature), there is no pleading with the Four Sacred Elements for respite. Only environmental stimulation, such as using fire (a source of heat) to melt ice, will allow the ice to become liquid again. The time to make requests is before the conditions emerge that threaten life. Wisdom to recognize changing conditions and, thus, wisdom to know when to make requests is a prerequisite to a long and well-lived life. Regardless of selfish human wants, the Four Sacred Elements will always behave according to their own dictates. This is recognized by Diné philosophers as one aspect of the Fundamental Laws of the Diné (1 N.N.C. §§ 201–206). These lessons are contained in Diné Creation Accounts (Zolbrod 1987). They are gifts from the Holy Ones (*Diyin Dine'é*) to the Diné.

Past scholars of European philosophical thought have linked Western philosophy to past and present political ideas. In similar fashion, linking Diné philosophy to contemporary political thought may yield interesting and useful conclusions. In Diné philosophy, four worlds have been traversed, which have culminated in contemporary events. (Some accounts state that there are five worlds, but Benally is comfortable leaving things at four worlds. For details of these events, see Benally 2006.) The four-world journey is presented in Figure I.1. Oral accounts of the emergence of the Diné into the fourth world were once "common sense." Common sense may not be so common anymore.

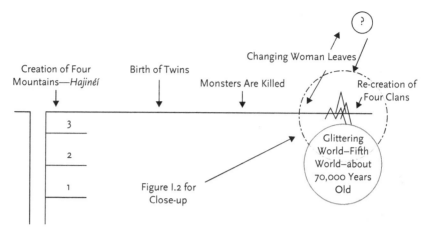

Figure I.1: Fourth World—White World—Important Events Applicable to Today

I.3. *SISNAAJÍNÍ* (MOUNT BLANCA) FOR INTERNATIONAL RELATIONS AND *DOOK'O'OOSŁIID* (SAN FRANCISCO PEAKS) FOR DOMESTIC AFFAIRS

Common sense is a funny phrase. The common sense written here is not very common anymore. Doing things because it is implied is antithetical to current Western models of education. Still, the young ones should be warned that it would be foolish not to learn from the implications of their world, the implications of their knowledge holders, and the implications of their time on earth. No one is going to beg the young ones to learn. They must be willing to do the work. There is a great deal of learning to be accomplished.

First we must address a caveat. I once overheard an individual from Navajo Nation lamenting how his people lacked philosophers like Socrates and Aristotle. As a result, he was confused on how a contemporary Diné government should be reformed. I was seated next to Avery Denny when this gentleman made the comment. I looked over at Mr. Denny and he looked at me; we shared a look of frustration. As will be made abundantly clear in Chapter 4, contemporary governing problems deeply involve the origin of the Navajo Tribal Council and its intended purpose. Like nearly every Indigenous nation in the lower forty-eight states of what became the United States, Navajo Nation was put under tremendous pressure to create governments with a singular purpose of signing land leases (Lerma 2014a, 108–146). A general pattern appears in which the United States promoted the benefits of Western-style governing hierarchies and created incentives for Navajo individuals to monopolize access to newly created tribal governments. Navajo Nation had this experience around the 1920s, and the trend continued across Indian Country into the late 1940s. Reforming tribal councils is not the goal of this research.

Rather, all scholars interested in reforming Indigenous governing institutions would be wise to heed a warning: nearly all Western philosophies of governing institutions inexplicably lead to the monopolization of resources (Lerma 2014a, 108–146). Another consequence of adopting Western institutions involves adopting heteropatriarchy along with "modernity." Prominent scholar Jennifer Denetdale correctly criticizes the recent push from Navajo Nation governing institutions to further marginalize women or any individual who cannot be clearly ascertained as "a man," meaning gay or transgender individuals. Her research on the Diné Marriage Act of 2005 finds great fault with an Indigenous nation bent on blindly supporting an amalgamation of patriotic sentiment intermixing loyalty to the United States and loyalty to Navajo Nation. These types of "with us or against us" mentalities not only work to render questions of gender invisible in mainstream society, but work to render gender unquestioned or unaddressed in Navajo Nation (Denetdale 2006b, 135). In another article, Denetdale is also critical of the term *traditional*, and for good reason. Many Navajo political leaders and influential voices have worked diligently to maintain their grasp on power by evoking a blanket and vague notion of being "traditional" (Denetdale 2006a, 10). While her work is specific to Navajo Nation, many other Indigenous nations have likely suffered, and will likely continue to suffer, from the marginalization of women.

Within Diné philosophy are various cycles of logic. This logic is quite specific in its balance regarding gender. Female and male must coexist and work together in order to make life. Each gender has its own special talents and no one gender is better than or superior to the other. Each is to be respected. These genders are in the philosophy. Yazzie and Denny have walked the walk in terms of applying Diné philosophy to contemporary problems. Figure I.2 is a visual expression of this book. To date, there has not been any other attempt to utilize the Sacred Mountains as a philosophy for contemporary governance. Figure I.2 is a two-dimensional model furnished by Denny (2010) as a way to organize the philosophy of contemporary Diné governance. Again, each mountain has both a male and a female spirit. Depending on the situation, Denny explains that *Sisnaajiní*, or the eastern mountain, can be female. *Tsoodził* male, *Dookʼoʼoosłiid* female, and *Dibé Nitsaa* male. *Dził Ná ʼOodiłii* is a both a female child and a male child. Diné philosophy does not ignore the female spirit. The Four Re-Created Clans were instructed to live within the boundaries of the Sacred Mountains. They were instructed to maintain their proper distance and nearness toward the Four Sacred Elements.

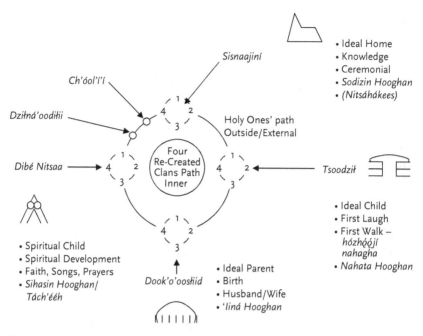

Figure I.2: Simplified Expression of Diné Governance

When an individual must leave the *hooghan*, he or she must behave in a way that is based on a cycle of philosophical ideals contained within *Dził Łeezh* in each of the Sacred Mountains.[4] Each Sacred Mountain has its own cycle or process for governing and maintaining proper distance and nearness toward the Four Sacred Elements. Humans are required to follow this pattern of behavior as they enter their homes and consider their needs. Specifically, they may ask themselves about their proper distance and nearness toward the Four Sacred Elements of the Diné: *Kǫ', Tó, Niłchí,* and *Tadidiin* (some have also stated the last element as both *Tadidiin* and *Nahasdzáán*). In English, these elements can be translated as fire and light, water, air, and pollen and earth.[5] Each of these elements is required for human life (*Bila 'ashdla' ei 'Iiná*) to exist, thrive, and otherwise continue. Each of the elements is a being with a life of its own, independent of any other beings (especially humans). If the people were to want it to be so, these basic tenets of Diné life could be the basis for contemporary Diné governance. Wisdom, or *Sá'*, is attainable through a lifetime of maintaining a balance. Elements, human life, wisdom, and so on are massively complex ideas, but again, they could be as simple as our distance and nearness toward the Four Sacred Elements (Begay and Maryboy 1998).

It is difficult to discuss the Diné philosophy of governance briefly. Oral accounts of Diné philosophy of governance are covered in Chapter 1, and even the account there is not nearly complete. It is likely that several individuals could write for a lifetime and still not capture everything there is to say about Diné philosophy. Diné governance is embedded within *Dził Łeezh*. One might superficially understand *Dził Łeezh* as a bundle of objects and abilities vested within the Four Sacred Mountains (Mitchell, Frisbie, and McAllester 2003, 170). *Dził Łeezh* can be carried and cared for by humans who have the ability to lead. Leadership is defined as a person's ability to keep his or her community within proper distance from the Four Sacred Elements. The relationship between the Sacred Mountains, Sacred Elements, and the home, or *hooghan*, will be discussed at length in Chapter 1. Some details about the ties across mountains and *hooghans* are mentioned later in this chapter. In short, all of these relationships must be maintained for an individual to be called upon to lead his or her people.

The characteristics needed for leadership have gone through a trial-and-error phase leading up to the emergence (Zolbrod 1987). Various animals attempted several types of leadership long ago. Each of these attempts failed to yield an appropriate approach to governance (Benally 2006, 1–40). To correct the failures of the past, the Four Sacred Mountains—*Sisnaajiní* (Mount Blanca), *Tsoodził* (Mount Taylor), *Dook'o'oosłiid* (San Francisco Peaks), and *Dibé Nitsaa* (Mount Hesperus)—were given to the Diné as a foundation for leadership (Mitchell, Frisbie, and McAllester 2003, 170; McPherson 1991, 15–24). Again, both the female and male spirit are within each mountain. Within each mountain are certain attributes for leadership. These attributes are also within *Dził Łeezh*. Future leaders must possess these attributes, or they will fail in their leadership duties (Denny 2010).[6] In other words, without *Dził Łeezh*, it will not be possible for leaders to attain proper distance and nearness toward the Four Sacred Elements.

Diné philosophy is based on life in the home (Roessel and Johnson 1974, 53–57). The traditional Diné *hooghan* contains tools for governing distance and nearness toward the Four Sacred Elements. Denny says that an ideal life takes place within an ideal home. This means that both woman and man must respect and acknowledge their inherent talents. The *hooghan* is a scaled-down model of *Diné Bikéyah*, or the traditional homeland within the Sacred Mountains (Mitchell, Frisbie, and McAllester 2003, 170; McPherson 1991, 15–24; Schwarz 1997, 20). In other words, the ideal home is modeled after the universe. Within the universe, the star people, or *Sǫ' Dine'e*, also first displayed the ideal relationship among female and male stars arranged in constellations. Note that there are many stories about leadership and the *hooghan*. Only a portion of these stories are summarized in this book. Still, these stories form the basis for Diné leadership philosophy.

Denny advised that a leadership initiative ought to start with the eastern-facing slope. Hence (as shown in Figure I.2), each Sacred Mountain's eastern-facing slope is demarcated with "1," which creates a pattern for the Four Re-Created Clans to follow. It is up to the *Diyin Dine'e*, or the Holy Ones, to follow the external path beginning with *Sisnaajiní* (Mount Blanca). Humans should follow the internal circle beginning with *Dook'o'oosłiid* (San Francisco Peaks), because humans should start with their real-life problems. This process will be discussed in greater detail in Chapter 1; it relies on Figure I.3 for explanation. The philosophy inherent in the Sacred Mountains' pathway outlines the foundation for what Western scholars tend to call international relations.

Denny (2010) furnished Figure I.3, which explores the necessary conditions for leadership at home—that is, domestic politics. The mountain model (*Dził Nahat'á*) is also a *hooghan* model for living. *Dził Łeezh* is embedded within the *hooghan*. In the *hooghan*, it is necessary to begin in the east and move sunwise south, west, and north. Diné philosophy introduces *Dziłna'oodiłii* (Doorway Mountain) and *Ch'óol'í'í* (Chimney Mountain) into the *hooghan* model. Denny teaches that a person (male or female) must have a home, a spouse, children, and *Dził Łeezh* to qualify as a leader. These leadership roles are not attained by a campaign. Rather, the community recognizes good individual leadership. Denny is alluding to the fact that, as a leader of a home, as a successful manager of the traits inherent in the *hooghan*, one has proven that he or she can lead beyond the *hooghan*.

Certain facts are inherent in the *hooghan*. It is necessary to exit the *hooghan* to sustain life within the home. The Four Sacred Elements do not automatically deliver themselves within the home. They need to be gathered if they are too far away. They need not be gathered if they are

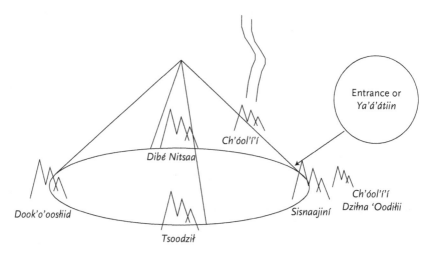

Figure I.3: Diagram by Avery Denny—Leadership within the Home

abundant in proximity to an individual *hooghan*. Hence, the only constant is change, and the relationship must be one of maintaining proper distance and nearness toward the Four Sacred Elements. When people exit the *hooghan*, they turn to the Sacred Mountains for guidance. They are specifically aware of their needs. They understand their imbalances with regard to the Four Sacred Elements. Collectively, life within the *hooghan* and life outside the *hooghan* are templates for leadership within the bounds (and beyond the bounds) of Navajo Nation. The unasked question is how these lessons can assist contemporary Diné governance—in other words, how can contemporary Diné leaders facilitate institutional access to the Four Sacred Elements? Framing how Diné philosophy may guide contemporary leaders is clearer if it is presented in the language of contemporary political philosophy.

To summarize, Diné philosophy has at least two inherent approaches to governance and leadership—domestic politics and international relations. Assume that domestic politics takes place within the *hooghan*. International relations take place outside of the *hooghan*. Past research fails to explore the two approaches and overlooks the international politics of Navajo Nation. In terms of the Four Sacred Elements, scholars should ask how domestic leaders can better coordinate access to these Elements. For international politics, readers should ask how leaders can better negotiate access to the Four Sacred Elements with colonial actors such as the United States. Past iterations of Diné philosophy utilize, at the very least, two approaches embedded in Figure I.2.

A process for contemporary international relations should take the form that the Holy Ones used when dealing with the non-Diné world (Denny 2010). Although this applies to all humans, the Diné who seek guidance from the Holy Ones must abide by the path first followed by the Four Re-Created Clans. Denny points to the Holy Ones' pathway as the cycle to restore the world from the brink of disaster. Comparatively, if Diné philosophy has restored balance at least four times in the past, the process of restoring balance to Diné governance today should be a very light task. As Denny (2010) states, however, "We have the solutions that no one wants to hear."

Denny implies that it may make more sense to deal with the non-Diné world by beginning in the west where *Dookʼoʼoosłiid* (San Francisco Peaks) faces the east. This is noted in Figure I.2, in which *Dookʼoʼoosłiid* is labeled with the numeral 1. Again, *Dookʼoʼoosłiid* represents a current-day assessment of life. Internationally, various threats to maintaining a proper relationship with the Four Sacred Elements are occurring now in real life. This implies that past plans for maintaining good relations with the Four Sacred

Elements are not working anymore. As a result, real-life events are going to put future regeneration processes at risk. But the first step to correct any of these problems is to allow a new idea (fire or spark) to deal with our daily mismanaged relationship with the Four Sacred Elements.

Moving sunwise, the process goes through *Dibé Nitsaa* (Mount Hesperus), *Sisnaajiní* (Mount Blanca), and *Tsoodzil* (Mount Taylor). This process will be elaborated upon in Chapter 1. For our purposes, we need to merely understand that Diné philosophy has embedded within it the necessary conditions for good governance and good politics. In other words, Diné philosophy inherently provides a path to maintain proper distance and nearness toward the Four Sacred Elements.

I.4. WHAT TO EXPECT GOING FORWARD

Before proceeding to a summary of the chapters, it may be helpful to critically consider this book's organization. Figure I.4 is an illustrated version of that organization. It is based on Diné philosophy. As will be further articulated in Chapter 1, each mountain is associated with a thought process. *Sisnaajiní* is associated with the birth of thought. *Tsoodzil* is associated with planning. *Dook'o'oosłííd* indicates lived life experiences. *Dibé Nitsaa* indicates reflection, rebirth, or regeneration. The cycle renews in the birth of thought. It is based on cosmic cycles in the universe. Specifically, it is based on the earth's rotation on its axis. At the dawn is a spark or sunrise; at midday the sun is in a mid-sky position. During the day, the sun tracks across

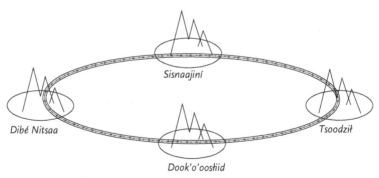

1. *Sisnaajiní*—For Thinking—Chapter 1
2. *Tsoodzil*—For Planning—Chapter 2
3. *Dook'o'oosłííd*—For Living—Chapter 3
4. *Dibé Nitsaa*—For Rebirth or Regeneration—Chapter 5

Figure I.4: Book Organization Based on *Dził Nahat'ááji*, or Mountain Planning Way

the sky when life is lived outside until sunset. At night, many life beings go to sleep to regenerate themselves for a new dawn or spark. Each chapter is a nested cycle within this larger cycle represented by Figure I.4. Each mountain also can be thought of as a cycle within the larger cycle. For example, *Dibé Nitsaa*, being associated with regeneration, can also have a cycle of regenerating thought, regenerating plans, regenerating life, and regenerating regeneration. This last one might be difficult to understand, but it really means allowing a space for regeneration to occur within the cycle of life. Many chapters in this book reflect this pattern, while some do not.

Readers are not required to read this book in any particular order. In many ways, readers may find this organization a bit jarring. I have attempted to organize this book based on Diné philosophy. This means that chapters may appear "repetitive." One thing that is absolutely clear is that I have dispensed with organizing this book based on time. Readers will note that I discuss "a history" of Diné international interaction *before* I discuss concepts of traditional Diné governance. I also fail to comprehensively discuss the problems of contemporary Diné governance until Chapter 4. Readers will note that Chapter 4 is a clear departure from Diné thinking. This departure is intentional. I also could just as well place the activity of contemporary Diné knowledge holders and elected officials in a number of different places within this book. Instead, I have attempted to be loyal to Diné philosophy as I have been made aware of its tenets. I won't state that this book is organized "correctly." I invite readers to read the chapters in any order they wish. I hope that this section will better orient readers to the forthcoming chapters and help them digest this research.

This book uses a unique conglomeration of research methodology practices. Sometimes Avery Denny uses a whiteboard to draw his ideas. I have attributed many figures drawn in the Introduction and in Chapter 1 to Mr. Denny. These probably constitute the closest tie readers may have to traditional Diné thinking in two- or three-dimensional form. Many chapters, though not all, are organized based on Diné thinking, as outlined by Diné mountain philosophy. In the interest of transparency, be advised that the figures introducing book and chapter organization are my own interpretation of Diné philosophy. Readers may infer what they wish from this disclosure. All other figures within each chapter are based on concept building (Goertz 2006). Concept building is used to identify necessary conditions and identify potential data in support of a condition's presence or absence. It is also used to diagnose problems in contemporary institutions of Diné governance. Still, a handful of figures, mostly in Chapter 5, express Diné philosophy using set theory (Ragin 1987). I have elected to utilize visual guides to express Diné philosophy, but they are not a part of Diné philosophy in and of themselves. They may be used to identify any set of complex relationships in social science research. My goal in using these tools of expression is to get beyond the limits of English in expressing Diné philosophy. My alternative would be to use similar methods as those exhibited in Justice Raymond D. Austin's work, where he admittedly "glosses over" Diné terms in English (2009).

I understand Diné philosophy as revolving in cycles. It is based on *Diné Bi Beehaz'áanii Bitse Siléí*, or the Declaration of the Foundation of Diné Law. More specifically, the basic movement of the sun in the sky is based on *Nahasdzáán dóó Yádiłhił Bitsąądęę Beenahaz'áanii*, or Diné Natural Law (Navajo Nation Council 2002). We might better understand this as the patterns exhibited by the rotation of the earth within the universe. From a Diné point of view, it might also be understood as a living Mother Earth as she communicates her needs to a living Father Sky (Griffin-Pierce 1992). My research with many knowledge holders dictates that projects take on a perspective laid out in the Diné Natural Law. At the dawn is a spark or fire in the east also known as the sunrise, which seems to be an ideal time to talk about a new dawn of normative Diné thought. This talk should be unspoiled by the reality of contemporary daily living. I will refer to this thought process as a *Hajinéí era*, or a time before Diné thought was impacted by colonial actors. I think of this as happening sometime after Diné began interacting with colonial actors, but I do not mean to imply that there is a "pure" form of Diné thinking. This would presume that Diné people emerged in a vacuum, and this is not correct. Chapter 1 is an attempt to capture an awakening at the dawn before we remember some of our life problems.

By mid-morning Natural Law states that humans should begin to use their thoughts, a gift from the Holy Ones, or *Diyin Dine'é*, to plan their day, their days, their months, their seasons, their generations, their lifetimes, and the subsequent lives of their children, grandchildren, and so on. Within our plans emerges the reality of life problems. And so Chapter 2 reflects these emerging problems. Humans ought to be sure they are correctly situated in their lives by ensuring that their fire is kept properly, that they have sufficient water (not too much or too little), that they have proper ventilation for their home, and that they have planted sufficiently for their season. Obviously, people rarely awake in the morning to discover things are perfectly situated. This is why Natural Law states how humans ought to plan for disruption. Chapter 2 begins to outline the details of Diné disruption by settlers. I next turn to real living and breathing concepts of Diné governance. Perhaps this is how things were in the *Hajinéí* era before disruptions of a genocidal nature emerged within the traditional homeland. Only at this point, it seems to me, are contemporary problems relevant, and I turn to a chapter on what we might call "self-termination" (Lerma 2014a, xiv). This chapter questions whether Navajo leaders of the twentieth and twenty-first centuries have unintentionally worked against the interests of Navajo Nation, giving away remaining vestiges of sovereignty. Finally, the remaining chapters focus on "regeneration," in which life is reconsidered. This is the place where previously articulated life plans attempt to correct themselves and realign with normative Diné philosophy. Diné philosophy will hopefully make more sense after reading Chapter 1.

Chapter 1, *Sisnaajiní* (Mount Blanca)—Philosophy of Diné Thinking, explores traditional institutions and how humans can utilize one of many cycles that exist in Diné philosophy. What are the main normative precepts inherent in Diné philosophy? This chapter will introduce (or reintroduce) the four directions as understood by Diné knowledge holders. These four directions—1-east, 2-south, 3-west, 4-north—are situated within nature. Diné Creation Accounts state that these directions are the very basic components given to the five-fingered earth-surface people as a canon of knowledge known as Natural Law or the Fundamental Laws of the Diné. This information allows readers to simultaneously think about their lives and their own governance systems as they find them today and as they expect to find them tomorrow. More concretely, Chapter 1 outlines how contemporary people may maintain their proper distance and nearness toward the Four Sacred Elements, independent of real-world challenges.

Chapter 2, *Tsoodził* (Mount Taylor)—Interrupted Planning in the History of Diné Governance, reviews traditional institutions and the disruption of Diné governance from its form before written history to its current incarnation. It is based on the assumption held by many knowledge holders involving a drift away from Diné philosophy as outlined in Chapter 1. It assumes that interaction with colonial actors has forced the Diné to adopt some negative components from colonial actors and other Indigenous nations, causing a disruption in contemporary lives. It ties contemporary calamities, including a current reliance on heteropatriarchy, to the displacement of Diné philosophy as the key guiding force in the Holy Ones', or *Diyin Dine'é*, path toward prosperity. The most severe barriers to maintaining the proper distance and nearness toward the Four Sacred Elements emerged during international colonial interaction. This discussion will highlight the importance of future leaders planning for a catastrophic change, while simultaneously reflecting on their current situation within the context of disruption.

Chapter 3, *Dook'o'oosłiid* (San Francisco Peaks)—Living Concepts of Diné Governance, serves two purposes. First, it describes how traditional ways of governing based on notions of *Naat'áahji* likely operated in effective ways. This chapter relies heavily on Chapter 1 and information carried by knowledge holders. It will push the boundaries of social science research by illustrating many of the key components of Diné philosophy. It will work to tie Diné philosophy to illustrations of "thinking in three dimensions." By "breathing life" into a static page, the hope is to encourage all interested individuals to breathe life into their own projects as we work toward a common goal of improving contemporary life. Knowledge holders assume that living a good, long, and wisdom-filled life is a consequence of following paths toward healing and protection while maintaining proper distance and nearness toward the Four Sacred Elements. The second purpose involves laying a foundation for comparison in Chapters 4, 5, and 6.

Chapter 4, Tearing Down *'Iiná Hooghan*—Concepts of Modern Navajo Nation Governance, considers how traditional institutions demand that a frank discussion take place about the recent evolution of Diné governance. While other chapters mention many contemporary concerns, this chapter was written to provide a clear and objective analysis of contemporary Diné institutions of governance. It highlights a very narrow purpose in constructing the Navajo Tribal Council and ties the evolution of this governing body to contemporary problems. It also works to demonstrate a clear break from the Diné philosophy of leadership and an adoption of Western institutions of top-down hierarchy. There is clear evidence of self-interest today. This self-interest diagnosis examines how some contemporary leaders have monopolized access to the Four Sacred Elements rather than facilitated equal and equitable access. The remedy may be to reconsider the role of contemporary leaders and their ability to govern access to the Four Sacred Elements independent of their particular philosophical preferences.

Chapter 5, *Dibé Nitsaa* (Mount Hesperus)—Regenerating Concepts of Diné Governance, reflects on the contemporary role of traditional Diné governance as it exists in various facets of contemporary Diné institutions of governance. Today there are many facets of Diné governance that mix both Western and Diné knowledge. One consequence of this mixing involves how some self-interested politicians lean on any premise that just so happens to support their predetermined conclusions. In a more positive light, this chapter is much more focused on attempts by contemporary knowledge holders and elected officials to reintegrate Diné philosophy into the twenty-first century. This chapter discusses how the stage is set to rediscover Diné philosophy as a foundation for future leadership.

Chapter 6, *Dziłná'oodiłii* (Doorway Mountain) and *Ch'óol'í'í* (Chimney Mountain)—Self-Generating Traditional Diné Institutions in the Face of Colonial Interaction, asks how traditional institutions exist today— perhaps they exist because colonial practices failed to destroy them, or maybe because traditional institutions are designed by the Holy Ones to survive catastrophic events. This chapter works to provide empirical evidence of Diné knowledge survival in the face of genocidal activity meant to eliminate it. It works to provide a theory of resilience that is applicable not only to the Diné but to all Indigenous peoples that have survived colonial onslaught. Survival of traditional Diné institutions, as expressed in Chapters 1 and 3, may have occurred so that future humans can use them to resolve their contemporary problems or to re-create their world. Humans must enter and exit only to return home to a sanctuary of Diné philosophy. We cannot expect the Four Sacred Elements to make themselves available if we continue to work toward a path of Sacred Element commodification.

Chapter 7, *Atsa* (Eagle) and *Ma'ii Tso* (Wolf)—Search from Above, Search from the Earth, discusses how traditional institutions of governance exist today. We need to better understand the metaphorical attributes of the eagle to search from above and simultaneously search the earthly surroundings by way of attributes possessed by the wolf. These attributes can be applied to searching for more equitable ways of coordinating the maintenance of proper distance and nearness toward the Four Sacred Elements. Perhaps this is the starting point.

Moving forward, it is useful to consider the following overarching perspective: for governance to function, it must have a foundation in philosophy, institutions to distribute directives, and humans (agents) to carry out directives. For the purposes of this work, Diné philosophy will be the philosophical foundation. This is a unique assumption.

Second, and most noteworthy, is the fact that there is *not* currently an operational institution by which Diné philosophy can distribute directives from the Holy Ones to the humans. The executive branch does not discuss nearness and distance from the Sacred Elements. The legislative branch also is quiet about the Sacred Elements, as is the judicial branch. Rather, while each of the branches of government may discuss the Fundamental Laws of the Diné, they may not have the ability to take the philosophy and inject it into contemporary policy. This book will, I hope, begin the conversation to build such institutions—although it will not contain the definitive answer on how to distribute the Diné philosophy to those willing to follow it. Rather, it will leave it to human agents to find their own pathway through institution-building strategies offered here.

Finally, in terms of Diné philosophy, one might consider this work as a communication between those who inhabit Mother Earth and those who guide from Father Sky above. I pray for my own proper access to the Four Sacred Elements now. I also pray for readers to fully understand tenets outlined here as they are meant to understand them. Without a proper setting for the mind, body, soul, and consciousness, one should expect very little from the information contained here. For many reasons, some will remain critical of an attempt at a traditional approach to governing. With more correct settings, however, one's ability to grasp concepts contained here may be expanded.

Many *Hataałii* (literally singer, but more "imaginatively" medicine people) reference *sin, nahagha, nitsákákees,* and *nizaad,* or songs, teachings, thinking, and words. Their collective goal appears to be setting the stage for a good interaction among all humans, plant people, animal people, Mother Earth, and Father Sky. All of these entities maintain good relations with the Four Sacred Elements *except* humans collectively. A fitting comment deserves attention as we proceed. We are trying to come together now (in our minds) for a common goal. We all must contribute to our common goal of understanding. An elder once said that common goals and understanding are also required for carrying out an Indigenous ceremony properly. We all need to set the stage correctly so that everyone is of a good mind, body, soul, and consciousness. If we can set the stage right, we can accomplish amazing things together. In fact, if we can all think about the exact same thing at the exact same time for two or three seconds, a miracle will occur (Wilson 2008, 69). I now pray for a miracle:

> *Sistsiji Hózhǫ́,* or beauty in front of me
> *Shikishli Hózhǫ́,* or beauty behind me
> *Shiyaagi Hózhǫ́,* or beauty beneath me (Mother Earth)
> *Shik'igi Hózhǫ́,* or beauty from above me (Father Sky)
> *Shinaadę́ę́ Na Tso Hózhǫ́,* or beauty all around (across the horizon)
> *Shizéé'dee Hózhǫ́,* or speaking one's thoughts with beauty
> *Nanita Sa'ah Naaghai*
> *Nanita Bikeh Hozhoon*
> *Hózhǫ́ Nahasdlii*
> *Hózhǫ́ Nahasdlii*
> *Hózhǫ́ Nahasdlii*
> *Hózhǫ́ Nahasdlii*

CHAPTER 1

Sisnaajiní (Mount Blanca)

Philosophy of Diné Thinking

Figure 1.1 depicts the organization of this normative chapter on Diné philosophy. It is supposed to be as pure a thought as can be expressed. This is an immense challenge because it will appear in English, outside of the ceremonial context, and I assume there is such a thing as a "pure thought." Readers will note that our guide is "life," or *'Iiná*. We will begin with thinking on life. We then begin thinking on our plans. We live our lives and allow ourselves to regenerate our lives. We can assume or imagine that the only pressure on Diné at this time period, in the post-*Hajínéí* era, would be other Indigenous peoples and potential miscommunication between Mother Earth and Father Sky creating unexpected climate phenomena.

Evidence and scholarly publications suggest that a nonunified body of Diné philosophy does exist (Austin 2009; Benally 2006; Bobroff 2004–2005; Gorman-Keith 2004; Lee 2007, 2006, 2008; Nielsen and Zion 2005; Parsons-Yazzie et al. 2007; Wilkins 1987, 2003; Yazzie et al. 2008). Much of the philosophy has been discussed as myth or legend (Farella 1984; Levy 1998; Zolbrod 1987). Many Diné scholars discuss what might be called cornstalk philosophy.[1] Like any other body of philosophical thought, however, Diné philosophy is not uniform. In fact, regional differences continue to exist today (Denny 2011). What follows is *not* a story, a myth, a history, or a legend of secrets. What follows is a living examination in which the only constant is change. Most of the information in Chapter 1 I learned in my work with Diné Policy Institute, or DPI. The information here is from countless conversations with Avery Denny and Robert Yazzie.

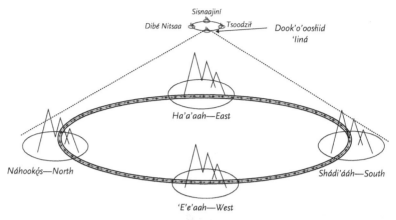

Sisnaajiní
Dibé Nitsaa — Tsoodził — Dook'o'ooslííd
'Iiná

Ha'a'aah—East

Náhookǫs—North

Shádi'ááh—South

'E'e'aah—West

1. *Sisnaajiní*—Thinking about Life—Re-Creating the Four Clans
2. *Tsoodził*—Thinking about Regeneration—A Plan for Life in the Fourth World
3. *Dook'o'ooslííd*—Thinking about Thoughts—Living in the Fourth World
4. *Dibé Nitsaa*—Thinking about Plans—A Philosophy of Regeneration, Renewal, Rebirth

Figure 1.1: Normative Diné Philosophy—A Lifeway Process

The information is also from various DPI advisory circle meetings related to specific topics such as the Navajo constitutional feasibility study, the Navajo Nation Council reduction, and Navajo food sovereignty.

There is nothing in this text that will be inconsistent with previous discussions of Diné philosophy. This is possible because past scholars, including Diné knowledge holders who have never written anything down, have implicitly taught their pupils to think in three dimensions as well as along time and space continuums. These dimensions are varying levels of magnification, such as a person might find in an online map, where one can zoom in on a specific area or pull away and see an entire region or hemisphere. A three-dimensional vantage point implies a geographic perspective within the four directions (east, south, west, and north) and within various elevations within the Six Sacred Mountains. And while the geography has remained relatively constant, at least during the last few hundred years, the people (plants, animals, humans, and the Elements) move constantly through time and within space. Readers should be very clear about one assumption: time continuums and space (geographic) continuums are *not* metaphors. This book is meant to access, both literally and metaphorically, a very narrow space in time before colonial actors began encroaching upon the Diné traditional homeland. If these writings are successful, readers will be deliberately carried within the Six Sacred Mountains and within the *hooghan* model for a good life (*'Iiná*). This challenge is immense and will probably never be complete. Full comprehension cannot come in a few hundred pages.

One key feature of this research involves attempting to clearly state assumptions. There could be some assumptions that have leaked into the research, and that is a weakness of many authors. One way to offset such a weakness is to attempt to disclose as many important assumptions as possible. Below is a list of some important assumptions:

1. Diné knowledge is gendered. It requires both female and male contributions for life to live and exist. No one gender is better than or superior to the other. We might call this equality across genders and equity within genders. A female will have equity in her talents endowed to her by the Holy Ones. The same is true of male equity.
2. A Diné philosophy *does* exist.
3. It is not necessary to comprehensively understand Diné philosophy except to realize that it is much broader than a philosophy of Diné governance.
4. This book discusses a subset of Diné philosophy that reflects Diné philosophy of governance.
5. There is no unified single body of Diné philosophy of governance, and this research does *not* propose to be *the* authoritative source.
6. Diné philosophy is complex. Just as a physicist cannot introduce all that there is about physics in a few pages, the same is true of Diné philosophy and Diné philosophy of governance.
7. The author is writing within the limitations of the English language and within the limits imposed by Diné philosophers. These limits are daunting. Still, there is much to be gained in reviewing what can be understood about Diné philosophy and what carriers of Diné knowledge deem shareable.

To rely on pan-Indigenous philosophy would eschew the opportunity to explore the way some traditional Diné teachings discuss problem solving. *Diné Bitsáhákees*, or Navajo thinking, is explored here from a general point of view. It will be evident later that there is a great deal of overlap between Diné thinking and Diné philosophy of governance.

General theories of European governance are also explored. Past research has assumed that a given European philosophy will explain Indigenous behavior. In contrast, exploring Diné governance based on the assumption that Diné philosophy will explain Diné behavior is possibly a novel yet very simple idea. However, because Diné leaders must interact with colonial actors, contemporary Diné leaders must understand the colonial actors they will interact with today and tomorrow. Thus, it is necessary to understand how and why colonial actors behaved as they did in the past and how they interact with the Diné in the present.

It is worth noting that Western philosophy of governance explains, in very broad terms, some of the aspects of contemporary Indigenous governance and practices that were "adopted" by (or forced upon) the Diné. As a consequence of concerns raised here, readers cannot understand past, present, and future Diné governance unless they understand, as best as is possible, the various philosophies that have impacted contemporary Diné governance. This assumption also implies that without understanding the various philosophies, the future direction of Diné philosophy cannot be fully understood.

1.1. DINÉ INDIGENOUS KNOWLEDGE

Diné knowledge scholars, such as Robert Yazzie, Raymond D. Austin, and Avery Denny, to name a few, teach that Diné knowledge protects itself. In other words, if someone is not meant to carry the knowledge, it will avoid that person (Austin 2009, 56). This teaching implies much more than "meant to carry" can express in English. Again, it is very important that readers take this journey we are embarking upon together seriously. In my heart, I'm trying to play a small part in carrying out a miracle. As others have argued, if we can all think about the same thing at the same time for just a few seconds, a miracle will take place (Wilson 2008, 69). Part of the prerequisite for a miracle is the correct mindset. Failing to take Diné knowledge seriously ensures that what follows will not make any sense to readers. One example from my personal experience may help to illustrate this point. I have witnessed and at times assisted the Honorable Robert Yazzie as he prepared for a talk on some aspect of Diné knowledge in some place in the world. On one occasion I saw him trying to prepare in what I would call impossible conditions. He was asked to discuss the Fundamental Laws of the Diné in about twenty minutes. I remember him sitting at his desk looking frustrated. He said he needed a break as he rose from his desk. He walked toward a sofa in his office and adjusted a pillow on one end so he could lie down and close his eyes. Just as he was adjusting his legs on the sofa, I realized that his challenge came from what I would call a matter of disrespect. How could anyone request such a massive task without allotting the appropriate time? No one would *ever* dare ask or assume that Albert Einstein could explain everything that there is to know about physics in twenty minutes. This same level of respect should be extended to carriers of Diné knowledge.

What is Diné knowledge? Luckily, we don't need to know exactly what Diné knowledge is; however, we must know some things about it. The discussion of Diné knowledge in the Introduction notwithstanding, Diné knowledge explorations should mitigate, as much as possible, the influence of Western philosophy. Keeping Western influence to a minimum gives us an opportunity to understand what it means to think more organically, like the Diné, as Holm et al. defined it in 2003 (Lerma 2012).

1. Does our focus come from our place territory within the Six Sacred Mountains? How will we relate to the Four Sacred Elements within the place territory?
2. Does our focus come from our sacred history in relation to the Six Sacred Mountains? How does sacred history teach us lessons about the Four Sacred Elements?
3. Does our focus use specific language about the Six Sacred Mountains? How will we discuss our relationship with the Four Sacred Elements?
4. Does our focus require some assumptions about a mountain-based ceremonial cycle? How do we ceremonially manage our relationship with the Four Sacred Elements?

Focus matters tremendously when attempting to apply any knowledge, especially an unfamiliar knowledge, to a contemporary problem. The focus here will be centered on Diné knowledge as it relates to the Six Sacred Mountains and the Four Sacred Elements. Each of the Four Sacred Elements is associated with a particular direction. Each direction is nested within a *hooghan* living model, which is associated with a particular Sacred Mountain. These directions are tied to a mountain individuals may not be able to physically see, yet the direction is also at the front door.

Denny explains that individual humans have an opportunity to personalize their relationship with themselves, their relatives, Mother Earth, and Father Sky. Being mindful of Diné knowledge protocols, it can be written in English that there are practices for striving toward beauty and balance. Figure 1.2 illustrates the relationship an individual adult female or male may wish to establish and nurture with all life on earth and within the universe.

The two adult humans illustrated in Figure 1.2 find themselves, perhaps, in the center of their world. They have their feet planted on Mother Earth under Father Sky. The illustration represents both female and male humans but can be simplified by focusing on only one. Any human may face the east in anticipation of the dawn. What follows are some details related to all that exist on Mother Earth. Some of the details are illustrated while others are omitted due to space limitations.

3. Mother Earth
Shimá Naahadzaan
Beauty Beneath My Feet
Shiyaagi

Fire—East
Spark of an Idea

4. Father Sky
Yadiłhił Hastiin
Beauty Above My Head
Shik'igi

1. Beauty Before Me—*Sitsiji*

Pollen
North
Regenerate
Life in
Dormancy

Water
South
Planning

2. Beauty Behind Me—*Shikishiłi*

Air—West
Living Up to Plans

6. Speaking with Beauty
Shizéé'dee

5. Beauty All Around Me
Shinaadéé Na Tso

Figure 1.2: Diné Lifeway

One of the most fundamental aspects of Diné philosophy involves the four directions. East, south, west, and north are embedded within the *space* of a home and within the Six Sacred Mountains. The four directions are associated within *time* during daily life and during a lifetime. Diné directions (space) are *Ha'a'aah*, or east, *Shádi'ááh*, or south, *E'e'ahh*, or west, and *Náhookǫǫs*, or north. These directions are noted in Figure 1.2. Directions ought to be acknowledged in a sunwise direction (time), starting in the east. Each direction is associated with a color: *Ha'a'aah* with *łigai*, or white, *Shádi'ááh* with *dootł'izh*, or turquoise, *E'e'ahh* with *łistoh*, or yellow, and *Náhookǫǫs* with *łizhin*, or black. These colors are also related to the Four Sacred Elements.

The Four Sacred Elements are *K'ó, Tó, Niłchí*, and *Tadidiin* or *Nahasdzáán*. In English these are fire, water, air, and pollen or earth. The Four Sacred Elements are noted in Figure 1.2. They are embedded in living spaces within the *hooghan* and within the Six Sacred Mountains. Readers will note that four of the Six Sacred Mountains are illustrated in Figure 1.2, but they are not labeled to avoid crowding the illustration. This embedded character implies three dimensions from the vantage point of a human facing east to greet the dawn. Readers can note these principles illustrated in Figure 1.2 by following the numbers: (1) east is in front or forward; (2) west is behind or in the past; (3) the earth is beneath the feet; (4) all degrees are above in the sky; in other words, (5) 360 degrees are all around (east, south, west, and north). The Four Sacred Elements are literally embedded in this geographic space. They are also embedded in time within daily activities and within the span of a human life. All colonial actor interaction time, treaty-making time, and so forth share a common thread of being linked by the presence of the Four Sacred Elements. In another sense, the Four Sacred Elements are part of every second of an individual's existence.

Both Denny and Yazzie have stated numerous times that *Ha'a'aah*, or east, involves *K'ó*, or fire and sunlight. Readers may note fire, the east, etcetera, in Figure 1.2. Denny often discusses how the Four Sacred Elements might order themselves, perhaps according to § 5. *Nahasdzáán dóó Yádiłhił Bitsąądęę Beenahaz'áanii*—Diné Natural Law (1 N.N.C. §§ 201–206). Natural Law can also be understood as the way Mother Earth and Father Sky interact with one another through atmospheric changes, lightning, rain, and wind, as well as night and day cycles. One could call this Diné climatology yet even this depiction might be narrow. Denny talks about how the Natural Law was first introduced to humans.

Fire is a spark, a thought, and humans need a spark to have a thought. The spark is given to humans as *Yołgai saad*, or white shell world language. *Sháá á shzhiniidi'ááh*, or the south, involves *Tó*, or water. Water is moisture, and humans need moisture on their tongue to make a sound. The spark and light is the idea, and the moisture is the expression of the spark vocally. Readers will find this information illustrated in Figure 1.2. The moisture is given to humans as *dootł'izhii saad*, or turquoise world language. *E'e'ahh*, or west, involves *Niłchí*, or air, which is illustrated in Figure 1.2. Humans need air to push the spark out of their bodies with their lungs. They need the moisture on their tongue to vocalize the spark. The air is given to humans as *Diichiłi saad*, or yellow world language. The least intuitive aspect of the elemental philosophy involves *tadidiin* and *nahasdzáán*. This is illustrated in Figure 1.2 on the north. All aspects of life require the regenerative process. Both pollen and earth reflect a return to regeneration for starting the process anew. Put another way, the process really does not end, because it is a contained cycle. New ideas, new moisture, and new breath all reflect on earlier observations. The elements for regeneration are given to humans as *saad*, or dark world language. This philosophy is embedded within the Sacred Mountains (1 N.N.C. §§ 201–206).

Each direction is associated with a Sacred Mountain that outlines the area within which the Diné are supposed to live according to the teachings of the *Diyin Dine'é*, or the Holy Ones. Living within the boundaries of the Sacred Mountains should allow individuals to retain their proper distance and nearness toward the Four Sacred Elements. To the east is *Sisnaajiní* (Mount Blanca). To the south is *Tsoodził* (Mount Taylor). To the west is *Dook'o'oosłiid* (San Francisco Peaks), and to the north is *Dibé Nitsaa* (Mount Hesperus) (Parsons-Yazzie et al. 2007, 275). Figure 1.2 omits two more Sacred Mountains for the moment. Oral accounts and 1 N.N.C. §§ 201–206 address *Dził na'oodiłii* and *Ch'óol'í'í*. These mountains will be discussed later. Readers should be mindful that Figure 1.2 is tremendously incomplete, far beyond the omissions noted in the preceding few paragraphs. The enormity and totality of Diné *'Iináji*, or lifeways, derives from traditional teachings about how to live individually, as a family, and as a group of relatives.

Moreover, Diné traditions highlight a process of problem solving. This is especially true if individuals foresee that they will have too much or too little contact with one or more of the Four Sacred Elements. The path of the four directions reflects the patterns in a person's life, not only during a daily cycle but also through the stages of maturity (birth, adolescence, adulthood, and elderhood). The notion of time and a lifeway path are omitted from Figure 1.2 to avoid crowding in the illustration. The stages are about time as a cycle of repeated daily events. Just as the elements are required daily, they are also required long term over a lifetime. Daily time cycles are all embedded within a life-long time cycle. People can think of birth and early life as a thinking stage, in which an individual is considering what the senses are detecting. Senses assist a person in learning what can be accomplished during a day, and, more generally, during the course of a lifetime. In adolescence, a person begins to make plans for the moment, for the day, and for life. As an adult, these adolescent plans are actualized in a manner consistent with Diné teachings. As the person ages, he or she may reflect back on specific life experiences so as to pass on to others what has been learned. It is possible, if there were more space, to illustrate birth in the east, adolescence in the south, young adulthood in the west, and elderhood in the north. Subsequent figures will illustrate notions of time and maturity.

The above process can also be applied to a moment of activity. Diné teachings state individuals should treat their day with the same discipline they do their lifetime, because within a day there is a life cycle, or *'Iináji*. Early dawn, the rising of the sun, encourages a person to plan activities with an idea about what can be accomplished and what needs accomplishing. During the day, these plans are put into action. By sunset, that person is reflecting on the day's work and how the daily tasks might have been performed more effectively and how they might be improved upon on a future day. If the tasks have been successful individuals should reflect on how the lifeway might be applied efficiently to another similar situation. Thus daily routines should involve maintenance of proximity toward the Four Sacred Elements. And, as discussed above, these teachings are linked to the four directions.

Traditional Diné teachings hold that the four directions (within the *hooghan,* within the Six Sacred Mountains, and so forth) also represent a thought process for Diné people to follow (*Diné Bitsáhákees*). This is a lot to absorb at once. Readers should note that the "Mountain Model" illustrated in Figure 1.2 is simultaneously a blueprint to build a home, or *hooghan.* To be clear, these teachings are also embedded in every word in this chapter. At some point, this chapter may appear repetitive, yet the aim is to represent cyclicality. Many anthropological accounts fail to capture Diné lifeways as a cycle. Much of the existing research written since the early 1990s (manuscripts, dissertations, theses, books, journal articles, presentations, and curricular materials) involves notions of *Nitsáhákees, Nahat'á, 'Iiná,* and *Sih Hasin,* or NNIS (N.N.C. §§ 110). NNIS is yet another cycle that could be embedded in Figure 1.2. Within all of these examples of Diné philosophical research is a space for the Four Sacred Elements. They all can be tied to the Six Sacred Mountains even if the examples do not mention these entities. What follows is, I hope, a simple but clear paraphrasing of *Diné Bitsáhákees.*

Readers may, again, refer to Figure 1.2 to understand the relationship between NNIS and the directions. We have reviewed how each thought process is associated with a direction. People are taught to begin the thought process to the east (greet the dawn) with *Nitsáhákees,*[2] or thinking. Next, moving sunwise to the south, they begin *Nahat'á,* or planning the activity. Then they continue to the west and begin *'Iiná,* or living the plan. Finally, they move to the north and enter the *Sih Hasin* phase of reflecting on the operation (regeneration), so as to learn from their mistakes and triumphs (Parsons-Yazzie et al. 2007, 275). Again, it may be illuminative to tie *Diné Bitsáhákees* to maintaining proper distance and nearness toward fire. Do people need fire only to cook today, or will they also need fire for heat in the winter? Failing to account for enough fire will cause problems, or fire will be too far away. An individual must think about his or her needs for fire. For example, assume there is not enough firewood. Hence, the individual creates a plan that the day must be spent collecting more firewood. Next, the person must live that plan, chop wood, and haul it to the home. It must be properly stored and dried. Finally, the individual may relax and consider the day's activities. It is a time for regenerating oneself with sleep. The process begins again at dawn, when more thoughts on the day ahead may come into being. Did this individual keep a proper nearness and distance relationship with fire?

These teachings of how to properly gauge and access the Four Sacred Elements are general and applicable to a diverse set of problems or tasks that people face daily. This is true for individuals and for those who must lead many others. Readers may refer to Figure 1.2 and take note of the two individuals (female and male) as the center for the Diné lifeway process. The process also lends itself to long-term goals, which might involve governance. Other nongovernance examples may further clarify *Diné Bitsáhákees*.

For a concrete nongovernance example outside of the home, Diné philosophy can be applied to obtaining a college education. Gorman-Keith applies *Nitsáhákees* to the "predominant theory about Navajo college students" so as to consider what is assumed about Navajo college students by people of European origin (*Bilagáanaa*) (Gorman-Keith 2004, 2). Many Diné scholars may personally experience their lives within and beyond their individual exposure to Diné philosophy. A common theme appears to be a striving for balance within the extremes found in pressure for success in the European world while remaining true to Diné philosophy. Gorman-Keith and others refer to this balancing as *Hózhǫ́ǫ́jí*, which is glossed in English as "beauty way." *Hózhǫ́ǫ́jí* is yet another cycle embedded within what has already been discussed in this chapter. Figure 1.2 not only could be reillustrated to depict a path toward beauty by following the principles articulated in numerals 1 through 6, but could also be depicted in the arrows that point toward the sunwise pattern of birth through regeneration and rebirth. This is yet another cycle within various other cycles. Denny advises that we carefully reconsider the role of *Hózhǫ́ǫ́jí* only because it is a bit too narrow. It might be more accurate to interpret other research on *Hózhǫ́ǫ́jí* as an attempt to represent '*Iinají*, or the Diné lifeway, which implies *Hózhǫ́ǫ́jí* among other complex principles. While other scholars' reasons for choosing the phrase *Hózhǫ́ǫ́jí* may be implied and, therefore, less than clear, it is consistent to state that going toward beauty contributes to living a good and long life.

As Gorman-Keith describes it, part of the *Nitsáhákees* process involves the introduction of an Indigenous worldview, which is contrasted with the scientific method (as understood by Western culture) (Gorman-Keith 2004, 23). Readers may wish to grant some leeway and assume that Gorman-Keith may imply the fire or spark associated with the east. In contrast, a pan-Indigenous worldview is first introduced as a broad, all-encompassing theory. Next, the Diné philosophy of education, which is directly linked to the general Diné philosophy of life, is placed within the broader pan-Indigenous theory. In other words, a person applies the *Nitsáhákees* process of thinking things out before he or she takes a step toward planning an operation. Thinking can also be a spark or an idea needed for the next phase.

Next in Diné philosophy is *Nahat'á*, or planning things out (Parsons-Yazzie et al. 2007, 275) The principle of *Nahat'á* can be linked to *Hózhǫ́ǫ́jí*, or moving toward beauty, as a means of attaining a college education (28). Again, the process of moving toward beauty, as depicted in Figure 1.2, is also consistent with moving toward the Diné lifeway. It is worth reminding readers that although many scholars do not point out the role of water, they may wish to imply the role that this important sacred element plays in planning. These principles involve a daily process to benefit people in both short-term (daily) and more long-term planning. Yet another cycle for planning that is not depicted here involves long-term planning by the week, by the month, by the season, by the year, by stages of a human life (birth, adolescence, adulthood, elderhood), and so on.

A third aspect of Diné philosophy involves 'Iiná. 'Iiná might be translated as "life," but it has a much deeper and more complex meaning (Parsons-Yazzie et al. 2007, 275). 'Iiná is the process of carrying out one's plans (Cody 2009). In real life, in real time, humans need to breathe life into their plans and make them come alive. The totality of Figure 1.2 is literally 'Iináji, or the Diné lifeway. Breathing involves air or, perhaps, a method of exchanging oxygen for carbon dioxide. It is clear in the minds of many knowledge holders that breathing is the basis and perhaps the most immediately available empirical observation for the Diné lifeway. To live is to breathe, to do, and to carry out your ideas and plans. Individuals are supposed to literally live up to their plans and their thoughts that have given birth to their current day and life. Humans can also literally breathe life into their daily plans. This might be similar to "suscitation" (similar to resuscitation, but it is not necessary to restart a life if an individual is already alive).

The cycle is made complete in Diné philosophy via reflection (regeneration), or Sih Hasin. With regeneration comes sustainability, dormancy, and rebirth. Here lies the opportunity to look back on what a person has accomplished. People are instructed to think about what went well to be able to implement such a strategy again in similar situations. They are also instructed to mull over what went wrong. Mistakes offer reasons for modifying past plans. In other words, people recognize what actions were wrong so that they can have a better strategy in mind when encountering a similar situation. Sih Hasin allows for "deconstruction and adaptation from a different time" (Gorman-Keith 2004, 147). Within reflection comes regeneration and renewal. Figure 1.2 depicts the regenerative process briefly, tying the process to pollen. A person literally goes to sleep in order to wake at dawn and start the process again with a new spark. Within sleep and dormancy are the seeds or pollen to regenerate life again at the dawn. This process goes on for a lifetime. When it is carried out correctly, a human should grow from birth to adolescence, adolescence to adulthood, and adulthood to elderhood. Elders regenerate their teachings by instructing the youth.

Unfortunately, only limited examples have been published in dissertations and theses that are not widely available. One area that has yet to be fully explored involves the opening prayer shared in the Introduction. Remember that we are now trying to set the tone for a ceremony. If we have the correct conditions, and we all think about the same thing at the same time for just a few seconds, perhaps a miracle will occur (Wilson 2008, 69).

The most direct tie to the Diné lifeway is through the individual. In the Introduction, I close with the following principles of the Diné lifeway, which are worth repeating here:

> *Sistsijį Hózhǫ́*, or beauty in front of me
> *Shikishli Hózhǫ́*, or beauty behind me
> *Shiyaagi Hózhǫ́*, or beauty beneath me (Mother Earth)
> *Shik'igi Hózhǫ́*, or beauty from above me (Father Sky)
> *Shinaadę́ę́ Na Tso Hózhǫ́*, or beauty all around (across the horizon)
> *Shizéé'dee Hózhǫ́*, or speaking one's thoughts with beauty
> *Nanita Sa'ah Naaghai*
> *Nanita Bikeh Hozhoon*
> *Hózhǫ́ Nahasdlii*
> *Hózhǫ́ Nahasdlii*
> *Hózhǫ́ Nahasdlii*
> *Hózhǫ́ Nahasdlii*

These principles center the human within all of creation, as illustrated in Figure 1.2. Mother Earth is at one's feet and Father Sky above one's head. These principles should allow a person to approach the world with humbleness and respect for all of creation. *Sistsijį Hózhǫ́*, or beauty in front of me, asks the Holy Ones (*Diyin Dine'é*) to ensure positive encounters. For example, we can once again consider the Sacred Element of fire. You want enough fire to eat and stay warm, but not too much fire nor too little. *Shikishli Hózhǫ́*, or beauty behind me, involves remembering where a person has been in life so as to have a good example to follow. It is instructive to recall an instance when too much or too little fire disrupted a path toward beauty. Someone may have been burned or was uncomfortably cold. This is also a place to ensure that one leaves beauty behind when one has walked on to the next destination. This requires exercising care in handling fire. *Shiyaagi Hózhǫ́*, or beauty beneath me, seeks strength from the earth by acknowledging its life-giving abilities. From the earth come the basic elements to have fire. From the earth emerge all of the Four Sacred Elements. Humans ask for life-sustaining properties. Fire must be fed with elements from the earth. *Shik'igi Hózhǫ́*, or beauty from above me, recalls a relationship with Father Sky.

Individuals can and should acknowledge the gifts received from the sky, such as water and air. "Gifts from the sky" can be understood as part of the climatological process of water becoming a vapor, rising in the atmosphere to change into a liquid, and falling as rain. In other words, individuals should be thankful for things such as rain. Still, because the gifts are not permanent, and there is an ongoing need for more of these gifts in moderation, it is appropriate to ask for gifts to assist in one's plans—and then to acknowledge these gifts as being precious: they cannot be taken for granted. *Shinaadę́ę́ Na Tso Hózhǫ́*, beauty all around, is an acknowledgment and appreciation for everything in a person's environment. It is the basis for keeping a proper distance and nearness toward the Four Sacred Elements. This acknowledgment must be made in a sunwise direction so as to ensure continued balance in the process of planning. *Shinaadę́ę́ Na Tso Hózhǫ́* is applicable within the walls of the *hooghan* and within the bounds of the Six Sacred Mountains. It asks that all that is encountered be of a good nature. In other words, a person asks that the fire needed for a day be delivered based on the needs for the day. Completing the cycle, *Shizéé'dee Hózhǫ́*, or speaking thoughts with beauty, is a process in which an individual implores the *Diyin Diné'e* to provide a path where all of his or her words, thoughts, and actions reflect all aspects from *Sistsijį* to *Shizéé'dee* (Cody 2009; Gorman-Keith 2004, 28–29). This means that individuals should maintain thoughts of prosperity when they use fire for their daily life. Abusing fire will lead to no good either immediately or down the road.

Diné lifeway principles seem especially cogent for the governance problems currently faced by Navajo Nation. How can adaptation of what was traditionally useful to the Diné impact current and future policy? It appears *Diné Bitsáhákees* requires leaders to facilitate access to the Four Sacred Elements for all individuals. Reflecting on how the contemporary Diné might adapt their traditional governance institutions to fit contemporary problems could yield interesting results.

It is important to question the definition of contemporary Diné governance as simply referring to post-1922 councils. We must not assume that contemporary Diné governance was meant to meet the citizens' needs. Many Diné scholars correctly point to the post-1922 government as the point when heteropatriarchy took root in contemporary Diné governance. This is a clear negation of the gender equality and equity inherent in Diné philosophy. It might be useful to ask what purpose contemporary Diné governance was designed to carry out. Perhaps, normatively, the best answer might be that traditional Diné governance must facilitate access to the Four Sacred Elements.

In fact, it is timely to call everything related to Diné governance into question because research on Diné philosophy and its impact on governance has never before been conducted. This approach is akin to the organization of an introductory book on political science. Many Euro-American books on political science begin with the philosophical roots of European culture. An encyclopedia about the philosophical roots of Indigenous or Diné governance would probably take one hundred years to draft and would still leave out a great deal of information. Obviously, space here limits the discussion.

Western society benefits from its own cultural norm of writing down its philosophies. Indigenous cultures tend to retain such knowledge orally. This might be known as songs, prayers, Creation Accounts, and other specific words only used in certain settings and during certain seasons. Certainly, Diné traditional knowledge about governance and leadership is orally retained, and it is necessary to contemplate (and acknowledge) how academia currently lacks information about Diné political philosophy.

The author proposes that scholars rethink the definition of Diné political philosophy and focus on the Four Sacred Elements. It is time to dismiss the common assumption that European philosophy has a cultural monopoly on "Truth" with a capital T. Previous attempts by the United States to solve the "Indian Problem" for Navajo people has involved imposing a "Truth" about leadership. Rather, it is time to put Diné knowledge to work. Diné knowledge can be the frame that holds together a contemporary Diné governance philosophy. While no one individual "thinks" indigenously by virtue of his or her hereditary makeup, it still benefits those interested in solving social ills in Diné communities to explore critically what it means to rely on Diné philosophy of governance.

The specific language used to govern the Diné remains with elders or otherwise qualified knowledge holders. The knowledge meant to govern remains intact someplace in the sacred history, in *Diné Bikéyah*, or Navajo land, in the ceremonial cycle (*Naach'id*), and in specific words, phrases, and songs. In short, Diné Indigenous philosophy is likely the basis for traditional Diné governance. We will now briefly explore this intersection.

1.2. FOUR RE-CREATED CLANS—FOURTH WORLD CYCLE

A key concern for many non-Diné thinkers is that the holistic view of Diné philosophy is difficult to manage and navigate. How does a person know what aspect of the philosophy is appropriate for a given problem? While the answer to such a question is not readily available, Denny (2011) does provide some guidance on a general philosophy of governance based on Diné thinking. Figure 1.2 reflects a great deal of embedded information. Some of the information is what political theorists might call normative Diné theory. In other words, Figure 1.2 contains a great deal of information regarding the way government *should be* according to Diné philosophy. Expressing Diné philosophical ideas in English is difficult. The English language leaves readers with the impression that once they reach the end of an explanation (such as in this chapter), they have come to an end point in the philosophy itself. Hence, it is useful to remind ourselves that Diné governance philosophy is not linear. It is a cyclical pathway. As mentioned before, the Four Sacred Elements are crucial not only to daily living but also throughout a lifetime. Since the Four Sacred Elements move constantly, individuals must also move daily throughout their lives. In other words, there is no way to *finally* capture all the fire a person needs—even after years of labor. The cyclical process requires repetition as a mechanism for system maintenance. Without maintenance, or continued adherence to the process, human-based government could descend into chaos, just as fire can burn everything to the ground. Like all Diné philosophy, the notion of how Diné governance *should be* originates from Diné Creation Accounts. We will focus on these stories in terms of how they discuss access to the Four Sacred Elements.

The story of normative Diné governance is not a tale of linear history. When non-Diné cultures tell their stories of how government ought to be, they do not rely on a history of intellectual thought alone. Rather, they rely on their intellectual predecessors. For European philosophical thought, these are individuals such as Socrates, Machiavelli, Locke, Habermas, and others. All philosophies of normative governance are replete with inductive and deductive reasoning even if the distinction is sometimes not readily apparent. Unfortunately, no Indigenous philosophy has ever been treated as a true normative philosophy with all the nuances, sophistication, trappings, and characteristics that have been afforded philosophies of other (especially European) cultures.

Compounding this omission is the cultural prescription that Diné philosophers (such as medicine people) not claim personal credit for traditional knowledge. No humans created the knowledge carried today. The Holy Ones created the songs, the prayers, the ceremonies, and the specific words. Only certain special humans have been able to learn these protocols and pass them along since time immemorial. Many are wise to acknowledge how this practice leaves doubt about the source of information. Still, Western intellectual thought calls the very legitimacy of such information into question (Smith 1999). Concerns about the legitimacy of Diné knowledge are distracting. The legitimacy of any knowledge must be measured using a metric created by the culture being assessed. One remarkable quality of Diné knowledge is its consistency. For millennia, *Hataałii* (medicine people) have been able to consistently deduce conclusions based on their traditional knowledge. One concrete example is that the Diné are still here today. They have not burned themselves out of existence! They managed to maintain their proper distance and nearness toward the Four Sacred Elements. Who are Western scholars to judge such consistency as less than legitimate? These issues are just a few of the concerns that must be acknowledged before exploring normative Diné philosophy.

What follows is a superficial and truncated account of Diné creation. This knowledge can also stand on its own as legitimate Indigenous creationism. Exploring some tenets of Diné philosophy will give readers a better understanding of Diné leadership and governance within the context of the emergence, or *Hajíneí*—how a society can organize protocols for managing a relationship with the Four Sacred Elements.

Long ago, the Four Clans were re-created at the beginning of the fourth world. These clans are, according to some versions of the Creation Accounts, called *Kinyaa'áanii, Tó'áhaní, Tódich'iinii,* and *Hashtł'ishnii.* (Some accounts say these are not the original clans, but the debates are not relevant here.) The clan system is currently used to organize people along varying levels of responsibility. During an introduction to a relative one has never met, both individuals will share their four clans. Some times, the individuals will discover that they share a clan. When the common clan is discovered, a relationship is also discovered. Relationships imply responsibility and obligation. Again, this relationship has always existed since time immemorial and at least since the clans were re-created. For the purposes of this book, it is best merely to know that clan responsibilities involve ensuring that one's relatives have adequate supplies and access to the Four Sacred Elements. No one individual or family should have the opportunity to monopolize access to the Four Sacred Elements. Clan relations work to offset monopolization. When the Four Clans were re-created, the people (Diné) were instructed to live within the bounds of the Sacred Mountains. Figure I.2 is a two-dimensional representation of the Sacred Mountains. At first, there were only Four Sacred Mountains. Later, two more mountains were added to furnish humans (*bíla' 'ashdla'*) with the *Dził Łeezh*[3] necessary to govern themselves properly. All of these occurrences set the stage for managing a human relationship with the Four Sacred Elements.

In 2011, during a lecture he delivered at Northern Arizona University, Denny discussed the manner in which humans should approach questions of governance according to Diné philosophy. Denny's comments involved a series of inductive decisions.[4] The pathway, beginning with *Sisnaajiní* (Mount Blanca), was the course followed by the Holy Ones, said Denny. He surmised that since the path of the Holy Ones is not meant for humans, it did not make sense for humans to attempt to duplicate such a pathway for the purposes of domestic Navajo governance. Put another way, humans are tasked with maintaining their proper distance and nearness toward the Four Sacred Elements and not with re-creating clans. Rather, Denny suggested that contemporary domestic Diné governance should follow a path outlined by the history of the Four Clans and their re-creation. In short, the path should begin at home. The path should begin with the Four Sacred Elements and start to build from there.

Within each of the Four Sacred Mountains is the essence of *Diné Nitsáhákees*. We can follow each mountain and its inherent *Dził Łeezh* through the process of *Diné Nitsáhákees*. We can start with *Sisnaajiní* (Mount Blanca), like the Holy Ones did long ago, or, as Denny suggested, we can begin with the *Dził Łeezh* inherent in *Dookʼoʼoosłiid* (San Francisco Peaks).

Notice how Figure 1.3 indicates that the cycle for *Diné Nitsáhákees* begins with the eastern slope. Also notice that embedded within Figure 1.3

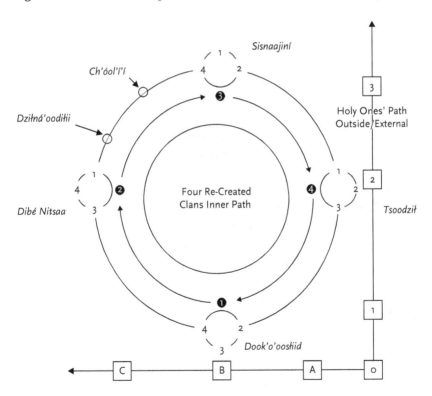

Readers may utilize figure 1.3 in the same fashion you would a map. By cross referencing the scales on the right and bottom, readers can join the intersecting letters and numbers to locate a specific location on a sacred mountain

Figure 1.3: Close-Up of Process for Normative Diné Governance

is a less obvious cycle. The Four Re-Created Clans have clear instructions in this diagram, but the instructions are subtle. We can see an eastern slope of *Dook'o'oosłiid* demarcated with the numeral D1. But less obvious is a southern slope of *Dibé Nitsaa* (Mount Hesperus) demarcated with the numeral N2. This position represented by numeral N2 highlights at least two ideas. It represents the *Nahat'á* (planning) stage of thinking involving the *Dził Łeezh* inherent in *Dibé Nitsaa*. The southern slope also represents the *Nahat'á* stage of the path followed by the Re-Created Clans. This inner circle pathway continues on to the western slope of *Sisnaajiní* (Mount Blanca) and completes one cycle on the northern slope of *Tsoodził* (Mount Taylor).

Here it must be reiterated that once the cycle is completed, the story does not end. The process of governance must be continually worked through or it will no longer function. For good governance to have a long and sustainable life filled with wisdom, the humans must breathe life into their own future institutions.

1.2.1. *Sisnaajiní—Nitsáhákees dóó Kó'*

Following the *Dził Łeezh* traits inherent in each of the Four Sacred Mountains is the recommended pathway by which the Diné of yesterday and today can and should govern themselves. The *hooghan* associated with the east and *Sisnaajiní* is Mount Blanca, which is called the *sodizin hooghan*. This is the origin of *Diné Nitsáhákees*. It is the spark or idea that started it all. Some have linked this spark or idea to the sunrise light (*'adinídíín*) as it shines in through the eastern-facing *hooghan* door. The process for governance in terms of *Nitsáhákees*, or thinking, involves a point of beginning or perhaps renewal. Here an individual can begin to understand the components necessary for an ideal home. This is also the place to look for the birth of new knowledge. Such new knowledge may be new to the individual or it could be new to the world, but it may be difficult to measure which is which. The *sodizin hooghan* is also the place for ceremonial and spiritual renewal and beginnings. *Sodizin hooghan* is ideal for beginning the process of governance. The *Dził Łeezh* inherent in *Sisnaajiní* possesses the tools needed for individuals to think about future governance ideas. *Sisnaajiní Dził Łeezh* is associated with beauty way, or *Hózhǫ́ǫ́jí*. This is a multifaceted approach.

Diné philosophy of governance requires that an individual explicitly think not only of yesterday (*Tzoodził*) but also of today (*Dook'o'oosłiid*) and tomorrow (*Dibé Nitsaa*). A person may interpret yesterday, today, and tomorrow literally or metaphorically. In other words, longer increments of time can be encompassed in these terms. An individual may look to last year or to the last decade or century, or he or she could look forward to another year, decade, or century. In thinking of future policy, a person must again follow the pattern of thinking (*Nitsáhákees*), planning (*Nahat'á*), living (*'Iiná*), and regeneration (*Sih Hasin*). Ideally, readers by now should be able to see all of these nested cycles within Figure I.1 (see page 12) even though the labels are not explicitly typed. Here, an individual can utilize the *Dził Łeezh* to consider the future of specific policies and government functions based on the current and future conditions being experienced. In *Sisnaajiní* a person can find the answers to questions that have yet to appear or to impact the population. By utilizing *sodizin hooghan*, individuals with well-attuned abilities (perhaps medicine people or knowledge holders) are able to foretell events for the benefit of the whole community.

1.2.2. Tsoodził—Naha'tá dóó Tó

To the south and associated with water is *Tsoodził* (Mount Blanca). For the spark to take off, it needs water and moisture. Its *Dził Łeezh* contains its own special attributes. *Nahat'á* literally means planning. Here we can find use for contemporary governance in terms of creating plans for current and future problems. The attributes in the *Dził Łeezh* contain the necessary elements for the ideal child. Here an individual will find the lessons needed for and the problems associated with raising a child properly. For example, the first laugh and the first walk are found here. The child is gaining abilities that will serve him or her for life. Greater amounts of forethought are needed to ensure the child's long life. Here, again, the function inherent in the *Dził Łeezh* can follow the pathway of thinking, planning, living out, and reflecting on specific plans.

1.2.3. Dook'o'oosłiid—'liná dóó Niłchí

It is worth mentioning that the following paragraphs could, again, also be illustrated in similar fashion as was done with Figure I.1. This is more evidence that the nesting of cycles within cycles is seemingly infinite. The various inherent traits are represented by the different *hooghans* associated with each of the Four Sacred Mountains. As Denny (2011) explained, an individual must start with *Dook'o'oosłiid* (San Francisco Peaks) and *'Iiná* (living the plan) for a number of reasons. We may interpret this to be consistent with a Diné lifeway. Understood simply, *'Iiná* is not possible without the Four Sacred Elements *Kǫ́*, *Tó*, *Nítch'i*, and *Naahadzaan or Tadidiin* (fire, water, air, and earth or pollen). The Four Sacred Elements are the basic building blocks of life. They each contribute to negating the seven monsters, or *Yei'ii Tsoh* (hunger, thirst, lice, indolent poverty, sleep, old age, and death), allowed to live (Benally 2006, 14). For example, fire can be used to resolve hunger issues. Yet the most cogent interpretation of the Four Sacred Elements is that each can give life, and each can take life away (Cody 2009).

The key to preserving life is to maintain the proper distance from the Four Sacred Elements. *'Iiná hooghan*, or the lifeway hogan, is illustrated in Figure 1.3 at *Dook'o'oosłiid*. The lifeway hogan is a very important tool for maintaining a proper distance and nearness toward the Four Sacred Elements. The way *'Iiná hooghan* is managed could be considered a metaphor for life within the Six Sacred Mountains. That said, many knowledge holders carry out their lives in this way today. For some, there is no metaphor. Figure I.3, the *'Iiná hooghan*, explains that the Six Sacred Mountains are representative of how a person should live life within the *'Iiná hooghan*. Within the *'Iiná hooghan* are four posts that represent the Four Sacred Mountains. The posts follow the same pattern laid out by the Four Sacred Mountains: *Sisnaajiní* for an eastern post, *Tsoodził* for a southern post, *Dook'o'oosłiid* for a western post, and *Dibé Nitsaa* for a northern post. The entry way for *'Iiná hooghan* represents *Dziłná Oodiłii*. Diné were given this mountain as a way to enter and exit their home. The sixth mountain, *Ch'óol'í'í*, represents the chimney. This mountain was given to the Diné so they could cook, keep themselves warm, and release exhaust smoke from their homes. Again, boiling things down to the daily life routine may be helpful. Operating from the *hooghan* on the basis of maintaining a proper relationship with the Four Sacred Elements is key.

Within the *'Iiná hooghan*, an individual is experiencing life as it happens. Fire, water, air, and pollen are operating in tandem by the second, minute, hour, and day. A person can look back to see what has been planned. How have fire, water, air, and pollen been accessed, gauged, and assessed? Is there too much or too little of any element? A person can look forward to see what may come around the corner by monitoring abundance and deficiencies in any of the Four Sacred Elements today. A person can question whether past plans remain relevant for life today. A person can look to the future to see if current life is in need of change as new obstacles emerge. As stated before, life begins in the home. What is in the home?

Being an ideal parent is a prerequisite for being a leader. Denny (2011) explained that within the *'Iiná hooghan*, which is connected to *Dook'o'oosłiid*, or San Francisco Peaks, a person will find the embodiment of the ideal parent and adult: someone who exhibits exceptional leadership qualities at home. If an individual cannot successfully manage his or her home, then there is really no point in that person trying to lead the community. So the community notices if an individual, of either gender, maintains a good distance and nearness toward the Four Sacred Elements. The *'Iiná hooghan* is literally where an individual lives his or her life; it is where the Diné people make a good life for themselves, their spouses, and their children. It is where a good relationship with the Four Sacred Elements thrives. An ideal parent has experienced birth and childrearing firsthand.

If an individual is called upon to lead the community, that person should do so willingly. Individuals are expected to have full understanding that there is more to the leadership role than merely the perks of the job. Indeed, heavy lifting is required of individuals through obligations to the community via *K'é*, or clan relationship, and *K'éí*, or descent (Austin 2009, 92–94, 153–156). The *'Iiná hooghan (Dook'o'oosłiid)* is utilized by the Diné as a home. Each area of the *'Iiná hooghan* is dedicated to specific uses during a day (and simultaneously during a lifetime). Things are kept orderly. Ideally, an individual will visit a specific area of the *'Iiná hooghan* each day. At the conclusion of a daily cycle, that individual will have visited all areas of the *'Iiná hooghan*. The consequences of not visiting all areas within a single day may imply an imbalance. For example, if an individual does not visit the eating area of the *hooghan*, that person will implicitly be starving himself or herself, and this is going to lead to a period of imbalance. (In common-sense terms, if you don't eat, you get hungry!) It could also mean that the individual has failed as a parent to feed his or her children. If there is nothing to cook, it may be because activities outside of the *hooghan* have not yielded any food. In the simplest of terms, without fire, there cannot be cooked food. Alternatively, an individual may have food but have failed to cook it. People carry out their lives based on plans (*nahat'á*) and thinking (*nitsáhákees*) in the *hooghan*.

1.2.4. *Dibé Nitsaa—Sih Hasin dóó Tadidiin*

Completing the process, but not actually stopping, requires a bit of an adjustment in thought for some accustomed to an end point. Hence, I introduce the "final" stage of the process known as *Sih Hasin*. The *hooghan* associated with *Dibé Nitsaa* (Mount Hesperus) and *Sih Hasin* is called the *Tách'ééh*, or sweat lodge *hooghan*. It is closely associated with *Tadidiin*, or pollen. The spiritual realm of Diné existence is here. There is a male and female *Tách'ééh hooghan*. A back story excluded here explains how the Diné population, in general, but not universally, utilizes the female *hooghan* for spiritual needs. The embodiment of the spiritual child resides within the *Tách'ééh hooghan*. Just as with pollen, it is a space for regeneration and renewal at various levels. Within *Tách'ééh hooghan* are the necessary conditions for an individual's spiritual health and well-being through regeneration. The *Tách'ééh hooghan* is a place for spiritual development throughout life. Spiritual truths are revealed (logical inductions), and logical deductions based on previous learning can be confirmed, disproven, or otherwise refined. A person will learn faith in aspects of life he or she may not be capable of observing within the *Tách'ééh hooghan*. The attributes of *Tách'ééh hooghan* work in ways that not all individuals will be able to understand. As with the other *hooghans*, *Tách'ééh hooghan* attributes are contained in *Dził Łeezh*.

The *Dził Łeezh* of songs and prayers are stored in *Dibé Nitsaa*. Perhaps this is the spiritual pollen of the people for regeneration. Such a *Dził Łeezh* bundle is associated with the protection way, or *Hashkéjí*. Not all individuals are equipped to bear the responsibility inherent in carrying certain aspects of Diné knowledge. To understand or carry such knowledge of specific songs and prayers may (and, more likely than not, does) require the carrier to utilize such knowledge for the well-being of others. Carrying Diné knowledge can be an onerous task. Such responsibility is inherent in the *K'é* relationship (Austin 2009, 92–94).

Within *Tách'ééh hooghan* an individual can reflect on life and his or her actions. Did that person behave correctly? If so, is the past behavior still warranted? If not, what should the new course of action be? If that person behaved incorrectly, what will be done to resolve the imbalance in the future? Such considerations are the embodiment of *Sih Hasin*. Once again, reflecting on ideas or concerns is not the end of the process. The regenerative process has no ending point even beyond life. A person must go back to the first step or the potential for chaos is likely.

Collectively, it is possible to interpret all of the above by referencing Figure 1.3, a close-up version of Figure I.2 with a reference grid on the margins. Denny (2011) has made an inductive leap, but the deductive consequences still make sense. First, a person begins to the west at *Dook'o'oosłiid* (San Francisco Peaks), as it is a good place to begin a process for thinking about everyday life. This location can be found by looking at 1B in Figure 1.3. A person can think about life as it is today, how it was yesterday, how he or she would like to see it tomorrow, and how that person's spiritual side interprets all three aspects of life. Then, the individual can move forward to the north and *Dibé Nitsaa* (Mount Hesperus), or 2C. The spiritual aspects of a person's current life, past events, and future events require reflection. An individual reflects to discover what truly works well, what needs adjustment, and what needs to be abandoned—all with consideration toward what the future may hold. People can ponder, plan, live with, and reflect on current living situations from a spiritual point of view.

Once a better direction on a spiritual level is located, moving to *Sisnaajiní* (Mount Blanca), located at 3B, is next. Here an individual thinks about how to implement spiritual lessons in a less abstract (more concrete) way. A person may ponder, plan, live with, and reflect on the birth of new ideas. Here it is possible to begin to exercise what social scientists might call counterfactual analysis, meaning readers may imagine an alternate reality (Brady and Collier 2004; Griffin 1993; Roese and Olson 2014; Tetlock and Belkin 1996). A person can imagine a future in which a certain policy change occurs. What will the consequences be? Will there be too much damage? Will changes reflect the needs of the people? Will changes be practical? Will the benefits of a policy serve an elite few? An individual can think, plan, live out, and reflect without ever doing anything that harms people. The place for imagination with purpose is here.

Finally, an individual can move to *Tsoodził* (Mount Taylor) at 2A and consider the plans that have been made at the previous stage. Serious consideration about how to implement policy takes place here in terms of thinking, planning, living out, and reflecting (regenerating) on consequences. With a well-articulated plan, a person can then live with that plan in the here and now (life). Inherent in the process is cyclical repetition (regeneration) in which one lives with current and future plans simultaneously.

1.3. NORMATIVE PHILOSOPHY BEGINS AT HOME

The philosophical roots of Diné thinking have been introduced in very basic terms and in terms of a policymaking approach. More specifically, they have been introduced in terms of the Four Sacred Elements. Recognizing these limits is crucial because they are quite debilitating to the philosophy itself. The main issue, which probably cannot be resolved here, is how to connect a very abstract philosophy to very real problems. It is hoped that thinking about *Diné Bitsáhákees* in terms of the Four Sacred Elements helps bring abstract ideas to the ground (earthly) level. Some examples based in real life may help illuminate the philosophy further. Examples are too numerous to comprehensively list. Instead, consider applications to corn, uranium, and each element as a common-pool resource.

Cornstalk philosophy might also make these tenets of Diné philosophy clearer. The life cycle of corn follows a trajectory first articulated here in concert with the dawn. There was a spark or idea or maybe even a lightning strike pointing out an origin for a single, nonspecific, first cornstalk. While color can be a major indicator in Diné philosophy, we can limit our understanding to white corn and leave it be. A human will take a poker stick (*gish*) and poke a hole in the ground. The hole is filled with corn pollen. The hole is then covered with dirt. This is a cycle within a cycle. In the pollen we can find all the necessary conditions for a fully mature cornstalk. However, it's just corn pollen—a powdery yellowish-white substance. Embedded in the pollen is the very DNA of a cornstalk. This DNA is the plan for that cornstalk life cycle. It has within itself regenerative qualities to produce another generation of corn. It begins with a root. That root will burrow into the earth and search for the Sacred Elements. Perhaps it began with a thought (fire) from a human planting the pollen. Still, the corn needs sunlight to spark its life. The roots will form and search for the other elements. The corn will search for water and carbon dioxide and will eventually mature into a cornstalk that provides more pollen. The roots will do their best to avoid too much or too little spark. The corn will need sunlight for photosynthesis to occur. It will need darkness to grow. Too much water will drown the corn. Too little will dehydrate it. Too much wind could blow it down. Too little carbon dioxide will limit or stop the corn ears' budding. The ancient humans and the contemporary knowledge holders know these simple facts of life.

Then again, life is not so "simple" anymore. One of the more contemporary issues faced by Navajo Nation involves the hundreds of abandoned uranium mines on the Navajo homeland. Many of the knowledge holders have offered interpretations of uranium as a monster put down by the Hero Twins. This part of the Diné Creation Account has not been discussed in this book but can be explored elsewhere (Benally 2006). Other accounts suggest that the monsters roaming the earth made life for humans very difficult. The Hero Twins, named Born for Water and Monster Slayer, learned protection songs, protection prayers, and protection methods from their father the sun. They used their father's methods to eliminate the monsters. Readers should recall the previously mentioned seven monsters allowed to live. Perhaps, the knowledge holders theorize, one of these monsters not allowed to live was uranium. Uranium was once buried within Mother Earth. She contained this monster after the Hero Twins put it and the others down. In this sense, uranium has been deprived of air, one of the Four Sacred Elements. The Holy Ones' warned the humans never to dig up the bodies of the monsters again. If they violated this edict, they would again suffer the harm of the monster. The knowledge holders surmise that uranium was dug up in violation of the Holy Ones warning and is now roaming the earth again. This is an enormous problem without a current solution. Still, it is very simple. Uranium, deprived of air, cannot harm. It is just another example of applying Diné philosophy to a contemporary problem. Still, these applications can be put even more simply.

That fire, water, air, and earth/pollen are here and now is without question. Yet every home in Navajo Nation does not always have access to these Sacred Elements. Not every home has fire in the winter. Not every home has electricity (fire or spark). Still, policymakers have failed to bring these utilities to all citizens who want them. Even more problematic, there are stories of families that do receive electrical service but do not want it. One should not assume a family without electricity is somehow deprived. The same is true of running water. Policymakers continue to fail at protecting water from environmental contamination. In 2015, the Animas River was inundated with gold-mining contaminants. Some reports state that up to 3 million gallons of polluted water broke free. Many Diné farmers remain very concerned (Laylin 2015). On the subject of air, we may look at this in terms of contemporary air quality. Diné citizens remain exposed to many unknown environmental pollutants in their air. Yet another monster released to the surface? Earth/pollen is the foundation for all of these calamities to coalesce into a damaged environment. Avery Denny typically responds to questions with a simple answer, "It's already there." Your questions are already in place and your answers are already in place too. Nearly every, or perhaps all, of the world's and Navajo Nation's problems boil down to this: something is out of balance; something or someone is too close to or too far away from at least one of the Four Sacred Elements. The challenges only seem daunting because the imbalance has been allowed to continue unabated for a century or more.

There are several research questions that can help us explore what traditional institutions of Diné governance offer to understanding challenges faced by Navajo Nation today and tomorrow. These include:

(1a) Does Diné governance need reform? Do the Diné people have a good relationship with the Four Sacred Elements?

(1b) Is there a lack of cohesion between pre-1923 and post-1923 governance approaches?

(1c) Do these two styles of governance need reconciliation?

(1d) Does either a pre-1923 or post-1923 government function better at maintaining a proper human relationship with the Four Sacred Elements?

(2)   What components make up traditional and contemporary Diné governance?

(3a) Should Diné governance step toward formalizing international ties with nations other than the United States?

(3b) If so, how?

(4)   What would a contemporary Diné governance structure look like?

(5)   Could future plans integrate traditional governance norms and existing governance institutions in the way that the peacemaker courts have done?

These questions are incredibly broad, but they must be addressed. The question of governance touches on a vast section of Diné philosophy. By looking at these questions one step at a time, the scope of this research will be more manageable.

Some knowledge holders believe the framework for normative Diné governance follows the process outlined in this chapter. Yet much debate surrounds the various interpretations of such a complex process. There is room for many facets of Diné philosophy to coexist alongside other interpretations. Many interested individuals respect the diversity of Diné philosophy, while others criticize what appears to be a lack of coherence (Austin 2009, 58–59). In the end, the goal of this book is to visit (or revisit) one potential interpretation. Rather than debate about who is correct, it is more productive to focus on the inductive and deductive decisions that have been described. Are the deductions logical? Do they fit the current problems of the Diné? It is not easy to come up with an answer. But one way of exploring the issues raised here would be to revisit the history of Diné governance in a timeline fashion. Could reflecting on the history of Diné governance with the normative philosophy of the Diné in mind better explain what happened in the past? In other words, did colonial interaction disrupt Diné access to the Four Sacred Elements? Some knowledge holders say yes. Most have yet to even ask the question.

CHAPTER 2

Tsoodził (Mount Taylor)

Interrupted Planning in the History of Diné Governance

Figure 2.1 continues the theme of following Diné thinking. Interaction with colonial actors may be understood as a moment when many Indigenous peoples, particularly Diné, experienced tremendous pressure to reinvent themselves. These new methods of living, probably too numerous to list, wound up in Diné thinking, Diné planning, and Diné life, causing immense disruption.

What follows here is a truncated history of Diné governance. The purpose of this history of Diné leadership is to focus on how recent events (in the period of interaction between colonial actors and the Diné) have impacted accessibility to the Four Sacred Elements. Note that there are some gaps involving the period between 1868 and 1923. Attempts have been made to fill non-Native history gaps with Diné accounts of their own history. Wherever possible, the Diné accounts are placed within a time frame.

The focus of this chapter is to better understand Diné thinking through the interpretation of Diné Creation Accounts, Diné interaction with colonial actors, Diné interaction with resource-extraction corporations, and the Diné need to eventually regain control of their sovereignty. All of these concerns can be boiled down to access to the Four Sacred Elements. Since Western perceptions of important historical events largely determine the content of existing archives, there are minimal referential ties to Diné philosophy and geography in this chapter.

The first section looks at the traditional stories involving *Naat'áanii* and their obligation to their people and their creator. A detailed account

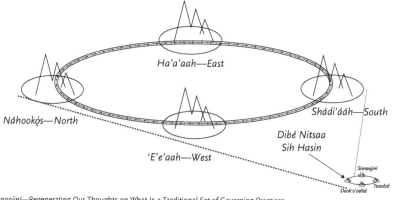

Ha'a'aah—East

Náhookǫs—North

Shádi'ááh—South

Dibé Nitsaa
Sih Hasin

'E'e'aah—West

Sisnaajiní
Tsoodził
Dook'o'osłííd

1. *Sisnaajiní*—Regenerating Our Thoughts on What Is a Traditional Set of Governing Practices
2. *Tsoodził*—Regenerating Our Plans, Learning How to Break Treaties
3. *Dook'o'osłííd*—Regenerating Our Lives with Settler Colonialism
4. *Dibé Nitsaa*—Regenerating Ourselves and Trying to Leave a Future for the Next Generation—Seeds of Modern Government

Figure 2.1: Regenerated Life Interrupted—Interaction with Colonial Actors

of these stories can be found in AnCita Benally's dissertation (2006). The brief account here is intended to simply set the context for looking at the research questions. These stories should be understood from the perspective of securing proper distance or nearness toward the Four Sacred Elements, or, alternatively, of maintaining a good and proper relationship to the Four Sacred Elements. This relationship is a Diné precept.

One might call what follows a timeline-style history of Diné governance. As is widely known, colonial actors began encroaching on Diné land when they arrived, forcing Diné leaders to change their way of life and style of leadership. Unfortunately, this interaction disrupted Diné access to the Four Sacred Elements. To gain insight into Diné leadership, this chapter will look at treaty negotiations. The treaty record will be supplemented with accounts and oral narratives of the same time period. The intention here is to see how Diné thinking permeated the colonial actor interaction period and to understand how European philosophies of war and peace are inconsistent with Diné thinking (and vice versa). The interaction period had a major impact on how Diné leaders facilitated their people's access to the Four Sacred Elements.

The primary documents, made up mostly of treaties, letters, and negotiation notes, suggest that a meeting of the minds rarely took place between Diné leaders and colonial actors. In fact, colonial actors failed to show much respect to the Diné leaders. Even after the last treaty between the two entities commenced (during the underinvestigated period between 1868 and 1923), the Diné philosophy of leadership was once again at work. But it is worth noting that there was a concerted effort to stop international interaction, as reflected by the ending of the *Naach'id* after the return from the Long Walk.[1] The 1868–1923 period is also notable because a great deal of the pre-1868 Diné leadership was replaced by Navajos handpicked by the United States. This period was followed by the introduction of corporate interests and the Business Councils. The quickly changing and seemingly haphazard institutions, which survive in modified form today, mark a deviation from traditional notions of Diné governance and leadership. Each of these phases of Diné governance can be discussed in terms of how it impacted the people's access to the Four Sacred Elements. Therefore, there is a need to revisit Diné history to ask, again, what impact Diné governance philosophy might have on contemporary governance.

2.1. TRADITIONAL DINÉ GOVERNANCE—REGENERATING COLONIAL ACTOR THINKING

Indigenous political philosophy is the driving force behind any accurate scholarly work on pre-Colombian Indigenous governance. Some prominent research on Indigenous philosophy includes Deloria 1973, 1979, 1988, 1997, 2006; Holm 1989; and Holm, Pearson, and Chavis 2003. However, the lack of dialogue about what constitutes Indigenous political philosophy is the major shortcoming of almost every publication on Indigenous governance (Blackhawk 2006; Wilkins 2003). There are many reasons why the dialogue about Indigenous political philosophy is hindered. In part, it is because it adheres to strict disciplinary lines. This chapter will span multiple disciplines, drawing on academic research written by historians, political scientists, lawyers, and linguists. At the risk of being "too general," there is at least one method of "essentializing" what it means to be Indigenous and what it means to be Diné. The notion of thinking in three dimensions simultaneously about a ceremonial cycle, place territory, specific language, and sacred history may be all that is required to think Indigenously (Lerma 2008, 2012, 2014a; Holm 1989; Holm, Pearson, and Chavis 2003). In fact, any group of individuals who collectively think along these lines can be defined as "a people." Germans, Italians, and Arabs (among many others) all have their roots in a ceremony, a place, a language, and a history (Deloria 1997). Intersecting the idea of peoplehood with specific Indigenous peoples through the concept-building approach can create quite robust findings so long as focus is carefully maintained (Sartori 1970; Goertz 2006). Readers are reminded of the discussion of Diné peoplehood in the Introduction as it relates to the Four Sacred Elements as well as how these elements all relate to Diné language, history, ceremony, and place.

The commonly recounted story of Diné governance starts with the first interactions between colonial actors and the Diné. Spanish, Mexican, and American treaties all hint at a history of confusion as European colonists attempted to rid themselves of the Diné by means of European-style warfare. When European warfare failed, treaties were made with whomever the Europeans assumed (by virtue of willful blindness or ignorance) were Diné representatives under a European-style notion of nationhood. This led to confusion: the Diné functioned neither hierarchically in the way a European state functions nor through the coercive enforcement of guidelines outlined in treaties (Deloria and DeMallie 1999, 70–71).

On the surface, it appears that the Diné did not have a government that extended beyond the limits of what some call a "natural community." In other words, they were considered a "local band" only large enough to live in a region defined by geographic barriers (Wilkins 2003, 68). Evidence to support the "local band" theory is consistent with the trail of broken treaties between the Diné and colonial actors. Examining one treaty negotiation highlights the confusion and ulterior motives that were at play.

The first treaty ratified by the United States is representative of the endemic problems referenced above. The treaty of 1849 led to problems because the Diné signatories, Mariano Martinez and Chapitone, were minor headmen from regions unknown to scholars today. Evidence suggests that they were selected to sign on behalf of the Diné because Narbonna, a major leader (a *Hózhǫ́ǫ́jí Naat'áanii*), had recently been killed. (Narbonna's assassination is discussed in more detail later.) In the wake of Narbonna's passing, other major *Naat'áanii* linked to Manuelito refused to participate in the negotiations (Wilkins 2003, 74). Hence, the legitimacy of the treaty must be called into question. Nonetheless, the treaty language regards the Diné signatories as representatives of Navajo Nation:

> The following acknowledgements, declarations, and stipulations, have been duly considered, and are now solemnly adopted and proclaimed by the undersigned: . . . Mariano Martinez, Head Chief, and Chapitone, second Chief, on the part of the Navajo tribe of Indians. (Wilkins 2003, 225; Deloria and DeMallie 1999)

Not surprisingly, problems emerged when differing bands of the Diné did not agree to the terms of this treaty. Second, some bands may have been unaware that a treaty was being signed between *themselves* and the United

States. How could these bands have been legitimately expected to agree to the treaty terms or to comply with them? Another interpretation may also explain noncompliance. That some bands were merely aware of a treaty signed by minor members of a group of people who might share linguistic and geographic traits is a questionable premise upon which to base a nation-to-nation treaty agreement. This example is offered to make a larger point about the inability and/or unwillingness, for whatever reason, of colonial actors to truly understand traditional Diné governance. If colonial actors fail to understand Diné philosophy, there is no way to acknowledge the importance it places on properly engaging with the Four Sacred Elements.

While it may seem odd to discuss the history of the Diné out of chronological order, the reason for organizing the history this way is to put the myth of Diné history on the table only to dispel it or at least call it into question. A seminal discourse on Diné leadership philosophy is contained in Benally's 2006 dissertation entitled *"Diné Binnahat'a,* Navajo Government." This work offers a detailed account of the link between Diné Creation Accounts and the impact thereof on leadership qualities. The scope of this book limits the discussion to key points. For example, the word *"Naat'ááhjí"* is used to describe the leadership way (Benally 2006, 1). *Naat'ááhjí* literally means that an individual is going toward leadership, but it is probably best understood as a path that an individual takes to become a traditional Diné leader. *Naat'ááhjí* also means following a path that allows for an equal and equitable relationship with the Four Sacred Elements for all. Because there are various levels of Diné leadership, it is unclear which level actually applies to governance (1). Regardless, the Diné word for leader is *Naat'áanii,* or "one who speaks or orates and moves his [or her] head about" (1). No clear distinction is drawn between a leader who governs versus a leader who performs other tasks. Yet within the story of *Naat'ááhjí* there are the philosophical roots of traditional Diné governance:

> The position of *Naat'áanii* was so basic to the beginnings of the earth-surface people that sacred narrative cannot be told without their presence. To assure the survival of those beings who would eventually progress to *Nihóókáá' Din'é'é Bíla'ashdla'ii*—the Five-Fingered, Earth-Surface People, order was necessary. Humanity was not meant to exist in chaos and disorder so the role of *Naat'áanii,* leaders, was instituted. (Benally 2006, 2)

There probably is no simpler example of *Naat'ááhjí* in practice than an individual's responsibility to maintain a proper relationship with the Four

Sacred Elements not only in an individual and family context but also for a community. This Diné philosophy of governance was revered by all Diné at least up until the time of interaction with Europeans. The story of traditional Diné governance is founded in "exceptional" leadership qualities of particular individuals. An "exceptional" leader is one who can consistently guide his or her people toward a good and proper relationship with the Four Sacred Elements.

Accounts of the origin of Diné leadership discuss how certain individuals were appointed to lead the community. The first Diné leaders were the Holy Ones (Benally 2006, 3), or *Diyin Dine'é*. The knowledge bestowed upon the Holy Ones are the teachings used to train *Naat'áanii*. Today, these teachings are called Navajo Common Law (4). They appear to outline a protocol for a proper relationship with the Four Sacred Elements. Several existences or "worlds" were traversed before the *Hajinéí*, or the emergence of the five-fingered people onto the earth.

The five-fingered people were led by First Man and First Woman, and their rank was equal and complementary (Benally 2006, 5). It appears that, in tandem, First Man and First Woman properly maintained a good relationship with the Four Sacred Elements for a time. The story concludes that women leaders will continue to lead, and that men will carry out the decisions as complementary equals (9). In other words, women were tasked with acknowledging imbalance in the day-to-day proximity of the family to the Four Sacred Elements. A woman would typically assess the situation from the vantage point of the *hooghan*, or home. Daily assessment of proximity to the Four Sacred Elements meant that sometimes a male would be instructed to go outside of the *hooghan* to obtain what was needed to maintain the proper proximity. Again, this daily routine led to a good day and culminated in a good life—also known as *Sa'ah Naaghái Bik'eh Hózhóón*. This aspect of complementary halves might better be understood as *Ałch'į' Sila* (Cody 2009).

The story continues, describing the increasingly more difficult tasks that humans encountered—always in connection with maintaining a proper relationship with the Four Sacred Elements. Through it all, Diné leadership philosophy always guided the community to the correct answers to avoid chaos (Benally 2006, 10). In this way, balance and harmony became the preferred way to maintain human society. Hence, the proper relationship to the Four Sacred Elements has always been regulated by the proper nearness or distance toward the Elements.

Denny and Yazzie have discussed on several occasions, both privately and in public lectures around the world, how proper relationships are key to a good life. The proper distance means that there are bad outcomes

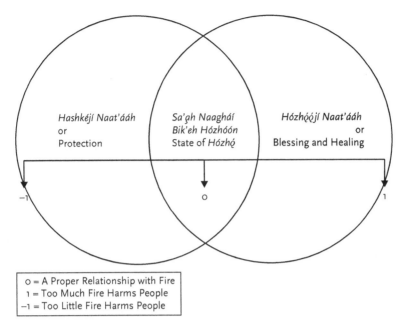

Figure 2.2: Concept Continuum of Any of the Four Sacred Elements, Such as *Kó*, or Fire, and How It Relates to *Sa'ǫh Naagháí Bik'eh Hózhóón*.

in exposure to the extremes. Here notions of *Hózhǫ́ǫ́jí* and *(Hashkéjí) Naayéé'jí* find their basis, and they remain today as a system used to balance distance and nearness toward many things in life, such as the Four Sacred Elements.[2] Figure 2.2 is a representation of proper distance as it applies to any of the Four Sacred Elements. The concept continuum represents some complex ideas. First are protection songs, prayers, and stories. Returning to the example of fire, individuals must learn to protect themselves and their families from fire. Protection ways can be harsh at times. Still, protection is not enough. People also must bless and heal themselves and their families to ensure that fire is used to promote long life. The converse is also true: people cannot properly handle fire, or any of the other Four Sacred Elements, with only blessing and a healing way. Protection is also needed because fire cannot be contained; it moves, and it is free. Fire requires a proper relationship to allow humans to keep their life in proper order. The songs and prayers given to the Diné for healing and protection are to be utilized to maintain *Sa'ǫh Naagháí Bik'eh Hózhóón*.

In other words, even if there is no problem, the balance must be maintained by using songs and prayers. If an imbalance does occur, known as *anáhóót'i'* or the emergence of a problem, the songs and prayers become even more important. This *anáhóót'i'* may be considered in degrees of urgency. As Figure 2.2 illustrates, it is possible to theoretically measure the distance from 0, or *Hózhǫ́*. Perhaps there is an approximate cutoff point at which a situation is no longer *Hózhǫ́* and becomes a matter of *Hóxchǫ*, also known as drifting away from *Hózhǫ́*. This is certainly an area needing further study (Austin 2009, 62–63). For analytical purposes here, any distance toward –1 or toward 1 requires maintenance. When maintenance of *Hózhǫ́* is neglected or impacted by a larger issue (an unexpected event), the level of urgency increases. In other words, when a situation drifts closer to a –1 or a 1 on the scale of maintenance, it becomes imperative to increase the level of urgency regarding attention to the problem. Figure 2.2 shows the concept continuum of any of the Four Sacred Elements. This model assumes that the Four Sacred Elements move, and it is the responsibility of earth-surface people to react accordingly. Leaders, therefore, were instructed how to maintain their society and political order by using *Hózhǫ́ǫ́jí* and *(Hashkéjí) Naayéé'jí* (Benally 2006, 11). In this way, traditional teachings gave rather clear, though difficult, instructions about maintaining proper distance and nearness toward the Four Sacred Elements. The stories go on to outline how things can go wrong.

One version of the story describes a feud between First Man and First Woman in which each had illicit affairs and brought forth children outside of their marital union. This led to fighting among the Diné. The story embodies the result of genders not working together to complement one another in their relationship with the Four Sacred Elements. First Man and First Woman reconciled eventually, but they had to deal with the consequences of their misdeeds, that is, the children born out of wedlock. One of the illicit affairs took place between White Shell Woman and Sun Bearer. White Shell Woman gave birth to twin boys known as the Hero Twins. The boys set out to slay the other children born of illicit affairs, but seven of these were spared when they pleaded for mercy. The seven remaining were hunger, thirst, sleep, lice, indolent poverty, old age, and death (Benally 2006, 12–14). It is said that the *Kinaalda* of White Shell Woman is the basis for *Hózhǫ́ǫ́ji*, and the acts of the Hero Twins ushered in *Naayéé'jí (Hashkéjí) Nahaghá*.[3] Note how each was necessary for the Diné to exist in balance and harmony: one destroyed while the other healed society. Both are necessary ways of governing and maintaining a good relationship with the Four Sacred Elements.

Another aspect of traditional Diné leadership involves ensuring that obligations, responsibilities, and benefits are shared and distributed according to Diné ways. This notion is maintained by virtue of *K'é*, which is loosely translated as "clan." Clan organization ensured, among other things, that people knew not only what they were responsible for doing but also to what they were entitled (Benally 2006, 16).

Traditional stories of existing in and traversing various realms (based on the teachings of leadership skills) can be taken literally or figuratively. For those who take these stories literally, and many still do, the question must be asked: "Why have such a process of leadership if there are no central Diné leaders?" The answer hints at the context for understanding the *Naach'id*, or the only remaining knowledge that has been shared regarding centralized Diné governance. Put another way, maintaining a proper relationship to the Four Sacred Elements impacted many Diné beyond a space a *Naat'áanii* might oversee. Hence, there must have been some way in which multiple *Naat'áanii* could coordinate the maintenance of a good relationship for all with the Four Sacred Elements.

Historical documents indicate that a *Naach'id* met occasionally to deal with issues that impacted more than one group of Diné, each of which was led by a single *Naat'áanii*. Several *Naat'áanii*, between twelve and twenty-four, would get together to discuss issues that impacted all Diné (Wilkins 2003, 70–71; Benally 2006, 28). *Naat'áanii* might be translated as the Western term "headman" (Benally 2006, 28). Scant details reveal that the *Naach'id* may have met every two to four years, while other records suggest the meetings were not so regular (Wilkins 2003, 71). All records agree that a *Naach'id* was called during a period of crisis regardless of the number of years since the last *Naach'id* (Wilkins 2003, 71; Benally 2006, 28). Again, any situation in which distance or nearness toward the Four Sacred Elements impacted several *Naat'áanii* appeared to be a good reason to hold a *Naach'id*. Some secondary sources state that the crisis at hand indicated which *Naat'áanii* set the agenda.

During periods of war, it is said that the *Naayéé'jí Naat'áanii* set the agenda. During periods of peace, the agenda was set by the *Hózhǫ́ǫ́jí Naat'áanii* (Wilkins 2003, 71). But perhaps the division was not this exacting. Since Diné philosophy requires that both approaches complement one another, it might be best to reconsider the notion of one group being in charge. Instead, it might be better to assume that crises merely allowed one group or the other to set a tone or inform an agenda. One of the most detailed accounts of how the last known *Naach'id* was carried out comes from Raymond D. Austin's dissertation "Navajo Courts and Navajo Common Law" (2007). Austin states that the last known *Naach'id* took place in the 1850s at *Tsin Sikaad* (Lone Tree), an area about 12 to 14 miles northeast of current-day Chinle (28). A large ceremonial *hooghan* was constructed with a diameter of 40 feet (29). *Hózhǫ́ǫ́jí Naat'áanii* sat on the south side of the *hooghan*, and the *Hashkéjí Naat'áanii* sat on the north side. Balance was maintained by having the families of the *Hashkéjí Naat'áanii* sleep on the south side of the ceremonial *hooghan* where *Hózhǫ́ǫ́jí Naat'áanii* sat during the *Naach'id*. Families of *Hózhǫ́ǫ́jí Naat'áanii* resided on the north side of the *hooghan* near where the *Hashkéjí Naat'áanii* sat during the ceremonial proceedings (29–30). This living arrangement may have been the result of wanting to stay consistent with the notion of *Ałch'į' Sila*. Further, Austin suggests it was also consistent with Navajo Common Law (30). Figure 2.3 is a three-dimensional illustration of the *Naach'id* based on the Austin description. Still, debate among scholars points to questions involving the purpose of the *Naach'id*.

AnCita Benally calls into question the academic record regarding the existence of the *Naach'id* in isolation, with no mention of another complementary and feminine approach to decision making. Given that the last *Naach'id* is said to have taken place prior to the Long Walk, Benally argues that the feminine aspect of leadership was solely relied upon when the Diné returned from their incarceration at Bosque Redondo (Benally 2006, 28–30). Her research points to the following interesting scenario:

> If war or a collective hunt was the purpose, *Naayééjí Naat'áanii* chanted [sang], said prayers, then silently, with only gestures, selected those who would participate in the hunt or war. Upon completion of their assignment, the selected group returned, reported, and revealed the results of their mission. (Benally 2006, 30)

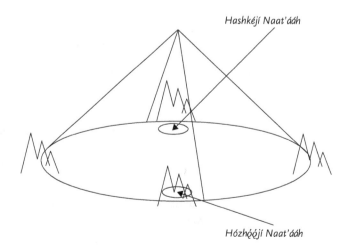

Hashkéjí Naat'ááh

Hózhǫ́ǫ́jí Naat'ááh

Figure 2.3: *Naach'id*, from Austin 2009, 10–11

Issues involving war and hunting are basically issues involving access to the Four Sacred Elements. The Diné wage war if other Native nations or colonial actors pose a threat. As will be argued later in this chapter, colonial actors proved to be one of the most powerful threats the Diné ever faced in their pursuit of a good relationship with the Four Sacred Elements. Yet there is no mention of the ways in which the Diné dealt with crises not related to war or hunting. Benally assumes that *Naach'id* gatherings might be related to what contemporary political scientists call issues of foreign policy. The ability to feed one's people is a foreign policy question today, because it requires that the state secure itself to the point that it can grow and distribute food to all its citizens. Again, this is clearly a question of access to the Four Sacred Elements, yet it differs because Diné philosophy precludes monopolization of any of the elements. Benally understandably wonders how the Diné dealt with issues related to internal or domestic crises. Benally links these issues to the domain of *Hózhóójí* and wonders how clans were adopted by the Diné. Since accepting refugees into a society today is probably best considered a domestic affair of immigration and naturalization, it makes sense that, at the very least, some form of gathering must have been convened to deal with adopting clans (Benally 2006, 32–33).

When examining the anthropological record regarding the Diné, women are notably absent. Could it be that anthropologists of the era were much more interested in recording the recollections of men? Since men run European cultures, it might be that European men simply assumed that Indigenous communities were the same. Therefore, no one bothered to talk to women regarding a female ceremonial gathering similar and complementary to the *Naach'id*. Deloria (2006) makes comparable arguments about the recording of oral stories of various Indigenous peoples.

Another factor that may have affected data gathering on female Diné leaders is that Diné cultural norms of the time would have prevented Diné women from being alone with a non-Diné man. Two precepts were at work. In the first place, Diné women were not to talk to a man who was not their husband or a relative. So unless a white male anthropologist was married or related to a Diné *Naat'áanii* woman, alone time would have been a violation of a cultural norm. A second consideration was that interaction with a person not related to the Diné was probably considered an issue of *Hashkéjí*, or protection way. Put in Western terms, dealing with a non-Navajo would have been a question of foreign policy. These occurrences conspired to obscure the female, complementary version of the *Naach'id*. One possible area to explore might be the beauty way (*Hózhóójí*). This book is the first attempt to explore a Diné philosophy of governance comparable to what exists for European governance philosophy. Understanding Diné philosophy of governance is necessary for those who want to understand why and how Diné governance is in its current condition. At the core, it seems clear to even the most novice observer that there are problems with contemporary monopolization of *any* one of the Four Sacred Elements. This approach attempts to highlight the foundation of traditional leadership, and in the process, it may uncover gaping holes that exist in contemporary Diné governance. It is said that the Holy Ones left the earth people with instructions on how to lead themselves. Diné *Naat'áanii* once knew how to guide their people and maintain a proper distance or nearness toward the Four Sacred Elements. These gifts and obligations continue today (Benally 2006, 38). While new challenges have presented themselves in the current era, there is little reason to believe that the original instructions are no longer relevant. In the end, it is clear that all humans, regardless of ethnicity, require fire and light, clean water, clean air, and pollen.

One unfortunate turn of events is that the record about interactions between the Diné and colonial actors has been dominated by the writings of the colonial actors. Therefore, it is difficult to give a balanced account of Diné international interaction with colonial actors. Still, the history of interaction will demonstrate the systematic monopolization of the Four Sacred Elements in the hands of non-Diné interests.

2.2. DINÉ INTERACTIONS WITH COLONIAL ACTORS— REGENERATING COLONIAL ACTOR PLANS

Diné interaction with non-Diné is a story of cross-cultural miscommunication. Historians would correctly state that there are absolutely no discussions of "sacred elements" in archival documents about treaty negotiations. Yet to ignore the Four Sacred Elements is to ignore Diné philosophy. On the other hand, some exploration of colonization philosophy is also instructive. A comprehensive discussion of colonization theory can be explored elsewhere (Getches et al. 2011, 43–73). The theory of colonization had practical consequences that had to be settled to the satisfaction of colonial actors, including the United States (64–73). A basic tenet of colonization theory concerned a civilized nation's right to discover land occupied or possessed by Indigenous peoples, including the Diné. Upon discovery, civilized nations could then claim the exclusive right to extinguish Indian title of occupancy by purchase, conquest, or abandonment (31, 98).

Hence, discovery is just the first step in the process of appropriating Diné land. What follows is a story of the postdiscovery attempts to appropriate

Diné land by extinguishing their right to occupy their own homeland, or *Diné Bikéyah*. Although historians may call this story a series of wars and treaties, followed by more wars and peace, from the Diné point of view, this is a story of international interaction. Therefore, the various colonial actors are fighting among themselves for the exclusive right to extinguish Diné occupancy and *not* for dominion over an already extinguished title. From the Diné perspective, this point of view is perplexing. A Diné critic might ask, "How do you extinguish a people's right to have access to the Four Sacred Elements of life?" Philosophically, without the Diné homeland, there can be no Diné. Perhaps it is more concrete to declare that fire, water, air, and pollen are independent variables. Life, or *'Iiná*, is the dependent variable.

There have been a total of nineteen treaties signed between the Diné and colonial actors. Given Diné philosophy, it seems very unlikely that all nineteen known treaties just happened to neglect the Four Sacred Elements. The gap between Diné philosophy and the treaty-making process suggests cross-cultural miscommunication. The Diné signed four treaties with Spain and six treaties with Mexico. They signed nine treaties with the United States, but only two were ratified by the U.S. Congress (Wilkins 2003, 21–22). These are the only *known* treaties. Yet the known treaties hint at a policy of confusion. Colonial actors, in an attempt to advance their interests, had a habit of handpicking Diné individuals to function as Diné leaders. Perhaps *Naat'áanii* clearly understood these interests as threats to a proper relationship with the Four Sacred Elements. An example of this is Diné headman Don Carlos. He was considered friendly to the interests of the Spaniards and was "civilized," in contrast to the rest of the people, who let themselves be dictated by "fear" or "profit" (Wilkins 2003, 72). This anecdotal evidence suggests that other interactions between colonial actors and the Diné were characterized by similar problems. One constant is that if non-Diné today continue to have a hard time understanding Diné philosophy, especially the importance of maintaining a proper relationship with the Four Sacred Elements, how can scholars expect colonial actors to have deliberately understood and then ignored them in nineteen negotiations?

2.2.1. Relations with Spain

What follows is a historical account of the international relations of the Diné with Spain, based almost exclusively on archival records. Treaties are evidence of failed attempts to extinguish Diné title of occupancy—in other

Table 2.1. DINÉ TREATIES WITH SPAIN

Date	Location	Purpose
1706	Santa Fe	Peace and alliance
1786	Rio Puerco River	Military alliance
May 12, 1805	Jemez Pueblo	Peace, trade, and alliance; exchange of prisoners
Aug. 21, 1819	Jemez Pueblo (?)	Peace; return of Navajo captives

Source: Wilkins 2003, 21–22.

words, Spain failed to conquer the Diné and needed a treaty to advance its interests. The known treaties between Spain and the Diné are listed in Table 2.1. Many questions remain about the motives of the Spaniards and the actual thinking of the Diné negotiators, but this information is practically nonexistent. None of the treaty negotiation archives mention the Four Sacred Elements. Where possible, the archival record is supplemented here with accounts of historical events of the era.

The Spaniards are said to have arrived by 1519 off the coast of Veracruz. By 1521, Spain had overrun what would become Mexico City and set up a colony christened New Spain (Foster 1997, 233). The general pattern of conquest was to subdue the Indigenous population by war and disease wherever possible. (The disease aspect of annihilation was an accident of *luck* for the Spaniards.) Nonetheless, the Spanish crown was unable to subdue all the Indigenous populations by use of military force. It is under these circumstances that Spain went into negotiations to appease the stronger Indigenous groups too far from Mexico City for military conquest. Another factor was that many Indigenous groups could not be overrun with military force. Spain, recognizing its relatively weak position, chose to appear strong and intimidating on paper, and thus Spain entered into treaties with the Diné.

The record of the first contact between the Diné and the Spaniards is scant. The first known contact apparently occurred in 1583 when Antonio de Espejo, a Spanish explorer, encountered the Diné in present-day New Mexico (Wilkins 2003, 203). It wasn't until the 1620s, however, that there was a documented treaty between the Diné and Spain. The earliest known peace treaty was arranged by a Spaniard named Fray Alonso de Benavides during his efforts to convert the Diné to Christianity. The historic account of this treaty dates back to the 1620s, and there is apparently no record of the negotiation itself (Brugge and Correll 1971).

Historians believe that extensive slave raids against the Diné began around 1620 and probably involved the Spanish invaders and other

Indigenous tribes of the Southwest (Wilkins 2003, 204). These raids obviously would have created a hostile relationship between the Diné and the Spanish government.

Evidence of a treaty is again found in 1706, yet no written form of that treaty survives. Scholars like Brugge and Correll are left to assume that verbal agreements were used to end conflict at that time. While Brugge and Correll conclude that there were no treaties between Spain and the Diné in the 1700s, they fail to note apparent discoveries made by Kappler as well as by Deloria and DeMaillie (Brugge and Correll 1971, 2; Deloria and DeMallie 1999, 133; United States and Kappler 1972; United States, Kappler, and United States 1971; United States, United States, and Kappler 1903, 1904).

Although there is no evidence of a treaty, historic Spanish documents suggest there was treaty-like activity. Documents indicate that the Spaniards believed there was a Diné conspiracy to cause harm to their colonial settlements. Examining these fear-based documents generates evidence of early forms of treaty making between the Diné and Spanish people. A letter to the governor of New Mexico, Don Juan Bautista, describes an alliance between the Diné and the Gila Apache and war waged against the Spaniards by both tribes (Wilkins 2003, 204; Deloria and DeMallie 1999, 133). The letter is also the first recorded instance in which the Spaniards handpicked a Navajo man as the supposed chief of the entire nation (Wilkins 2003, 205). The language indicates that the Spaniards saw themselves as the superior actor or sovereign of the area. The Diné were chastised for their "lack of confidence" and their "mistaken conduct in not declaring themselves openly and generally against the Apaches" (Deloria and DeMallie 1999, 133). The letter implies that the Diné would receive a "great benefit" by agreeing to declare allegiance to Spain in Spain's conflict with the Apache. The document goes on to indicate the need for an intermediary to handle any "misunderstandings" that might come up during the course of the agreement, but the term "misunderstandings" is never explicitly defined or elaborated upon. In the end, the Diné were expected to hold steadfastly to five named requirements:

1. That they maintaining, as they proposed, the required subordination and fidelity, the protection of the king would be sought and declared in their favor.

2. That to bring about the declaration of war against the Gilas, one of the chiefs named, with only Navajos and the interpreter, should set out on a campaign at the will of the governor at the end of July of this year; so that besides their performance in the past year, the enemies might have this new proof that the Navajos were now moving frankly and voluntarily against them.

3. That from the people who might not be included in this expedition, that chief should hold out those whom he might consider fit to go as auxiliaries with the monthly detachments of troops; this reinforcement he fixed right there at 30 individuals each month; for these individuals, the Navajo accepted with much gratitude the aid of horses and supplies dispensed by the Commandancy-General.

4. That from the moment the council was dissolved, they should go down to occupy their old camps to plant their seeds, and that, concerning the security which the governor guaranteed them in conserving the sustaining them in that situation, they could proceed to build sod huts.

5. Lastly, that for these ends proposed and to prove their acquittance, they received and assured on their part the life of the interpreter, offering to be directed by his advice. (Deloria and DeMallie 1999, 134)

The Spanish stance of superiority over the Diné is apparent in the five conditions of peace. Condition 1 demands subordination of the Diné. Condition 2 reflects a strategic military move on the part of the Spanish government: the Spaniards needed the Diné to become enemies of the Gila Apache people. This condition is written in such a way that it implies that all should implicitly understand the declaration of war between the Diné and Gila Apache. Condition 3 involves the giving of horses and supplies to the Diné in return for cooperation. Condition 4 requires the Diné to become farmers and stop moving around. It was an attempt to remake the Diné in the Spanish image. Condition 5 affirms that the Diné agree to the four previous conditions and agree to accept the advice of a Spanish interpreter (Deloria and DeMallie 1999, 134).

Although the Diné and Spanish authorities agreed to some type of terms, the conditions discussed here may not be the actual terms. There is limited evidence of a meeting of the minds, but there really is no way to know exactly what was lost in translation during negotiations. There also is no way to understand if any of the conditions were embellished when the letter to Governor Bautista was written. What can be established is that the language used was condescending toward the Diné. It was meant to impress a sense of Spanish superiority, and it included veiled threats as well as explicit promises of great benefits being bestowed upon the Diné if they lived up to the terms of the treaty. When one considers the actual military might of the Spanish forces in relation to the Diné, one can safely conclude that the treaty was more bark and less bite, an indication of the Spanish inability to conquer the Diné. Early treaties maintained the use of condescending language and made implicit and explicit threats with little ability to implement those threats. The first written treaty appeared in

1805 following a bitter, year-long war between the Diné and the Spaniards (Brugge and Correll 1971, 2). After one hundred Diné were killed, several bands of Diné sought peace (Wilkins 2003, 205). The representatives involved were Fernando Chacon, governor of New Mexico, and Cristobal and Vicente of the Diné (Deloria and DeMallie 1999, 144). A prior draft of a treaty was said to have contained harsh language. The draft called for limits on Diné territory, for the Spaniards to keep livestock they took during the war, and for the return of a disproportionately small number of Diné captives compared to the number of Spanish captives demanded in return. In addition, no gifts or food were given to the Diné when they visited Santa Fe to see the governor regarding acts of diplomacy (Brugge and Correll 1971, 3). For reasons unknown, this proposal was not used to make peace with the Diné. Some scholars suspect that Spain's actions yield the answer.

Chacon was removed from his post as governor prior to peace being reestablished. The argument is that the Spanish crown was not happy with the way Chacon handled the treaty-making process. He was replaced with Joaquin Real Alencaster (Brugge and Correll 1971, 3). The treaty of May 12, 1805, is a more cordial agreement, with language depicting reciprocal demands. There were five conditions in the treaty:

1. That at no time shall they [the Diné] make any claim to the lands of the site called Cebolleta.
2. That they shall restore to us the two children that they have handed over to me, and any other captives [who] are found in their power.
3. That they will make no alliance, treaty, nor communication with a nation or band hostile to us, and that on the occasions which might arise, they will also make war.
4. That if any of their nation commit a robbery or other damage on those of this province, their chiefs will hand them over that they may be punished.
5. That on our part we will permit them commerce, stock-raising, and planting of fields and other enterprises which they may wish to engage in, and that it will be presented to them as I have verified it to the Interpreter, Josef Antonio Garcia conforming to what they have solicited, in order to give notice among them in due time and that there is handed over to them, as has been handed over to them, the captain called Segundo and 16 prisoners more that existed in San Elecario, and that in case of there being other prisoners among them or among us they will be handed over reciprocally; and that receiving them under the protection of the King and in his royal name, they are to be made to understand that the violation of the referred conditions,

and to which fulfillment remains obligatory to the Nation in general, will be held to be formal declaration of War, and it will be attacked suddenly in order to destroy it entirely (Deloria and DeMallie 1999, 144).

The terms, in general, are far more neutral than those in the treaty described in the letter of 1786. Condition 1 reads like an agreement, ceding the area of Cebolleta, a place where Spain had established a settlement (Brugge and Correll 1971, 3). While condition 2 does not read as reciprocal, it should be read in reference to condition 5, in which sixteen prisoners are "handed over reciprocally" in return for the two children mentioned in condition 2. Condition 3 refers to an alliance between the Spanish government and the Diné. One could interpret this clause, in light of the last alliance made in 1786, as evidence that the Diné were now considered a military power capable of benefiting the Spaniards. Although the language is not reciprocal, in that Spanish warriors are not obligated to defend the Diné, the clause reads like a mutual agreement. Condition 4 is a jurisdictional clause allowing the Spanish government to punish Diné who committed crimes against the crown. The 1805 treaty is devoid of condescending language, which perhaps indicates that the nature of the relationship may have changed. War with the Diné may have forced the Spaniards to respect their enemy.

What can be ascertained by the two examined treaties is the change in the relationship between the Diné and Spanish people. A final treaty between the two nations was signed August 21, 1819, and it has been characterized as "one of the longest and most complex treaties ever made with the tribe" (Brugge and Correll 1971, 5). Here, the Spaniards elected to enter into a treaty with a *Naat'áanii* named Joaquin. Joaquin went to the Spanish officials in an effort to make peace. He also warned the Spaniards that other *Naat'áanii* were preparing for war because they remained angry over land encroachment. Joaquin's actions, which included moving away from other Diné bands and cutting ties, placed him in the position of traitor to his own people (Wilkins 2003, 72). Despite this situation, the Spanish officials considered Joaquin the "Chief of the Navajos," as is apparent by his signature at the bottom of the treaty of 1819.

A total of eighteen conditions are listed in the treaty, but these can be condensed. The treaty first established an intermediary, seemingly to prevent confusion concerning whom the Spaniards should address when problems arose. It is clear that the Spaniards wanted the Diné to name a leader in the same way that they made their own leaders known. This leader would be required to live near a Spanish intermediary to help solve problems before they escalated into a war. Punishment for crimes against the Diné by Spaniards, and vice versa, was to be meted out according to a negotiated agreement on a case-by-case basis. Yet this condition was dialed back in the next condition, which stated that if the offender was Diné, the person would be punished by the Spanish government because the Diné lacked the ability to properly punish individuals and extract compensation. Should the offender be Spanish, however, the Spanish government would decide what punishment and compensation were necessary.

Other conditions included backing away from war when conflict emerged between individual members of the two groups. Apparently, this was meant to prevent war arising from every single dispute that could break out between the Spaniards and Diné. We might assume from this condition that many past wars were over the dispute between few individuals. Condition 10 is the most interesting because of its condescending language:

> 10. In the name of the Sovereign (although with their ill-timed and senseless hostilities they have been made undeserving) there is conceded to the said Navajo Tribe the lands that until now they have made use of for planting, pastures and other uses that might be applicable to them, with such reforms as have been repeatedly proposed, they should observe peace and harmony with the Spanish, half-breed and Indian people of the province.—Agreed. With thanks. (Deloria and DeMallie 1999, 146)

Here the word *Sovereign* is used to describe only one group—the Spaniards—and not both. Although this is not a clear-cut case of a superiority complex, it does hint at the perspective the Spaniards had of the Diné. Then, the Spaniards assess the Diné as being undeserving of a concession due to "senseless hostilities." The concession seems to involve land that the Spanish officials admit they have no right to use because it historically belonged to the Diné.

The other conditions followed almost reciprocally. They allowed for the raising of livestock by Spanish people on Diné land, without the Diné having to cede land. If anything, condition 12 established an informal knowledge of boundaries the Diné have always considered relevant. Arrangements were made for the appointment of "hostages." These were the Diné individuals who were to stay with the Spaniards. These individuals would be replaced occasionally with other Diné individuals. The treaty even took jurisdiction over the Hopi by making the agreement that the Diné were not to disturb them. Condition 17 is interesting because the Spanish attitude is once again made apparent:

> 17. In just return this government expects a perpetual peace and sincere and cordial harmony, to which on its part it will contribute with great care,

rejoicing henceforth, so that saturated by so much kindness they will comfort themselves gratefully, and the Navajo general, the captain and other individuals will carefully flee from all that could alter such a beneficial situation, they will raise their livestock, will tranquilly cultivate their lands, and enjoy the fruits of their labors in abundance and the energetic protection of the Monarch of the Spains that loves them tenderly, desiring their happiness as the superior government. (Deloria and DeMallie 1999, 146–147)

This condition may prove slightly more difficult to identify as condescending due to the lack of direct language to that effect. However, since other passages in this same treaty assume superiority, it is unlikely that this position would be relinquished by the Spanish mid-treaty. The first suspect phrase is "beneficial situation." There is no evidence that the Spanish presence was really beneficial to the Diné. The next line hints at the Spanish need for the Diné to behave as Europeans by "tranquilly cultivat[ing] their lands." But the most obvious point of assumed Spanish superiority involves the statement that places the Spanish monarch in the role of "protector" of the Diné. It can be assumed that the Spanish represented themselves as the superior government. Moreover, since only one Naat'áanii signed the treaty and that single Naat'áanii was considered a traitor to other Diné, it is unlikely that the treaty of 1821 brought any lasting peace.

There is an idea worth noting in the three Spanish treaties discussed here. They all contain condescending language and empty threats against a Diné-based uprising. Furthermore, there are far too many loose ends. But what is clear is that the record indicates a superiority complex held by Spain—a European power with little or no capability of enforcing treaties. Little change in attitude could be expected from the Mexican government that would replace Spain. Those Indigenous groups out of the reach of Spanish rule were deferred to another time and place when Mexico gained enough power to subdue what it perceived as an obstacle between itself and prosperity: Indigenous peoples.

2.2.2. Diné Relations with Mexico

The Diné relationship with Spain had run its course by 1821. A coalition for the break between the Spanish crown and Spanish colonizers in Mexico City began emerging by the beginning of the 1800s. Today, Mexico celebrates September 16 as the date of Mexican independence. It was on this day in 1810 that Miguel Hidalgo let the Spanish crown know that an effort for independence was in place. Spain tried to maintain control of the colony by executing Hidalgo in 1811. Hidalgo's successor, Jose Maria Morelos, was also executed, in 1815. By 1821, support for independence was strong enough that Spain yielded to the pressure by relinquishing its control over its former colony (Foster 1997, 235). For the Diné, a new colonial actor had emerged and taken control of the exclusive right to extinguish their right to occupy their homeland. The newly formed Mexico inherited Spain's benefits and problems, which included the "problem" of the Diné. Purchase and conquest operations would again be fiercely opposed by Diné leadership. This opposition can probably be best understood as effective *Naat'áanii* ensuring that the Diné had proper access to the Four Sacred Elements. The Mexican government chose to interact with its enemies via war and diplomatic relations, that is, treaties to extinguish Diné (Indian) title. A list of Diné treaties with Mexico is included in Table 2.2.

The main theme of the period in which the newly independent Mexico attempted to exert control over historically Diné land is best conveyed by one word: chaos. Mexico experienced many problems, including corrupt

Table 2.2. DINÉ TREATIES WITH MEXICO

Date	Location	Purpose
Oct. 29, 1822	Zia Pueblo	Peace, trade, and return of all white captives
Feb. 12, 1823	Paguate Pueblo	Peace; return of all white captives
Jan. 20, 1824	Jemez Pueblo	Peace
June 18, 1824	?	?
1835	?	?
July 15, 1839	Jemez Pueblo	Peace, trade, and alliance; return of all white captives
March 10, 1841—draft of negotiating points—only known evidence of terms for next treaty (1841)	?	?
Sometime between April and May 1841	?	Peace, trade, and return of all white captives
May 8, 1841	Santo Domingo Pueblo	Peace, trade, and return of all white captives
Mar. 23, 1844	Santo Domingo Pueblo	Peace, trade, and return of all white captives

Source: Wilkins 2003, 21–22.

leaders such as Emperor Iturbide. Another issue involved an economic legacy that included a $75 million debt for the Mexican war of independence. Also, there was a fight for control of the country among status quo groups, such as the Creoles, the Vatican, and military leaders. The most obvious threat to the newly formed Mexico was the Mexican-American War and its impact on the Diné. There still existed the problem of "Indians" and raids into Mexican-occupied settlements (Foster 1997, 121). Again, treaties during this time do not mention the Four Sacred Elements.

During this period, Mexico continued using settlements established by Spain in what became the state of New Mexico. Areas of note include Pueblo of Jemez, Pueblo of Laguna, and Villa de Santa Fe, among others (Jenkins et al. 1974, 18). At the time of Mexican independence, the central government in Mexico was so unstable that many times New Mexico exhibited a more stable government. Nonetheless, problems persisted. One ambiguity was the lack of clear laws. With Spanish and Mexican laws not clearly defined, many people in power followed whatever governance method was convenient for their given situation. Thus, governors of the New Mexico Territory changed frequently, and that also meant that attitudes toward the Diné were chaotic.

In 1821, the Treaty of Cordova made all Indigenous peoples in Mexican territory citizens of Mexico. Facundo Melgares, governor of New Mexico, was the diplomat responsible for negotiating peace between the Spanish government and the Diné. He survived the transition to independence and oversaw the first treaty between the Diné and Mexico. During 1822, a delegation of thirteen *Hózhǫ́ǫ́jí Naat'áanii*, or peace-way leaders, approached Mexican government officials. Diné philosophy of governance indicates that had the delegation been interested in war, the *Hashkéjí Naat'áanii* would have been involved in the negotiations in part or exclusively. The Mexican officials killed the *Naat'áanii* for reasons unclear to us today (Wilkins 2003, 205). Primary documents from this period do not clearly indicate the impact that these killings had on the treaty negotiation process.

Secondary reporting of written negotiations indicates Melgares wanted much harsher language than appeared in the finalized version of the treaty of October 29, 1822. Some demands included a return of "apostates," which some scholars believe were Pueblo refugees under Diné protection. Additionally, boundary restrictions appear in negotiation documents unavailable to this researcher. All of these demands were enforced under threat of resuming war.

Past researchers point out that the actual treaty lacks the harsh language proffered in negotiation documents. Most intriguing is the elimination of boundary restriction language from the treaty (Brugge and Correll 1971, 7). One possible inference involves the inability of the Mexican government to enforce many of its own demands. Another inference is that the Diné recognized the impotence of Mexico, and so they successfully eliminated the boundary restriction language from the treaty. Such inferences are supported by the previously documented problems that Mexico inherited upon its independence.

The 1822 treaty still had condescending language that placed Mexico in an apparent position of power, even though that power was an illusion. For example, the treaty of 1822 stated that peace was granted by the Mexican government. A second clause indicated that past treaties would remain in force. Clauses three through seven toned down the harsh language and indicated a sense of parity between the negotiating parties. Such clauses included a stipulation that all parties forever "forget" the injuries caused and that the Diné remain at liberty to trade and travel within Mexican provinces (probably meant to specify the province of New Mexico) (Deloria and DeMallie 1999, 149). For reasons that cannot be ascertained, at this time a treaty was drawn up between the Diné and Mexico. Historical reports indicate that no war took place in 1823 between the Diné and Mexico. Moreover, histories of Mexico and New Mexico do not indicate any situation that would warrant peace negotiations or renegotiations. One apparent change was the appointment of Jose Antonio Vizcarra to the position of governor of New Mexico. One scholar, who was perplexed by the treaty, wrote, "The conditions demanded were so unrealistic that it can only be presumed that Vizcarra was trying to start a war" (Brugge and Correll 1971, 9). Yet with so many obstacles barring an expensive war, it is difficult to understand how such an endeavor was rationalized as being logical (Brugge and Correll 1971, 33–34).[4]

The treaty of February 12, 1823, demanded that all Mexican captives be returned by the Diné. It also stipulated that any Diné in Mexican custody be returned if the individual wished to return home. Other demands included the return of any and all items stolen from Mexicans by any Diné, Diné conversion to Catholicism, and the adoption of a settled, European-inspired lifestyle by the Diné. These demands were apparently not met, and a negotiated reply was recorded in the treaty. The Diné agreed to hand over the Mexican captives they had. They also claimed that they were "dying of hunger" and therefore could not return the items stolen in raids, but they stipulated that they would not steal from the Mexicans in the future. The final demand of conversion was sidestepped for four months pending a discussion regarding the matter among the Diné (Deloria and DeMallie 1999, 153). The fourth demand was not addressed in the four-month period, and Vizcarra went to war in response. Little is known of the outcome. A treaty was apparently concluded on June 18, 1824, but the text and terms have been lost. Peace was negotiated again in 1835, but no record of the circumstances leading up to the negotiations or the conditions of the peace are known (Brugge and Correll 1971, 10).

By 1839, another peace treaty was necessary between the Diné and Mexico. The circumstances leading up to the treaty are not well known. With seven well-defined clauses, the treaty took on a more "boilerplate" format than past treaties had exhibited. Demeaning language was used once again in the introduction. The Diné were described as being in a situation of "humiliation," which had led them to seek peace. No hint was given of the Mexican need for peace. The treaty called for a return to peace and commerce and a return of captives on both sides. Clause three assigned blame for the war to the Diné, stating that the Diné had to refrain from "disturb[ing] the order with the citizens of . . . New Mexico." Other clauses called for trade to resume, the punishment of Diné "murderers" by Mexico, and Mexican measures to punish guilty individuals for a Diné death. (The treaty said that Mexicans who caused a death would pay "30 sheep . . . for the dead man," and the guilty individual would be "punished according to law.") The language in the treaty implied that Mexican law would control all parties (Deloria and DeMallie 1999, 164).

Clause six of the 1839 treaty is interesting: it reads, "In case any Navajo Indian woman succeeds in escaping by fleeing from the house of her master, on arrival of the said woman in her own land, when it is verified, that she remain free and without any obligation of the nation to give anything for her ransom" (Deloria and Wilkins 1999, 140–141). Although admittedly a leap of inference, one potential hypothesis is that the 1839 treaty was dealing with the kidnapping of Diné women for use as servants by well-to-do Mexican citizens or some other form of slave trade. Evidence of such activity was more explicitly apparent on July 18, 1868, when the U.S. Congress passed Joint Resolution 83, prohibiting the peonage of Diné women and children for the purpose of serving Mexican elites (Deloria and Wilkins 1999, 141).

The final clause was an agreement to defend one another's nations from enemies. The language attempted to give the clause a moral imperative: if the Diné allowed others (colonial actors or other Indigenous groups) to invade either their own land or the land claimed by Mexico, such permission would be an insult to their honor as a nation. Arrangements were made for one or two Diné to live in the Cebolleta and Jemez settlements to facilitate communication—perhaps as diplomats do today—between the two nations. A simpler interpretation is that the two would be hostages.

The treaty mentioned that the Sahuanos, the Comanche, and "barbarous tribes" could be expected to invade Mexico (Deloria and DeMallie 1999, 165). A period of "peace" apparently existed for only one year, as reports of peace talks emerged again in 1840 (Brugge and Correll 1971, 11).

In 1840, the Diné held a *Naach'id* near *Tsé yí*, or Canyon de Chelly, with the intent to make peace with the Mexican government (Wilkins 2003, 206). It is unclear if peace was reached by April or May of 1841. The original signed treaty has gone missing, and scholars are left with a draft that cannot be taken as the actual terms of the peace agreement. A draft of the negotiations dated March 10, 1841, has been attributed to shaping the peace of April/May 1841. The March 10 document amounts to a list of demands laid out by the Mexican government. Such demands included a move for "peace and commerce," a handover of all Mexican captives in Diné custody, and recognition or acknowledgment by the Diné that the Mexican government was a "superior all[y]." One goal of the treaty was the removal of "all motives for resentment," presumably on the part of the Diné. A final goal was to impose Mexican law on Diné for crimes committed against Mexicans while making sure that if Mexicans committed a crime against the Diné, a "certain fee" would suffice (Deloria and DeMallie 1999, 165).

By 1844 a new treaty was needed. On March 23, 1844, the final known treaty between the two nations was recognized by the Diné and Mexico. A total of eight clauses, in which the seventh was deleted, delineated the same terms and conditions that the prior treaties outlined. The clauses called for peace and commerce, repatriation of captives, surrender of Diné thieves to Mexican authorities, and other directives. Clause five was unique in its request: "The Navajo Chieftains understand that if they again raid the Department, with only this act, even when they afterwards request peace, it will not be accorded to them, and war will be made continually upon them" (Deloria and DeMallie 1999, 172). Perhaps this is a clue into the reason, from the perspective of the Mexican government, why so many peace treaties with similar language have emerged from the period. Alternatively, a raid on the "Department" may have been a relatively new phenomenon that was so drastically costly that it warranted a single clause and the threat of perpetual war—an empty threat, to say the least.

With problems emerging on all sides, the Mexican government would not have a hand in the traditional Diné homeland much longer. By 1846, the United States' invasion to fulfill its goal of "manifest destiny" had been carried out, making the position of the Diné all the more complicated. On August 18, 1846, the change in sovereignty of the Spanish/Mexican settlements occurred. Historians suggest the transition was a peaceful process in which Brigadier General Stephen Watts Kearny declared that the formerly

Mexican territory was now a part of the United States of America and that the former Mexican citizens would be afforded the protection of the U.S. government (Jenkins et al. 1974, 33). It would take the United States and the Diné just four months to find it necessary to formalize an agreement between them.

2.2.3. Relations with the United States of America

The United States believed that a peace treaty with the powerful Diné would secure the Southwest Territory—although the past two colonial actors had attempted the same method and failed. (See Table 2.3 for a list of treaties with the United States.) It is worth reminding readers that the reason why the United States went to war with Mexico was to obtain the exclusive right to extinguish Diné (Indian) title and not to obtain the land itself. That right was secured in 1848, but the United States still had to extinguish title by purchase, conquest, or abandonment (Getches et al. 2011, 70, 98). For the Diné, access to the Four Sacred Elements remained keenly in focus. Some scholars have broken the U.S. treaty-making process into two stages. Stage one took place prior to 1849 and dealt mainly with regulating commerce among tribes (Deloria and DeMallie 1999, 60). Since the United States attempted to

Table 2.3. DINÉ TREATIES WITH THE UNITED STATES

Date	Location	Purpose
Nov. 22, 1846	Bear Springs (Ft. Wingate, NM)	Peace, trade, and exchange of prisoners
May 20, 1848	Monte Del Cuyatana (Beautiful Mountain), Navajo Country	Peace, trade, and return of all Navajo captives
Sept. 9, 1849	Canyon de Chelly, AZ	Peace, trade, and return of all Navajo captives
1851	?	?
July 18, 1855	Laguna Negra, AZ	Trade; established Navajo reservation boundaries
Nov. 20, 1858	Ft. Defiance, AZ	Peace
Dec. 25, 1858	Ft. Defiance, AZ	Peace; established Navajo reservation boundaries
Feb. 15, 1861	Ft. Fauntleroy, NM	Peace
June 1, 1868	Ft. Sumner, NM	Peace; established Navajo reservation boundaries

Source: Wilkins 2003, 21–22.

exercise control only after 1848, there was only enough time to create two treaties dealing with commerce.

The 1849 treaty between the Diné and the United States marks the second stage in U.S. treaty making, and it was meant to legitimize the U.S. claim to Diné lands (Deloria and DeMallie 1999, 60). The United States and the Diné entered into nine peace treaties between 1846 and 1868. These treaties were signed in 1846, 1848, 1849, 1851, 1855, two in 1858, 1861, and 1868. Of the nine treaties, only two were ratified by the U.S. Congress (Wilkins 2003, 72). Historians and other scholars are left with many questions concerning the attitude the Diné adopted with respect to nonratified treaties. Not surprisingly, none of these treaties mention the Four Sacred Elements.

The general view of the nonratified treaties is that either the Diné or the United States rejected the terms of the treaties in one way or another. But such a definition is problematic because rejection can be taken to mean several things. Due to lack of documentation, it is not known if a treaty was not given adequate attention by the U.S. Congress, the Bureau of Indian Affairs, or the Diné. Complicating matters is the fact that many agreements could potentially have been made between the Diné and various Indian agents and army officers that would not have been recorded or recognized by other agents of the U.S. government. As a rule, such low-ranking U.S. agents had no authority to enter into treaty negotiations with the Diné. Still another complication was the imposition upon some Indigenous groups, not necessarily the Diné, to not have written agreements (Deloria and DeMallie 1999, 1237). What's more, Deloria and DeMallie point out that nonratified treaties "provide evidence of the kinds of issues that affected people on the frontier and eventually created a need for a more specific legal relationship spelled out in a later treaty" (1238).

The first treaty between the Diné and the United States was established on November 22, 1846. The agreement was the commencement of a meeting between upwards of five hundred Diné and one hundred Americans (Wilkins 2003, 206). The agreement was short; it contained five articles. The length of the entire document was only half a page. It asked for a "firm and lasting peace." The treaty also defined the people of New Mexico and Pueblo Indians as Americans. Finally, the treaty promoted free travel to trade and sought assurances that full protection be granted by the host nation (Deloria and DeMallie 1999, 1264). Is it possible that free travel and protection were an attempt by *Naat'áanii* to secure proper access to the Four Sacred Elements? The language was balanced, with the two nations appearing as equals. The United States did not ratify the treaty.

A second treaty, which the United States also failed to ratify, was agreed upon on May 20, 1848. During this time, the Treaty of Guadalupe Hidalgo was signed between the United States and Mexico. In that treaty, Indigenous peoples were claimed to be under the jurisdiction of the United States. There were no Indigenous peoples represented at the negotiations (Wilkins 2003, 206). Theories of colonization factor in here, as other sources have indicated (Getches et al. 2011, 43–73). This second treaty may have been intended to replace the 1846 treaty and to gain approval by all parties involved. This treaty contained five articles, and the language was slightly harsh in only one instance, in which payment in the form of sheep was demanded by the United States for "expenses incurred . . . in this campaign." Some speculation about that article suggests that the sheep payment was merely compensation for the expenses of the U.S. expedition to meet and sign the treaty (Brugge and Correll 1971, 14). The rest of the language asked for goals similar to those of the 1846 treaty: firm and lasting peace, mutual trade, repatriation of prisoners, and so forth (Deloria and DeMallie 1999, 1264–1265). Again, these hint at securing access to the Four Sacred Elements. It is difficult to state for sure whether or not the nonratified status of these first two treaties led to the negotiation of the third treaty, which was ratified by the U.S. Congress.

The treaty of September 9, 1849, was the first U.S. attempt to legitimize its claim to Diné territory or to declare that Diné title was extinguished. The legitimization was made in terms of Western concepts of land ownership, in which the U.S. government would acquire a title to the land that it could then disperse in the form of grants to private developers (Getches et al. 2011, 64–73). The treaty was more complicated than previous treaties, and it had a total of eleven articles. Among the treaty's provisions was the establishment of jurisdiction over the Diné's historic homeland, calls for a cease of hostilities between the United States and the Diné, establishment of the United States as governing trade between the two nations and other outside parties, and an agreement with the Diné to turn over a Diné person accused of murder. Territorial agreements included a clause that stated that the United States would adjust territorial borders to best suit the Diné (Brugge and Correll 1971, 68–71). Perhaps the true reason the treaty was ratified by the U.S. Congress involved the clause that allowed the United States to adjust the territorial boundary at will with little opportunity for the Diné to contribute to such decision making. One might assume that the treaty was leading up to plans for the Long Walk. Yet all of the clauses imply a threat to *Naat'áanii* because they put the ability to maintain a proper relationship with the Four Sacred Elements in jeopardy.

It is believed, based on research involving the primary documents of the era, that the United States was growing impatient with the Diné's habit of defending themselves against slave traders and U.S. encroachment (Denetdale 2009, 29). It appears that the United States was attempting to establish itself as the only police force in the area, while extinguishing Diné (Indian) title. This would further threaten the ability for *Naat'áanii* to exercise their best judgment about access to the Four Sacred Elements. Although it is not explicitly stated, it seems that the United States was upset that the Diné did not turn to the United States when they were assaulted by other Indigenous groups and New Mexican citizens (Denetdale 2009, 26). Again, these kinds of assaults threatened the Diné ability to maintain the correct distance and nearness toward the Four Sacred Elements.

A second recurring problem involved the lack of coercive leadership among the Diné and the impact of Navajo Nation's unwillingness or inability to stop all people from raiding against non-Diné people (Denetdale 2009, 30; Wilkins 2003). There was no way that the 1849 treaty could last because Narbonna, *a Hózhóójí Naat'áanii*, was killed and scalped during the negotiation process (Denetdale 2009, 30–32). This assassination was a huge blow to Diné morale because, first, Narbonna's role was not to wage war. Second, Narbonna had a great reputation among his people for vociferously pushing for peace in the face of obvious instances in which the Diné were continuously taken advantage of, harassed, enslaved, and killed with little cause. With anger on all sides, the fighting continued. These events signaled chaos and a breakdown of the proper relationship with the Four Sacred Elements.

The treaty of September 10, 1851, has apparently been lost. The treaty was required because a different group of Diné were asked to agree to the terms set forth in the 1849 treaty (Brugge and Correll 1971, 17). The second group of Diné reportedly did not take the negotiation process seriously for reasons unknown. After discussing the treaty details, this Diné group determined that the 1849 treaty was entered into by a group of Diné who did not have the authority to negotiate for the "Diné Nation." The treaty was agreed to by this second group (72). Perhaps this treaty-ratifying process showed that the United States had learned from its past mistakes in treating the Diné as a single entity. A more sinister analysis is that the United States was simply covering as many bases as possible as it sought an agreement with the Diné that would allow the United States to do what was best for U.S. interests. Regardless, the United States did not ratify the treaty (17). There is more evidence that the Diné leaders did not take the U.S. treaty seriously.

By this time, Fort Defiance had been founded, and Manuelito was considered the main leader of the Diné. Evidence suggests that this was a title assumed by Manuelito only for the purpose of negotiating treaties with the United States. This raises the question, What does serving as a figurehead have to do with securing a proper relationship with the Four Sacred Elements? To his own people, Manuelito was still a *Hashkéjí Naat'áanii*. His role remained one of guiding the people to protect their good relationship with the Four Sacred Elements. A dispute over grazing land between Manuelito and U.S. army leaders became an eighteenth-century cold war. Each group escalated the tensions by grazing on certain lands and slaughtering each other's grazing cattle. Manuelito offered his resignation as "Chief" of his people. He no longer wished to serve as the figurehead leader for the purposes of negotiating with the United States (Denetdale 2009, 32–34). Perhaps he recognized that his role was futile since it had nothing to do with the Four Sacred Elements. All the while, the ambition of the United States remained undeterred as it struggled to protect its New Mexican citizens from many Indigenous peoples.

Because the United States was already systematically curtailing Indigenous peoples' way of life, it may not be a surprise that the next treaty was a giant leap in terms of its intended result. The treaty of June 18, 1855, was an attempt to set up a reservation for the Diné. The reservation would be a method of extinguishing Diné (Indian) rights to occupy their own traditional homelands. Then the United States would hold title in trust for the Diné. It is important to note the signatory for the Diné was not Manuelito but Zarcillos Largos (as "Head Chief"), probably because the former did not go along with the U.S. demands (Wilkins 2003, 207). Zarcillos did not agree with Manuelito's aggressive stance, as evidenced in the grazing dispute (Denetdale 2009, 34). Most probably, the idea that the United States was acting in the best interests of the Diné was a buildup from the previous two treaties. Yet when the United States could not back up its treaty talk, the Diné saw fit to protect themselves by war and raiding. In other words, the Diné saw fit to protect their access to the Four Sacred Elements. Alternatively, economic interests allowed some Diné to raid for their own personal well-being. This would have been seen as a monopolization of access to the Four Sacred Elements, and most likely, that action would have been considered inconsistent with Diné philosophy.

A total of ten articles detailed such concepts as keeping peace among the Diné and other Indigenous groups and both sides giving back any captives obtained during fighting. The language of the treaty was more legalistic than in previous treaties. The main objective was to establish a Diné reservation with parameters set by the United States. It was also stipulated that the boundaries could be changed at the discretion of the U.S. government. Unilateral decision making is consistent with U.S. colonization theory (Getches et al. 2011, 64–73). Payment was set at approximately $98,000 over the course of several years. It appears that the underlying goal was to make the Diné into farmers and sheep herders. Another goal was to remove the communal landholding concept in favor of individual ownership and "advance upon [Diné] civilization" (Deloria and DeMallie 1999, 1314). Archival records indicate that the treaty was not ratified due to complaints by New Mexicans that not enough land was ceded by the Diné (Brugge and Correll 1971, 18). A draft of the reservation design set forth by the United States in the June 1855 treaty appears in a document entitled "Articles of Agreement and Convention, July 18, 1855" (Brugge and Correll 1971, 73).

It is not entirely clear when the following events occurred. What is known is that war soon heated up again between the Diné and the United States. An unknown Diné man killed a slave belonging to a U.S. army representative, Major William Thomas Harbaugh Brooks. Some historians believe the murder was retaliation for the slaughter of Manuelito's cattle. Zarcillos reiterated the lack of enforcement mechanisms between a single Diné leader and men from other bands. It should be noted that racism played a role in the U.S. effort. Brooks, a slave owner and Southerner, believed that people of color were inherently inferior to whites and that the whites must force their laws on all people of color (Denetdale 2009, 33–34). It is believed that these events, among other skirmishes, preceded the next set of treaty negotiations. An armistice was declared on November 20, 1858, which was not ratified by the United States nor agreed upon by the Diné. Speculation is that the armistice treaty was never submitted to the U.S. Senate. Instead, the treaty served to detail the conditions for a later treaty agreed upon on December 25, 1858 (Brugge and Correll 1971, 18). The armistice was a thirty-day truce that allowed for further treaty negotiations, drafting, and signing. The armistice demanded adherence to rules set by agents, the return of stolen horses, and the delivery of a murder suspect into U.S. custody (Deloria and DeMallie 1999, 1336). The December treaty would include the armistice conditions and also set forth other conditions.

The treaty of December 25, 1858, formalized the armistice of the previous November. The treaty was a throwback to prior, less legalistic treaties that set forth demands agreed to by the Diné. There were no longer any demands for the United States to meet. The treaty imposed an eastern territorial limit on the Diné, with the threat of destruction of livestock found outside the boundary. The treaty also demanded that property that was lost or stolen by Diné had to be replaced. Finally, it demanded that there be a single leader for the Diné for the purpose, seemingly, of simplifying relations between the Diné and the United States (Deloria and DeMallie 1999, 1338). Reports indicate that the treaty was never presented to the U.S. Senate, and it was rejected by Diné representatives. Rejection by the Diné makes sense because all of the conditions threatened the maintenance of a proper relationship with the Four Sacred Elements. The overall assessment of the armistice and subsequent treaty is that it failed to change any Diné actions (Brugge and Correll 1971, 20). That this treaty was even drafted probably indicates that the previous treaty was too strongly worded and that the threats the United States made could not be carried out.

The last known *Naach'id* took place sometime in 1859. Although there is no way to know for sure, the discussion most probably centered on relations with the United States and how U.S. actions continuously threatened a proper relationship with the Four Sacred Elements. On February 15, 1861, a treaty was entered into between the United States and the Diné, but it was never ratified due to the start of the U.S. Civil War. Speculation abounds concerning the actual purpose of the document. It could have been an armistice drafted by soldiers to end a war, and submission to the Senate may never have been intended. Because of the U.S. preoccupation with Confederate rebels, the New Mexican and Ute attacks on the Diné continued unabated by U.S. governmental intervention (Brugge and Correll 1971, 21). The language of the 1861 treaty harshly called for the Diné to submit to U.S. authority. It also asserted a U.S. desire for the Diné to establish settlements west of Fort Fauntleroy (Deloria and DeMallie 1999, 1339–1340). (Fort Fauntleroy was renamed Fort Lyon and later the second Fort Wingate after the original Fort Wingate was abandoned [Global Security 2009].) Still, Manuelito and his warriors maintained war efforts. Perhaps they took seriously their role of protecting Diné access to the Four Sacred Elements. Alternatively, they realized they could monopolize their own individual access and enrich themselves.

As part of the treaty obligations set forth in 1861, the Diné would visit Fort Wingate to obtain food rations, feast, race horses, and generally commune peacefully. According to historical reports, during one of the horse races, it was discovered that Manuelito's saddle girth had been cut in an attempt to sabotage his racing abilities. The disagreement led to violence; U.S. soldiers indiscriminately murdered women and children who were in attendance (Denetdale 2009, 38). Meanwhile, these deadly conflicts in Diné Country coincided with the U.S. Civil War and the revival of the idea of removing Indians from their homelands. That the plan to remove the Diné was implemented during the U.S. Civil War may, perhaps, have prevented it from being as effective as it might have been otherwise.

Conjecture aside, it is clear that Fort Sumner was chosen as an intern-ment/concentration camp for the Diné and the Mescalero Apache. Fort Sumner was chosen in spite of, or perhaps because of, the fact that the land was prone to harsh summers and winters. It also had alkaline water and inadequate wood, and it was largely uninhabitable (Denetdale 2009, 39). Removing the Diné from within the Six Sacred Mountains was the clearest and most serious threat to their ability to maintain a proper relationship with the Four Sacred Elements, and all *Naat'áanii* understood this. The idea was to move the Diné to a land they did not know. Thus, confused, the old would pass away and the young would be educated as Christian farm-ers. Although it is not clear how effectively the message was disseminated, the United States stated that in exchange for the Diné's surrender, they would be given food, clothing, and shelter while awaiting marching orders to the Bosque Redondo reservation (Denetdale 2009, 40). The Diné called the subsequent march *Hwéldi*, or what contemporary historians call the Long Walk. The Diné refer to this time as *Nidahonidzoodą́ą́*, or the time of fear (Benally 2006, xv). Again, completely severing access to the Four Sacred Elements is just as serious as a mass execution, and all *Naat'áanii* understood this fact.

The U.S. campaign to remove the Diné was spearheaded by Indian fighter Kit Carson. Apparently, his plan was to go through Diné land and burn *hooghans*, murder people who did not surrender, and allow his soldiers to have their way with whomever they encountered (Denetdale 2009, 42). In other words, Carson attempted to sever all ties between the Diné and the Four Sacred Elements. As a result, many Diné probably did not consider surrender as an option and interpreted the behavior of Carson and his men as a war of genocide. (From the Diné philosophical point of view, it was clearly a war of genocide.) In what might be considered a form of guerilla warfare today, Diné warriors followed the Carson outfit and attacked when Carson's men let their guard down, thereby avoiding open European-style warfare. This activ-ity angered, humiliated, and embarrassed Carson (Denetdale 2009, 42).

Eventually, the Carson campaign followed many Diné into *Tsé yí*, or Canyon de Chelly. *Tsé yí* was a Diné stronghold and was known to protect its people well. There are many stories of people waiting in *Tsé yí* for years at a time while U.S. soldiers searched in vain. The Diné were capable of climbing up and down the canyon walls by using ladders constructed out of natural materials and pulling them away so the soldiers could not follow. *Tsé yí* is considered a gift to the Diné from the Holy Ones, or *Diyin Dine'é*. The area was a shelter, a place where the Diné could ask the *Diyin Dine'é* for help. In the end, however, the Carson slash-and-burn campaign took its toll, and more Diné had no choice but to surrender (Bighorse, Bighorse, and Bennett

1990). Many *Naat'áanii* decided that they would personally lead or accompany their people on the march to Bosque Redondo, and many "voluntarily surrendered." They likely knew that they would be needed by their people to secure their access to the Four Sacred Elements as best they could.

There was no relief coming for the Diné. Since wars of colonialism are quite profitable, the slave trade continued unabated, and more Diné surrendered and agreed to march east to Fort Sumner. Conflicting reports indicate that Barboncito joined the people on the Long Walk to ensure they had good morale (Bighorse, Bighorse, and Bennett 1990, 34–35). Less believable is that Barboncito was caught with a small group in *Tsé yí* and forced to join his people on the walk (Denetdale 2009, 45). Philosophical considerations may indicate that Barboncito went along voluntarily to ensure his people had as good a relationship as he could facilitate with the Four Sacred Elements. It was only after Manuelito and his group had held out as long as they could that they agreed to take the walk (Denetdale 2009, 46). Once again, Diné philosophy suggests Manuelito would only have gone along for reasons involving access to the Four Sacred Elements.

The incarceration period was bad all around. The details of the horrors can be located elsewhere (Denetdale 2009; Bighorse, Bighorse, and Bennett 1990). Ultimately, with no way to regulate a relationship with the Four Sacred Elements, there could be no Diné. Food was in short supply, and there were too many people (seven thousand Diné) for Bosque Redondo to support. Inhumane living conditions involved digging and living in a hole in the ground (Denetdale 2009). Two major conditions doomed the U.S. removal experiment. First, publicized evidence of the horrific conditions forced the U.S. government to supplement the concentration camp financially. Second, the U.S. army was not able to prevent individuals from returning to their homeland. Under threat of an all-out rebellion, the closing of the experiment commenced in 1868 (Denetdale 2009, 88). The next treaty formalized the end of the incarceration period. The creation of the Diné reservation within the area of their traditional homelands came next. It is difficult to know what *Naat'áanii* were thinking, but they must have been keenly aware that they would no longer be able to maintain their relationship with the Four Sacred Elements as they had prior to colonial actor interaction. It may have been time to mitigate the damage as much as possible by accepting the terms dictated to them by colonial actors.

The second and final treaty ratified by the U.S. government, known as the treaty of 1868, is probably the most famous of the treaties (Brugge and Correll 1971, 22). Table 2.4 is a list of the *Naat'áanii* who signed the treaty of 1868. The information was obtained from the Navajo Nation Museum Archive and is duplicated verbatim here (along with the original spelling).

Table 2.4. LIST OF *NAAT'ÁANII* WHO SIGNED THE TREATY OF 1868
WITH NAVAJO NAMES, CLANS, AND *NAAT'ÁANII* SPECIALIZATION

Name	Residence	History
BARBONCITO, Head Chief *Hastiin Dá'gháá íí* (Man of Mustache) *Naat'áá Hastiin* (Man with Black Feather) *Hozhoonzhi Naataani* (Peace Chief)	Canyon De Shea, AZ (Canyon de Chelly) *Ma'iideeshgiizhinii* (Coyote Pass)	First signer of 1868 treaty Head chief at Fort Sumner Youth warrior, peace chief, and medicine man Died March 16, 1871, after long illness
ARMIJO *Gish dilid'di* (Burnt Staff)	East of Chuska, NM *Kinyaa'áánii* (The Towering House)	Second signer of the 1868 treaty Chief and peace chief at Fort Sumner Died in 1882
DELGADO also known as DELGADITO *Diniihí Nééz* (Painful Tall Man)	Crownpoint, NM *Kinyaa'áánii* (The Towering House)	Third signer of 1868 treaty Only person who signed his name Originally Navajo enemy before 1864 Saved Navajos from Kit Carson Warrior chief Died in 1872
MANUELITO *Hastiin ch'ilhajíní* (Black Weeds leading from Water Edge) *'Ashkii Diyinii* (Holy Boy)	Manuelito Springs, NM *Bit'áá'nii* (Folded Arms People/ Within His Cover)	Fourth signer of 1868 treaty Head war chief before 1864 Peace chief Counselor after 1864 ca. 1818–1894
CAPITAN LARGO *Hastiin Bigódi Bijáá'* (Sits with Knees by Ears)	San Juan River *To'tsóhnii* (Big Water Clan)	Fifth signer of 1868 treaty Head and peace chief
HERRERO *A'tsidíí Sani* (Old Silversmith) or *Beshííłiini* (Metal Maker)	Wheatfields/Narbona Pass, AZ *Dibé'lizhini* (Blacksheep Clan)	Sixth signer of 1868 treaty Signed 1858 treaty at Ft. Defiance as head chief Died in 1870
CHIQUETO OR CHIQUITO *Łįįneeníįhí Bi'ye'* (Horse-Giver's Son)	East of Chuska, NM *Dibé'lizhini* (Blacksheep Clan)	Seventh signer of 1868 treaty Head chief and headman of warriors Died in 1874
MUERTO DE HOMBRE *Bi wosíí* (His Shoulder)	Chinle Valley, AZ *To'tsóhnii* (Big Water Clan)	Eighth signer of 1868 treaty Warrior chief Died in 1878

(continued)

Table 2.4. CONTINUED

Name	Residence	History
HOMBRO *Dichiin biłhe'hí'* (Dying of Hunger)	Ganado to Keams Canyon, AZ *Lók'aa' Dine'é* (Reed People Clan)	Ninth signer of 1868 treaty Head and peace chief
NARBONO also misspelled as NARBONA *'Ats áá bisłóní* (One Who Fights/Rip Tied to Saddle)	Tohatchi, NM *Nąnasht'ézhí* (Zuni Clan)	Tenth signer of 1868 treaty Head chief and sub-war chief
NARBONO SEGUNDO *Hastiin Dziłtá'nií* (Near Mountain Man)	Two Grey Hills, NM *Dziłtá'nií Dine'é* (Near Mountain Man)	Eleventh signer of 1868 treaty War chief and headman
GANADO MUCHO or AGNAS GRANDES Hastiin *To'tsóhnii* (Man of Big Water) or *Bibééghashíílani* (Man with Many Cows)	Ganado, AZ *To'tsóhnii* (Big Water Clan)	Twelfth signer of 1868 treaty Warrior in youth Head chief and peace chief Political leader and counselor Died in 1890

Source: Navajo Nation Museum Archive 6/07.

The treaty of 1868 contained thirteen articles in all, and it returned to the legalistic tradition contained in the previously ratified Diné-U.S. treaty of 1849. It is worth noting that there is a plethora of information contained in Table 2.4. Of special interest is the column labeled History. Although the information is incomplete, it is noteworthy that war and peace leader designations were assigned. There are six clearly noted peace-way leaders: Barboncito, Armijo, Manuelito, Capitan Largo, Hombro, and Ganado Mucho. Additionally, there are five identified war-way leaders: Delgado, Chiquito, Muerto de Hombre, Narbono, and Narbono Segundo. The individual not designated as a war or peace leader is Herrero. These facts often go with little further analysis, and such neglect is a shame. Oral accounts suggest that the Diné governed themselves with a balance between war-way and peace-way methods, which are also known as *Hózhǫ́ǫ́jí Naat'áanii* and *Hashkéjí Naat'áanii*. This balance is part of a larger philosophical understanding known as *Ałch'į'Sila* requiring a balance between war and peace methods of diplomacy. Table 2.4 may be the only empirical evidence in support of Diné philosophical underpinnings. This discussion may seem like a distraction or an aside. However, from a Diné perspective, this treaty was likely the latest in a line of sacred documents in which *Naat'áaanii* continuously and relentlessly worked to preserve their people's access to the Four Sacred Elements. From the U.S. point of view, however, it was just another legal instrument to extinguish Diné (Indian) title (Lerma 2014a).

The most important and notable aspect of the treaty was the formation of the Navajo reservation, a diminished land base within the traditional Diné homelands or within the Six Sacred Mountains. Again, reservation formation through treaty is a method of recognizing Diné title and then extinguishing that right of occupancy. Hence, the treaty of 1868, in the minds of U.S. policymakers, likely and finally extinguished Diné (Indian) title. With the Diné's title extinguished, the land title was assumed by the United States to be held in federal trust, which means that the title could not later be conveyed to an individual land owner (Lerma 2014a). The treaty was a typical U.S. reservation setup—complete with promises of supplies for establishing U.S.-style settlements and an agent to facilitate dealings between the United States and the Diné. Education in the ways of U.S. tradition was also deemed necessary to "civilize" the Diné. Eight separate limitations on the Diné were listed in the treaty. Most important are the railroad clauses that gave the United States right of way through reservation territory. Future land cessions were also said to require a three-fourths vote by Diné males (Brugge and Correll 1971, 88–98). While all of these clauses were probably clearly interpreted as threats to the maintenance of a proper relationship with the Four Sacred Elements, the treaty may have been the best option given the Long Walk experience.

A final nonratified treaty was an attempt to further individualize the Diné by forcing them to accept subdivisions of reservation land based on the size of individual families. In fact, to call this document a treaty overlooks the U.S. policy of ending treaty making in 1871 (Bighorse, Bighorse, and Bennett 1990, 104). The "Agreement with the Navajo" of March 27, 1874, reads like an addendum to the 1868 treaty. The change from calling the negotiated resolutions treaties to calling them agreements is a reflection of U.S. congressional squabbling over the ability to ratify treaties. Prior to 1872, only the U.S. Senate needed to ratify treaties. Some see the change in terminology as a further curtailment of Indigenous sovereignty (Wilkins 2003, 20). Still, it may also be viewed as the end of treaty making with the Diné and a shift in U.S. policy to consider the Diné a domestic political issue. In other words, the Diné were no longer considered a legitimate international actor by the United States. Perhaps weary over the prolonged struggle to cheat the Diné out of their weapons and land, the United States did not take much interest in the Diné until corporate interests discovered finite resources (such as oil) on the reservation in the 1920s.

2.3. EARLY RESERVATION PERIOD 1868–1923—REGENERATING LIFE AFTER WAR

The period from 1868 to 1923 in Diné history is relatively undocumented by historians. One exception to this oversight is the work of Bailey and Bailey (1999). Some major events in U.S. Indian policy occurred during this time frame, which still have some general impact on the Diné. But for the most part, the United States left the Diné alone, perhaps because it was preoccupied with other Indian issues, such as the war with Geronimo and the Apaches. This may have been the last historic period when Diné relations with their Four Sacred Elements were not at risk.

Several sources use "timeline" summaries to discuss the events of this era. In 1869, the U.S. Congress passed a statute in which all remaining tribes were settled on various reservations. This legislation was in line with the extinguishing of Indian title, passing title into federal trust, and holding title for the Indians' best interest as defined by the U.S. federal government. The idea of looking out for the best interests of Indians later evolved into Federal Trust Responsibility (Getches et al. 2011, 329–366). Each of the Indian reservations was given over to a Christian church denomination for further assimilation procedures (Bighorse, Bighorse, and Bennett 1990, 104).

Between 1878 and 1884, the Navajo reservation increased in size via several executive orders (Denetdale 2009, 124). The reason for the increases involves the fact that too many people lived in the space originally demarcated in the 1868 treaty. Also, many Diné found themselves living in spaces that were not technically a part of the reservation. Five separate U.S. actions established the current reservation boundaries (Wilkins 2003, 208). (The Navajo reservation now encompasses 8 million acres [Bighorse, Bighorse, and Bennett 1990, 104].) Post-1868 governing institutions were created just after the incarceration period concluded.

The Diné took steps to rejuvenate their way of governing upon returning to their traditional homeland. The rejuvenation process likely involved healing and protection songs and prayers to ensure that post-1868 governance would secure a proper relationship with the Four Sacred Elements. In the fall of 1868, a blessing-way ceremony was held at Window Rock for seven days. There were a total of thirteen leaders. Each leader received a *jish*, or bundle. The thirteen leaders were instructed to carry the *jish* through Window Rock four times. Afterward, the thirteen dispersed in the Four Directions to begin their lives again (Wilkins 2003, 79). All thirteen *Naat'áanii* proceeded to pick up where they left off in guiding their people in their future relations with the Four Sacred Elements. Indian agent documents of the time indicate four groups in relation to the agency. The area east of the agency was run by Manuelito. The area south of the agency was run by Mariano and Tsi'naajini Biye'. The area west of the agency was run by Ganado Mucho, and the area north of the agency came under the direction of Francisco Capitan (Wilkins 2003, 79). There was little European interest in the events on the Navajo reservation at that time. Hence, there was little reason to question or co-opt the organic leadership process Diné leaders utilized to begin governing again. It is interesting to note that there was no apparent record of a protection-way ceremony such as a *Naach'id*. Some scholars simply state that the last *Naach'id* was held before the Long Walk, and the ceremony must have been lost during the four-year incarceration.

But the story of the *Naach'id* is not so simple. One account mentions the last *Naach'id* taking place in 1859 (Austin 2009, 11). Many questions beyond the scope of this book remain about the *Naach'id*. Since the Diné were not to interact in war ways, why would they have a war-way ceremony upon returning to their homeland? Perhaps some of the Diné leaders were tired of war and only wanted to go back home in any shape they could. Perhaps *Naat'áanii* actually believed that there was no longer any threat to their relationship with the Four Sacred Elements. Another possibility is that war ways and war leaders were discriminated against or otherwise discouraged from continuing their practices. This would require beauty-way leaders to ignore their concerns about sacred element relations. While they were incarcerated, the unknown question of where the Diné would ultimately end up loomed heavily in the minds of Diné leaders. Some U.S. policymakers considered removing the Diné to current-day Oklahoma. The Diné leaders were probably aware of this plan while incarcerated at Bosque Redondo. It is known that they had a ceremony that foretold the Diné would return to their homeland (Austin 2009, 5). By 1868, that prophecy had been realized. After 1868, Diné leaders emerged with interests that happened to converge with U.S. interests.

One of the few accounts of the 1868–1923 period comes from Bailey and Bailey (1999). Here we learn that neither the Diné nor the U.S. officials wanted another war. The Diné primarily wanted to rebuild their destroyed political economy (Bailey and Bailey 1999, 27). One might interpret the economy-rebuilding interest as falling into the hands of *Hózhǫ́ǫ́jí Naat'áaanii* or peace-way leaders.

Diné leaders achieved their goal of rebuilding their political economy and, in fact, experienced economic prosperity shortly after returning to their homelands. This era of economic prosperity was the most successful that Navajo Nation had ever seen, and it has not been witnessed again (Bailey and Bailey 1999, 73–88). Of course, the unasked question is whether *Hózhǫ́ǫ́jí Naatʼáaanii* simply disregarded their philosophy and monopolized their individual and clan access to the Four Sacred Elements. This would mean that a growing interest among *Hózhǫ́ǫ́jí Naatʼáaanii* probably involved preventing Diné citizens from disrupting economic prosperity. In other words, if individuals questioned this monopolization, it could disrupt the status quo of economic prosperity. One way to disrupt prosperity was to create a hostile situation by Diné raiding non-Diné settlements. If some Diné continued to raid, it could have brought back the U.S. army. This would have stopped or at least decreased the level of economic prosperity for the majority of nonraiding Diné. This is a serious and underresearched process that cannot be fully addressed here. Suffice it to say, Diné leaders were keenly aware of the raiding issues.

A "Chief's Council" was formed at Bosque Redondo. This council was made up of Armijo, Delgado, Manuelito, Largo, Herrero, Chiqueto, Muerto de Hombre, Hombre, Narbono, Ganado Mucho, Narbono Segundo, and the principal chief, Barboncito (Bailey and Bailey 1999, 29). These leaders were dependent upon the U.S. army to regulate the wayward Diné who might engage in raiding.

This interest makes sense *if* one assumes that these twelve leaders each had an interest in his own personal economic prosperity. Some existing accounts support this assumption. For example, Manuelito and Narbono did resort to force in 1870 to recapture raided livestock (Bailey and Bailey 1999, 30). Another example comes from 1878, when forty "witches and thieves" were killed by Manuelito and Ganado Mucho (33). These events suggest a type of purging. They may also explain why the *Naachʼid* apparently went away after 1859 and why the subject of *Hashkéjí Naatʼáanii* is a touchy one today. Did the Navajo elite (peace-way leaders) purge themselves of their war leaders? Reexamining Table 2.4 may provide further evidence of a *Hashkéjí Naatʼáanii* purging. Note that the far-right column contains information about years when the signers of the treaty of 1868 passed away. Many of the *Hashkéjí Naatʼáanii* began passing away in the 1870s. Delgado walked on in 1872, Chiquito in 1874, Muerto de Hombro in 1878, and Herrero in 1870, but it is not clear if the latter was a war or peace leader. Many clearly designated peace-way leaders lived longer: Babroncito died in 1871, Armijo in 1882, Manuelito in 1894, and Ganado Mucho in 1890.

It could be that *Hashkéjí Naatʼáanii* were not content with the Chief's Council and its apparent disregard for protection-based relations with the Four Sacred Elements. As such, it may have simply been convenient for these war-way leaders to be shunned and, in the most serious situations, executed by an emerging Navajo elite made up of peace-way leaders. It is worth noting that individuals such as Manuelito changed from war-way to peace-way leaders during their lives. Could former war-way leaders have recognized a threat to their lives and changed their ways to live longer? Other loosely related research includes Martha Blue's *The Witch Purge of 1878: Oral and Documentary History in the Early Navajo Reservation Years.* The relationship between *Hashkéjí Naat'áanii* is beyond the scope of this research but warrants further study.

Time moved on, and new leaders emerged. At the same time, shifting U.S. policy involving the assimilation of Indians allowed for more coercive attempts to control Diné leaders. This was evident during the period between 1878 and 1910, in which the Indian agent appointed "Head Chiefs" for the respective groups (Wilkins 2003, 79). Manuelito was named the head of the first Navajo police force. The Navajo police operated as the only law enforcement, government-type entity that was recognized by the U.S. government (Denetdale 2009, 28). Later, in 1884, the United States replaced Manuelito with Chee Dodge, a bilingual Diné of mixed blood (Wilkins 2003, 79). Between 1901 and 1911, five agencies were set up. The agencies are still used today in modified form. In no particular order, these agencies are called Southern or Fort Defiance; Northern or San Juan, which was renamed Shiprock; Western or Tuba City; Western extension or Leupp; and Eastern or Pueblo Bonito, which later became Crownpoint (Wilkins 2003, 208). It is very questionable that the Four Sacred Elements remained a high priority among anyone with power respected by the United States. This neglect would not ever be implied, let alone acknowledged, after oil was discovered.

In 1921, oil was discovered on the San Juan Agency, or Shiprock (Wilkins 2003, 208). Discovery of oil was the impetus for the creation of contemporary Diné governance, which is still used in modified form today.

2.4. CONTEMPORARY DINÉ GOVERNANCE—REGENERATING TOMORROW WITH WESTERN GOVERNMENT

What follows will be a brief summary of the "democratic" era of Diné governance. This period of Diné history might be characterized as the point when U.S. corporations began to discover that valuable natural resources were present on the Navajo reservation. Alternatively, it could be that resource extraction corporations always knew of the finite resource deposits. It may be that it was only by the 1920s that the technology to extract the resources was fully developed. This is another area that certainly deserves further research. It should be clear by now that any attempt to extract and commodify raw materials based on the monopolization of the Four Sacred Elements is a clear violation of Diné philosophy. The U.S. government has a nasty habit of discovering things and appropriating them for its own enrichment (Getches, Wilkinson, and Williams 1998; Lukes 2005; Morgenthau 1948; Said 1978; Waltz 1979; Wilkins 1987, 2002b, 2003).

Euro-American-style governance was developed and presented to Navajo people open to, or unaware of, U.S. interests. The Diné leaders of the 1920s were selected in much the same fashion that was exhibited during the treaty-making era. They were selected by the United States to support governance restructuring, which ultimately reflected U.S. and corporate interests. More often than not, the legitimacy of approved government changes was questionable at best. This is the type of co-opted Navajo government that is willing to ignore the Four Sacred Elements and allow finite resource extraction.

The discovery of oil in Diné Country during the early 1920s was a major impetus for the formation of the 1922 Business Council (Wilkins 1987). The Business Council was organized so that oil and gas leases could be more easily obtained from the Navajo people. Recall that previously any changes required a three-quarters vote by all male Diné. The Business Council changed this process to focus on the distribution of royalties. Before the Business Council operated, royalties were only distributed to the region where oil and gas were discovered. However, this required the U.S. government and its corporate interests to obtain several "tedious" permissions. Reconfiguring a single Business Council would allow corporate interests to go to one decision-making board to obtain permission to extract resources on any land within the greater Navajo Nation. This was the main purpose for changing the royalty payment scheme (Wilkins 1987).

The Business Council was headed by three Navajos appointed by the U.S. Secretary of the Interior. It is simply not clear if these three Navajo men were aware of the future consequences the Business Council would have on relations with the Four Sacred Elements. On January 3, 1923, the Business Council was modified and tasked with assembling a committee to create the Navajo Tribal Council (Wilkins 1987). The January 3, 1923, model appears to have been hastily assembled in the wake of the Business Council model. This may be because the Business Council model was not accepted by the Diné people as a legitimate body fit to represent them (Wilkins 1987). Again, the question must be raised about whether this heavily concentrated business model was concerned with a relationship to the Four Sacred Elements. Also, the January 3 model established oversight mechanisms via some branch of the U.S. government. For example, delegates and alternate delegates were removable by the Secretary of the Interior. Also, the Navajo Tribal Council only met when the U.S. Commissioner of Indian Affairs was present. More modifications followed.

On January 24, 1923, the Navajo Tribal Council was formed (Wilkins 1987). Perhaps it is more accurate to state that the January 3 body was modified into the January 24 model. U.S. interests attempted to maintain control within the council. Navajo leaders, although it is not clear who these leaders were, eventually thwarted these attempts. In 1933, Navajo Nation revoked some of the U.S.-imposed oversight mechanisms. Specifically, the requirement that a "federal representative be present at council meetings" and the requirement that the council "convene at the liberty of the Commissioner" were revoked (Wilkins 1987).

The January 24 Navajo Tribal Council was less likely to represent U.S. interests. One might conclude that the Tribal Council body was hijacked by Diné citizens, as evidenced by several revocations that took place after its 1923 introduction. Over time, the scope of the January 24 model expanded to take on responsibility for Diné governance. Prior to these changes, the Tribal Council served as an advisory board to the U.S. Commissioner of Indian Affairs. It's likely that the January 24 model and its modifications would have remained in place had it not been for the Indian Reorganization Act of 1934.

The United States maintained an interest in pushing tribal governments into the envelope of a U.S. constitutional model of government. As a consequence, Navajo Nation created a Tribal Constitutional Assembly in 1938 (Wilkins 1987). Here it helps to understand federal Indian policy of the time. The Indian Reorganization Act of 1934, or IRA, was meant to bring Indians into the modern era by formalizing their governments (Wilkins 2003, 59). A better way to understand the IRA was that, during this time, the United States was operating under the false assumption that its own form of government was the most advanced government, and all other forms of government were inferior to its own. As a consequence, little attention was given to traditional Indigenous governance institutions. Many tribes adopted IRA-style constitutions, but Navajo Nation did not. Regardless of the Navajo vote to reject the IRA, the era was colored by the U.S. government's outlook on tribal governance. The U.S. government and the Secretary of the Interior offered rhetoric that IRA legislation would solve problems outlined in the Meriam Report (Meriam and Work 1928). The United States's one-size-fits-all approach was really meant to address natural resource extraction in Indian Country and, specifically, in Navajo Nation.

Four years after the IRA was passed, Navajo Nation put together a Tribal Constitutional Assembly tasked with writing a constitution. Navajo people were critical of proposed reform to their governance. Perhaps the majority of the Navajo constituency was recognizing that their "leaders" were being more heavily concentrated. The most obvious failure of the Tribal Constitutional Assembly was that it did not write a constitution that was accepted by Diné citizens. In addition, the U.S.-approval requirement imposed on the Tribal Constitutional Assembly was the most overt presence of U.S. interest. U.S. assessment meant that Tribal Constitutional Assembly resolutions could not take effect unless the U.S. Secretary of the Interior approved them. Less overt, but questionable at the very least, were the rules for participation as a council member. Any set of rules purporting to govern participation in any exclusive body must be scrutinized for their discriminating properties. According to Lukes (2005), rules for participation are always subject to power domination. Finally, we know that the original intent of the Constitutional Assembly was to write a constitution. When the object was not fulfilled, a much broader scope of governance was introduced by virtue of the Tribal Council voting itself into office (Wilkins 1987). Unclear in all of these changes is the impact that each Tribal Council has today. From this point forward, there is no manifest or latent mention of the Sacred Elements.

There is no clear answer regarding how the various council incarnations have complemented and conflicted with one another. This area certainly deserves further research. Diné governance functions adequately enough to prevent most Diné from violently overthrowing it (Wilkins 2002a). Nonetheless, there are many tough questions that have not been addressed. What follows is not meant to be a normatively clear description of contemporary Navajo Nation government. Rather, the next few paragraphs are included to point out how rapidly some of the names and institutions have changed over the last century.

Research of the primary and secondary literature produced ill-defined ideas of what constitutes contemporary Diné governance. One exception is David Wilkins' work on Diné governance (2002a). Prior to the 2011 Title II amendments, there was a Navajo Tribal Council; an advisory committee; a Tribal Council Code, which included a Bill of Rights; a description of Navajo government structure and power; an outline of tribal membership criteria; election laws; outlines for dealing with fiscal matters; various business and commercial statutes; land use/natural resource management criteria; and elements dealing with law and order (Wilkins 2013). The most prominent features of contemporary Diné governance involve the three-branch system made up of executive, legislative, and judicial branches.

Presumably, the legislative and executive branches are derivative of the various tribal councils. But without cultural norms, legitimacy is questionable at best. Given this stipulation, it is necessary to look at contemporary Diné governance in a different manner. The consequences of a Tribal Code, which allowed for rule by resolution, followed by the cementing of the "Rules for the Navajo Tribal Council" have been far-reaching. The changes to Navajo government created a situation in which individual Diné were able to secure an executive position. Executives could then consolidate power within the executive branch (Wilkins 1987). Power consolidation in the executive branch was later offset by legislative branch checks on executive power through CD 68–89. A judicial branch was also added. The relationships between the executive, legislative, and judicial branches were further modified by CD 68–89 (Wilkins 2013). Left unclear are the ways in which recent modifications have augmented, negated, or left unmodified previously articulated governmental actions.

What has been presented here is a condensed history of Diné governance. Notice the break between normative Diné philosophy and imposed policy practice. Stated more simply, the potential for considering relations with the Sacred Elements simply vanishes over time. Notice, too, how the interaction with non-Diné people created a situation in which past planning could no longer properly manage contemporary issues. In other words, real-life events could no longer rely on past experience. Also, the act of warfare, in terms set by colonial actors, is a big disruption for any culture or society. It is very difficult for any group, let alone a group like the Diné, who were not actively colonizing their neighbors for the sole purpose of extracting resources, to sustain war indefinitely. As has already been stated, the Diné's philosophical aim was to maintain a proper distance or nearness toward the Four Sacred Elements. Hence, it does not make sense that Diné leaders could continue to utilize their normative governance model to sustain warfare. European-style war involving ethnic cleansing has nothing to do with elemental relations.

One interpretation is that the interaction period, in terms of war and the economy, created a break in the process that was outlined in Figure 1.1. Denny believes that a fracture in the timeline caused the planning stages inherent in Diné normative philosophy to inadequately deal with interaction with non-Diné peoples. It was not possible for Diné leaders to fathom a fire that could have wiped out colonial actors. They probably could not bring themselves to waste moisture on an idea as insane as carrying out genocide against the United States. They simply did not have the air to even speak about such an unspeakable pathway. Because, in the end, how can humans wish to regenerate what is essentially a countergenocidal strategy? According to Denny, disregard for relations with the Four Sacred Elements explains the chaos that exists in Diné governance today. Still, it seems consistent to conclude that any existence at all is better than no existence whatsoever. It appears that had *Hashkéji Naat'áanii* been allowed to take control, we might not know the people who call themselves Diné. Denny goes on to assert that no non-Diné approach can adequately resolve the problems faced by the Diné today or tomorrow. It's one thing to take the word of an individual on matters of institutional relevancy. It would be quite another to explore how concepts of Diné governance might have operated in two dimensions and along conditions of necessity. What happens when the underlying conditions are not cared for? What happens when new institutions are installed with little thought about their necessary conditions?

CHAPTER 3
Dook'o'ooshiid (San Francisco Peaks)

Living Concepts of Diné Governance

Figure 3.1 could be the most organic depiction of Diné philosophy in practice. This chapter is an attempt to represent Diné thinking in two or three dimensions. It also attempts to follow Diné thinking in a cyclical pattern starting with a basic idea about a leader, providing a context for leaders working to protect their people, for leaders to heal their people after the need for protection has passed, and for how both protection and healing are necessary conditions for a good, long, wisdom-filled life. This is true not only for the individual but also for the community at large.

Each day people have an opportunity to carry out what they have planned. Life is in the present tense, and plans and thoughts are in the past tense. Protocols for life can easily be linked to protocols for behavior shaped by Diné institutions of leadership. Living concepts of Diné governance can be taken literally. From the Diné philosophical perspective, knowledge holders talk about breathing life into inanimate objects like a *hooghan* or a strategy for weathering a drought. Yet as interaction with colonial actors increased, perhaps *Hajíneí*-era institutions of Diné governance were no longer able to breathe on their own. Still, even the notion that the Diné had institutions of governance before 1923 may be a novel idea in some circles. This chapter focuses on two governance systems: (1) the living concept of *Hajíneí*-era governing institutions, which indicates that the Four Sacred Elements probably had an impact on bringing these institutions to life; and (2) the lifeless institutions of governance that emerged in the vacuum left after war and colonial actors harmed Diné political and economic institutions.

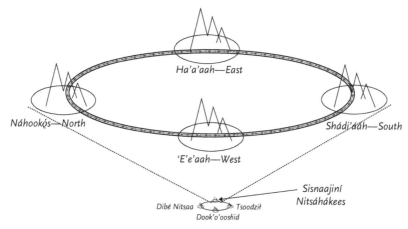

1. *Sisnaajiní*—Thinking Good Thoughts—Good Relations with the Four Sacred Elements
2. *Tsoodził*—Thinking Good Plans—Toward Knowledge, Age, Wisdom
3. *Dook'o'oosłiid*—Thinking a Good Life into Being—Acheiving *Hózhǫ́* One Minute at a Time
4. *Dibé Nitsaa*—Thinking Regeneration—Humans in Balance with Mother Earth and Father Sky for Generations

Figure 3.1: Living and Breathing *Diné Bibehazáanii*

Hence, there is an interesting interaction between life philosophy and the existence of institutions.

Institutions are part of a political science perspective that entails some general assumptions about the political environment. The institutional perspective is defined as one "that sees political interaction as depending on actors pursuing actions that are compatible with their interests and that are constrained by the structure of the situation in which they find themselves, especially the structure of political institutions" (Bueno De Mesquita 2009, 434). The institutional perspective can be applied to the maintenance of a proper distance and nearness toward the Four Sacred Elements in the following manner: *Naat'áanii* once took their role seriously. They were *actors* who governed (led) their people to maintain their proper relationship with the Four Sacred Elements. Maintaining good relations with the Four Sacred Elements was compatible with the interest of the Holy Ones. Perhaps the only point of debate involves *how* to maintain good relations. Did specific situations require healing or protection? Diné philosophy probably guided *Naat'áanii* in choosing the best course of action. The protection and healing practices allowed Diné progress from time immemorial until about 1861. The protection process was possibly ignored or discouraged by *Naat'áanii* after 1861 until the Diné either forgot or refused to openly utilize their protection philosophy. In any case, these institutions did exist and had a life of their own based on ceremony, place, language, and sacred history (Holm, Pearson, and Chavis 2003; Lerma 2012).

The analysis of Diné philosophy in this chapter is offered as a foundation for guiding future leaders who wish to reincorporate either Diné philosophy or some other Indigenous philosophy into their decisions and policymaking. Simultaneously, this chapter is also a response to the challenge offered by Shawn Wilson in *Research Is Ceremony: Indigenous Research Methods* (2008). Early research by Indigenous scholars involved stating the problem from an Indigenous point of view, such as in Deloria's *Behind the Trail of Broken Treaties* (1974). Later research by Indigenous scholars employed "mainstream" solutions. Today, Indigenous scholars are attempting to "decolonize" their worldview as they search for ways to rebuild their Native nations (Smith 1999). Wilson offered a fourth stage of Indigenous research that relies on Indigenous thinking and is perhaps similar to Cajete's (2000) or Begay and Maryboy's scholarship (1998). This chapter will attempt to use Diné philosophy in conjunction with the concept-building method to promote thinking in three dimensions (Goertz 2006).

3.1. TRADITIONAL DINÉ CONCEPTS—REFLECTING ON THE PAST

As was discussed in Chapter 1, it is possible to look back to past planning to better understand if those plans, as they were then implemented, are effective in governing lives today.[1,2] For example, yesterday's relationships with the Four Sacred Elements *must* play a role in how people plan for today and tomorrow. Because we can assume that even now *all* humans need a good relationship with fire, water, air, and pollen, this chapter will reflect on past concepts of Diné governance. Before exploring the relevance that traditional Diné governance has for contemporary issues, it is useful to understand the mechanics of traditional Diné governance more clearly. Previous chapters outline some of the patterns in Diné philosophy of governance and some of the disruptions that occurred during times of warfare and economic destruction. Diné philosophy states clearly that humans have a responsibility to maintain their proper distance and nearness in relation to the Four Sacred Elements (1 N.N.C. §§ 201–206). When the Diné interacted with the United States, it usurped and monopolized *Hajínéí*-era Diné institutions; the result is that since then the Diné relationship with the Four Sacred Elements has been neglected or perhaps overtly disregarded. Today, it seems clear that contemporary Navajo policymakers rarely, if ever, consider their relationship to the Four Sacred Elements. Some perspective on the function of *Hajínéí*-era institutions might assist those interested in reconnecting with the elemental philosophy of the Diné.

The concepts of Diné governance presented here are based on scant primary and secondary sources, which might not be completely accurate. Moreover, besides the author, there are no other scholars of Diné governance currently working with concept-building methods. The concepts presented here are designed to show how *Hajinéí*-era institutions of Diné governance were alive and responsive to the Four Sacred Elements. The goal of this chapter is to relearn how traditional Diné governance operated. It will answer this question: How did traditional concepts of Diné governance work to ensure that all people had a good and proper distance and nearness toward the Four Sacred Elements?

3.1.1. Concept of *Naat'áanii*

Oral tradition and some primary documentation point to the existence of *Naat'áanii*, or traditional headmen, in Diné society (Wilkins 1987, 41). These documents, of course, do not capture Diné philosophy, which is much more complex. In Figure 3.2, the five components of legitimizing a *Naat'áanii* have been compiled from descriptive research and rearticulated into a three-level view. In addition, there are conditions or traits that can be observed in the real world that verify the presence of individual secondary-level conditions (Goertz 2006, 30, 35, 62). The term *Naat'áanii* is a placeholder. One can change the name of the concept (to headman, for example), but so long as the conditions underlying the concept remain intact, the concept itself will not change.

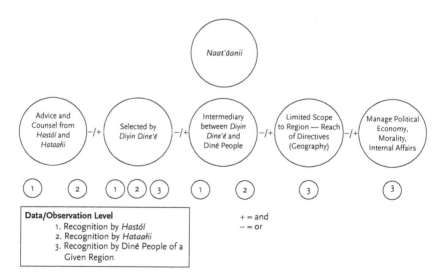

Figure 3.2: Three-Level View—Concept of *Naat'áanii*

One can consider the five traits of a *Naat'áanii* as necessary individually and sufficient collectively. In other words, if an individual does not possess the five necessary conditions, that person cannot be a *Naat'áanii*; each condition alone is not capable of representing the full *Naat'áanii* concept. Rather, all five conditions must be present. The most noteworthy ties between conditions and philosophy are ties to *Hastóí* and a *Hataałii* and a leader, as well as selection by an intermediary between the *Diyin Dine'é* and the Diné people. *Hastóí* are wise elders and a *Hataałii* is a singer/medicine man or woman. There is no way to empirically link any human being to the selection condition in a way that satisfies social scientists. However, Diné philosophy recognizes that the *Diyin Dine'é* are responsible for teaching the Diné to live by their tenets. Second, these tenets should be looked at as institutions of Diné governance that provide norms of behavior given various scenarios. These three conditions should be taken as the people of a particular era understood them. Yet how do we know they exist? While the causal pathway between these conditions and leaders may be unclear, other conditions are more observable. Below all the secondary-level conditions are connections between said conditions that can be observed by the average Diné citizen and that can be associated with the presence or absence of the corresponding secondary-level condition. We will consider one condition at a time as an example of the *Naat'áanii* concept design.

Putting "breathing life" concerns aside yields a more analytical (and dry) perspective on institutions of Diné governance. Starting from the bottom left of Figure 3.2, notice that the data/observation level is labeled one and two. The numbers one and two correspond to the recognition of the secondary-level trait by *Hastóí* and *Hataałii* (Wilkins 1987, 41). The corresponding secondary-level trait is "Advice and Counsel from *Hastóí* and *Hataałii*" (Wilkins 1987, 41). Thus, an analyst might observe the relationship with the Four Sacred Elements and institutional ideas as follows: *Hastóí* and *Hataałli* recognize the need to give their advice and counsel to a *Naat'áanii*. *Naat'áanii* cannot lead without this advice and counsel because they need to ensure that they are operating correctly and that the community remains in balance concerning its relationship with the Four Sacred Elements. By giving their advice to a *Naat'áanii*, the *Hastóí* and *Hataałii* verify the legitimacy of a particular *Naat'áanii*. If *Hastóí* and *Hataałii* lose confidence in the leadership of a given *Naat'áani*, they may stop giving their advice and counsel to that individual. For example, a *Naat'áanii* who invites an imbalanced relationship with the Four Sacred Elements will stop receiving the counsel of *Hastóí* and *Hataałii*. Such action would eliminate the secondary-level condition labeled "Advice and Counsel." By eliminating the Advice and Counsel condition, the legitimacy of the *Naat'áanii* is also lost. Community members will recognize this as a sign that they should also not follow the *Naat'áanii*. Continuing to follow a nonlegitimate *Naat'áanii* invites an imbalance (*hóxchǫ́*) with the Four Sacred Elements in the community. Hence, the concept of *Naat'áanii* does not exist as an investment in an individual. The ability to lead under the *Naat'áanii* system is invested in the seat or position.

Note that *Hastóí* and *Hataałii* also recognize (or do not recognize) that a given *Naat'áanii* is the intermediary between the Diné and *Diyin Dine'é* (Wilkins 1987, 41). Two outcomes of the relationship are worthy of note. First, the concept of *Naat'áanii* as described in Figure 3.2 illustrates the important roles that *Hastóí* and *Hataałii* provide in traditional Diné governance. More information on this topic is available in the Introduction and in Chapter 1. Second, *Hastóí* and *Hataałii* traditionally had a tremendous impact on governance by determining who the *Naat'áanii* were, because the *Naat'áanii* were relied upon by average Diné for various needs, including their management of relationships with the Four Sacred Elements. Still, *Hastóí* and *Hataałii* were not all-powerful.

The *Hastóí* and *Hataałii* did not have a say in every aspect of determining the legitimacy of *Naat'áanii*. As noted earlier, some of the secondary-level conditions are more directly observable, such as geography and regional scope. These conditions appear to have been solely determined by the physical space in which some Diné happened to live. In other words, the Diné of a given region invested in their own regional *Naat'áanii*. Once again, when the Diné failed to recognize a given *Naat'áanii*, the legitimacy of that *Naat'áanii* came into question. This might be better understood as a product of the institutional perspective applied to *Hajínéí*-era Diné leaders.

3.1.2. Concept of *Hashkééjí* (War) *Naat'áanii*

Another trait of traditional Diné governance is having governing specialists who focus their expertise on specific situations in times of war or peace. Again, it might be revealing to think of war-way leaders in terms of the institutions guiding their decision making in times of crisis. However, Denny and Yazzie, in personal conversations and public lectures, both state that the situation was more nuanced. The Four Sacred Elements point of view suggests that *Hashkééjí Naat'áanii* likely involved a protection language, songs, prayers, and a particular pattern of thinking. War-way leaders understood how to protect against things like too much fire. Protection way is consistent with war when violent challenges to relations with the Four Sacred Elements are imposed by colonial actors. Beauty way is consistent with regeneration and healing practices, also known as

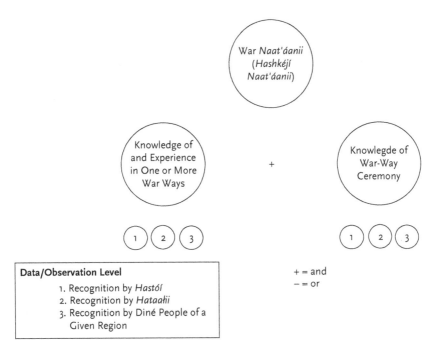

Figure 3.3: Three-Level View—Concept of *Hashkéjí Naat'áanii*

seeking peaceful resolutions to imbalances with the Four Sacred Elements. This innovation is represented by the traditional Diné governance institution involving war *Naat'áanii* and peace *Naat'áanii* (Wilkins 1987, 43). In the Navajo language, a war leader is called *Hashkéjí Naat'áanii*. Figure 3.3 is a representation of *Hashkéjí Naat'áanii* in a three-level view. It is very similar in format to Figure 3.2.

As an institution, the *Hashkéjí Naat'áanii* represents the basic level. There are two necessary conditions for legitimizing a *Hashkéjí Naat'áanii*: knowledge and experience in one or more methods of warfare and knowledge of at least one war-way ceremony (Wilkins 1987, 42). The primary and secondary research about *Hashkéjí Naat'áanii* is incomplete. According to Diné norms, the majority of *Hashkéjí Naat'áanii* knowledge is inappropriate for dissemination in book form, and that convention will be respected here. It is, however, worth reexamining the various issues raised in Chapter 2 concerning the possibility that war leaders were purged and how the relationship between war-way leaders and the treaty of 1868 unfolded (Blue 1988). Because of the lack of information, however, it is difficult to elaborate on institutional and Sacred Element issues.

The lack of information is evident in the vagueness of the secondary-level conditions of *Hashkéjí Naat'áanii*. Theoretically, it would be possible to create a highly informed concept of *Hashkéjí Naat'áanii* by discovering and sharing the various "war ways" in terms of experience and ceremony. This discovery process could fill in many blanks about institutional constraints (such as what constitutes agenda setting for war-way leaders) as well as processes for protecting proper relations with the Four Sacred Elements. In other words, it could be possible to establish a set of secondary-level conditions below "knowledge and experience" and "ceremony." This benefit will be useful when discussing early twenty-first-century iterations of Diné governance.

3.1.3. Concept of *Hózhǫ́ǫ́jí* (Peace) *Naat'áanii*

The most useful concept of traditional Diné governance is the peace *Naat'áanii* (*Hózhǫ́ǫ́jí Naat'áanii*). As an institution, the peace way is probably the best-known governance process that still exists today, because the judicial branch of the Navajo Nation government carries out peacemaking to resolve issues.[3] Figure 3.4 is the three-level view of the *Hózhǫ́ǫ́jí Naat'áanii*. The five necessary conditions for a *Hózhǫ́ǫ́jí Naat'áanii* are

1. To contribute to the sacred needs of Diné life and culture
2. To exhibit character
3. To be a good public speaker
4. To be charismatic
5. To contribute to the day-to-day needs of Diné life and culture (Wilkins 1987, 41–42)

Some of the conditions need further elaboration. Several knowledge holders, including both Denny and Yazzie, discuss how character is a function of being a fully formed adult. Thus, an adult has a lifeway *hooghan*, a spouse, and children, and he or she successfully manages day-to-day as well as long-term relationships with the Four Sacred Elements. To exhibit character is to live a good life in concert with a spouse as a complementary equal and an equitable partner. As Yazzie has repeatedly said in public lectures and in private conversations, the married life in Diné philosophy is a representation of *Ałch'į' Sila*. Denny has added that the relationship between Mother Earth and Father Sky is the ideal that humans can strive for on earth. If an individual is recognized as living up to the ideal, that individual is considered to have exhibited good character. Still, this is not enough to be a peace-way leader.

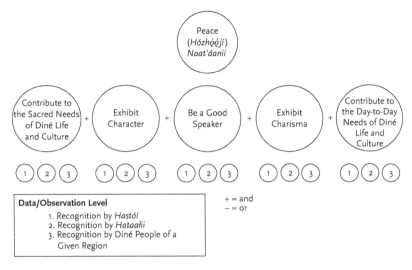

Figure 3.4: Three-Level View—Concept of Peace *(Hózhǫ́ǫ́jí) Naat'áanii*

Institutional conditions about being a good public speaker and displaying charisma also deserve some attention. Many knowledge holders exhibit these characteristics in their everyday life, yet they are not simply selling their ideas by any means necessary. These two conditions are inextricably linked to ensuring that peace-way leaders are advocating for a path that will bring all the people into proper relationship with the Four Sacred Elements. In English, being charismatic and having good speaking skills may appear to be superficial. Yet from the Diné perspective, these skills probably invoke a mastery of oral accounts about Diné creation, knowledge of ceremonial practices, an adherence to the norms of *K'é*, and a general respect for many issues, including the complementary (not hierarchical) nature of gender roles, as well as the equality of other community members and the weight of their concerns. All of these considerations, again, are guided by the institutional boundaries of Diné philosophy in practice.

In terms of institutions, all of the secondary-level conditions of a *Hózhǫ́ǫ́jí Naat'áanii* are recognized by the *Hastói, Hataałii,* and the Diné of a specific region. It bears mentioning that these "observations" are tricky from a non-Diné point of view but were very much respected by Diné at one time. As a function of Diné philosophy, each of the necessary conditions can be linked to maintaining good relations with the Four Sacred Elements. Sacred needs include ensuring proper distance and nearness toward the Four Sacred Elements. Personally keeping that relationship in balance is an indication of excellent character and charisma. Finally, day-to-day needs involve ensuring a community-wide good and balanced relationship with the Four Sacred Elements. Yet individual *Naat'áanii* have only so much reach. Institutionally, there is a mechanism for dealing with issues that span several geographical regions. At times it was necessary that several *Naat'áanii* meet for a *Naach'id* (Wilkins 1987, 41).

3.1.4. Concept of War and Peace *Naach'id*

One of the most interesting facets of Diné philosophy and governance involves the *Naach'id*. It is an institutional marvel. The *Naach'id* probably operated only when the need arose—similar in organization to a confederacy. In ceremonial terms, this means that the people from various communities likely came together to resolve a common dilemma such as drought or war. Denny has frequently stated that *Naach'id*-type gatherings could only operate if twelve or twenty-four *Naat'áannii* were willing to cede some of their agenda-setting abilities to the larger *Naach'id* body. Hence, scholars may wish to reexamine the *Naach'id* as a "Navajo Confederacy," in that each region would allow some of its sovereignty to be transferred to the ceremony for a limited amount of time. After the issue had been resolved, Diné leaders dismantled the central governing institution (*Naach'id*) and took their sovereignty donation back to their respective regions (Lerma 2014a). Primary records indicate the existence of a *Hashkéjí* and a *Hózhǫ́ǫ́jí Naach'id*. A *Hashkéjí Naach'id* and *Hózhǫ́ǫ́jí Naach'id* are depicted in Figure 3.5 and Figure 3.6, respectively. There are five necessary conditions of a *Hashkéjí* and *Hózhǫ́ǫ́jí Naach'id*:

1. A *Hashkéjí* and *Hózhǫ́ǫ́jí Naach'id* meets every two to four years or during an emergency that affects several regions.
2. Twelve *Hashkéjí Naat'áanii* are present, although some reports indicate that as few as six or as many as twenty-four leaders attend.
3. War is occurring.
4. Twelve *Hózhǫ́ǫ́jí Naat'áaanii* are present.
5. *Hashkéjí Naat'áanii* have the floor.

Note that the data/observation level involves recognition of all five necessary conditions by the *Hastói*, *Hataałii*, and the Diné of the respective regions of the various *Naat'áanii*. A *Hózhǫ́ǫ́jí Naach'id* (Figure 3.6) is very similar to the *Hashkéjí Naach'id*, with two exceptions: First, there is no state

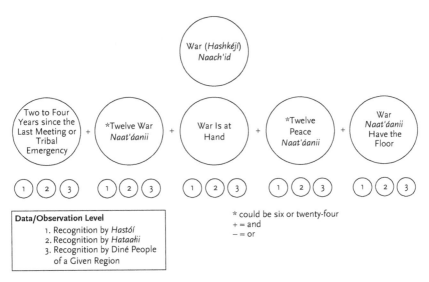

Figure 3.5: Three-Level View—Concept of War *(Hashkéjí) Naach'id*

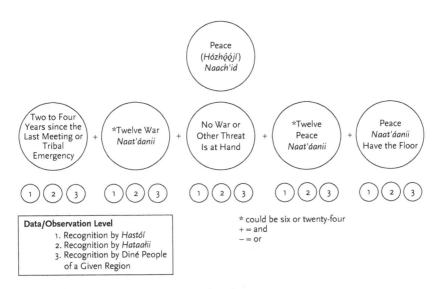

Figure 3.6: Three-Level View—Concept of Peace *(Hózhǫ́ǫ́jí) Naach'id*

of war, and second, the *Hózhǫ́ǫ́jí Naat'áanii* set the agenda. These institutional boundaries potentially worked as guides for managing relations with the Four Sacred Elements.

Managing a relationship with the Four Sacred Elements should bring out more nuances for interpreting conditions one and three. Condition one mentions an emergency. It seems consistent with Diné philosophy to assume that any condition that could potentially create an imbalance in the relationship of the people with the Four Sacred Elements is an emergency. Emergencies are likely measured in degrees, and the more severe the condition, the more likely one would encounter *anáhóót'i'*, or harm (Austin 2009, 62). Condition three is also impacted by considering the Four Sacred Elements. Cultural warfare is not the same as political warfare.[4] Cultural warfare, it appears, should also be considered a threat to the relationship of the Diné with the Four Sacred Elements. When external parties (other Native nations or colonial actors) threatened this access, the Diné protected their relationship by using a protection mechanism that included violence and warfare. Still, it seems consistent that after the protection way was followed, a follow-up healing process must have been required, too. Any extreme healing or protection action could lead to a condition of *anáhóót'i'*, and it should have been forecast and contained by the respective *Naat'áanii*. This discussion illustrates how three-level-view concepts can help elucidate traditional Diné governance. Ideally, these kinds of discussions should take place with knowledge holders present so they can comment on specific and relevant aspects of Diné knowledge. It might also be useful to contrast concepts of Diné governance with English descriptions of Diné governance to truly appreciate the difference.

These concepts of traditional Diné philosophy are offered as a foundation for future research. Many times Denny has discussed these ideas in English and in *Diné Bizaad* (the Navajo language), but his assumptions have been unquestioned by the audience. Do students think these teachings are just for recreational pondering? Do listeners who are familiar with these teachings see them as relevant within the ceremonial *hooghan* only but irrelevant to "modern" times? It is difficult to tell what audiences are thinking when aspects of Diné philosophy are discussed. What is clear is that audiences seem to be misunderstanding or perhaps underestimating the vastness of Diné philosophy. As a result, many of the questions asked of Denny are answered, "It's already there." In other words, the answers that people seek are inherent in the philosophy, and to arrive at some answers requires only simple deductive reasoning. The Four Sacred Elements are already there. The four foods (corn, beans, squash, and tobacco) are already there. The four directions are already there. The Sacred Mountains are already there. Yet people don't take the time to discover their own answers, which may be hiding in plain sight.

So where is this traditional thinking in Navajo governance today? Some historians argue that all of this philosophy disappeared sometime between the return from Bosque Redondo and the emergence of the Business

Council. Obviously, the author of this book would disagree. Diné philosophy may have simply gone underground while Navajo Nation "modernized" into a bureaucratic state beholden to finite resource extraction interests. If Diné knowledge holders are correct, the people of Navajo Nation can revive traditional Diné institutions by simply opening their hearts and minds to what is already there.

Tearing Down 'liná Hooghan

Concepts of Modern Navajo Nation Governance

Chapter 4 is a departure from the others because it must deviate from Diné philosophy's organization. It will likely never be known if the principle players who contributed to the "modern" Navajo government considered using Diné philosophy to build things. Perhaps they thought of the U.S. model and created a plan to implement a Western example, and now all citizens of Navajo Nation must live with the consequences. This Western model of Navajo government appears to have embedded itself on the backs of Navajo citizens, regenerating itself every few years in the shadow of one crisis or another. Figure 4.1 is a theoretical representation of what might be going on on Navajo Nation today. There is a mixing of Western philosophy and Diné thinking. It is unclear to what extent things shift from generation to generation. How scholars might "measure" the influence is probably unknowable. It is probably most important that readers fully understand that there is no dichotomous binary between one philosophy and the other.

4.1. CRITICALLY RETHINKING DINÉ NATION BUILDING—WHO IS MARGINALIZED?

Heavily supported by the United States, this modern Navajo government is likely subject to "policy concessions" due to foreign aid contributions. "Likely" can shift to "empirically measurable" should future researchers

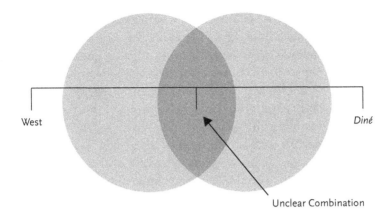

West   *Diné*

Unclear Combination

This is a *normative* representation of the post-1920 philosophical orientation of Navajo Nation government. The extreme points represent an unknowable pure philosophy. On the left is some unknowable "Western" philosophy. On the right is an unknowable pure *Diné* philosophy. The important section to focus on is the "Unclear Combination" of both philosophies. It appears inconsistent, and wherever the philosophies contradict, it seems the most powerful individuals happen to prevail.

Figure 4.1: The Potential Intersection between U.S. Governing Philosophy and *Diné Bibehazáanii* in Post-1920s Governing Institutions

collect appropriate data and demonstrate links between money and policy concessions. Typically scholars do not think of treaty obligations as "foreign aid," but I implore readers to rethink this idea. Just as it operates around the world, the United States may see benefits in foreign aid donations to its non-Indigenous citizens in the form of public goods. Should these goods be recognized as a value to the citizens, they are likely to reelect policymakers responsible for making the foreign aid donation. In turn, Navajo policymakers reap the benefit of foreign aid by distributing the aid to their winning coalition. The losers are the Navajo citizens who should benefit from a policy that their leaders give up to their foreign aid donor in exchange for aid. Case study research demonstrates a tie between U.S. influence and cheap natural resources (Needham 2014). This phenomenon likely impacts all Indigenous nations within what became the United States (Lerma 2014a, 124–146). It remains unclear if these concerns are on the radars of many nation-building experts.

It is now emerging, in scholarly circles, how impactful neo-liberalism as a dominant economic institution is not only on underdeveloped nations but on Indian Country as well. There are now some voices pushing back against the consequences of neoliberalism (Voyageur, Calliou, and Brearley 2014). Still, one of the most influential bodies of work appears to inadvertently promote conditions leading to even more neoliberal-style policy in Indian Country (Cornell and Kalt 2000; Jorgensen 2007). The impact of neoliberalism on Indian Country and on Navajo Nation deserves much more critical scrutiny (Lerma 2014a, 110–123). What's more, current research on Indigenous nation building and rebuilding has also neglected the immense impact that rebuilding currently existing institutions of governance has on marginalizing women (Denetdale 2006a, 2009). Ignoring these problems allows them to persist. Failing to truly and comprehensively learn from our elders about what it used to mean to govern from a traditional point of view only serves to maintain a status quo that, in general terms, works in support of colonial actors and an entrenched Indigenous elite.

The body of literature on rejecting colonial institutional constructs is growing (Lerma 2014a, 51–53). Some have argued, in print, that Indigenous nations are best served by returning to their own endogenous ceremonial processes for governing, while rejecting Western-style electoral politics (Alfred 2009, 29). There have been accusations that many tribal governments inadvertently, or perhaps intentionally, adopt the negative baggage of Western institutions during their constitutional reform processes (Moreton-Robinson 2006, 384). Critical Diné scholars have pointed out how the current Navajo Nation institutions have worked to marginalize women or those who do not concretely identify as male (Denetdale 2006a, 2009). Proponents of the current Navajo Nation government appear uncomfortable with or incapable of addressing these legitimate concerns. As leaders, they are accountable to their citizens to address this legitimate question: Did Navajo Nation adopt attitudes involving heteropatriarchy around the same time it created the Navajo Tribal Council? Again, critical scholars correctly assign blame to Western notions of patriarchal white sovereignty, wherein a line of logic can be traced back to colonization. Navajo land was claimed by several colonial actors, including the United States, based on the assumption that Navajo people could not own their own land. It was convenient for the United States, a colonial actor, to transfer the sovereign claim from a monarchy to the modern U.S. state, thus claiming Navajo Nation. Western political theorists argued for the creation of a social contract between men and a state. Most Western philosophers implied or stated that this contract was for the benefit of *white men* exclusively, thereby marginalizing women and people of color, including Indigenous people (Moreton-Robinson 2007, 87–88).[1] Notwithstanding a handful of exceptions, this is also broadly true of Navajo Nation today.

The politics of tradition appear alive and well in Navajo Nation. The debate among traditional knowledge holders involves the role that women have played throughout the Diné Creation Accounts. Traditional knowledge holder Maybelle Little gave a talk in my tribal government class. She discussed the role of *Sǫ Dine'é*, or the Star People. She adamantly reiterated how women were not to lead. She was specifically referencing Navajo presidential candidate Linda Lovejoy (Little 2010; Kracker 2010). This does not mean the debate is settled. Many knowledge holders allow their knowledge to coexist with others' knowledge even if the information is contradictory (Austin 2009, 58). Many other knowledge holders refute this notion that women cannot or should not lead, citing Changing Woman as a leader, among others. Dr. Herman Cody added some information on the role of women when he stated that a woman typically walked behind a man. This was not an indication that the woman was lesser than a man. Rather, it was a reflection on how the man was supposed to "take the bullet" for the woman should they encounter danger on a journey (Cody 2009). Mrs. Little referenced similar ideas when she stated that the male Star People were required to take the bullet for the female Star People (Little 2010). Oddly, there have been some accounts of the separation of the sexes, an episode within the Diné Creation Account in which the women get blamed for the creation of the monsters (King et al. 1943, 20). However, it seems the majority of other accounts hold both genders at fault for their misdeeds.

Due to the contradictory accounts, it appears many public office candidates in Navajo Nation have carried out at least two strategies. Either they have selectively cited traditional Diné knowledge when it suits their needs, or they have remained silent so as to avoid any controversy. The result is that misinformation about Diné Creation Accounts has been disseminated as "traditional" (Denetdale 2006a, 10). We should expect other nations to grapple with debates on "what is traditional" or to otherwise default to tradition when a special interest just so happens to coincide with doubt. Many nations are finally addressing gender issues in the twenty-first century (Barker 2011, 189–223; Coulthard 2014, 147–176). Hence, future Diné policymakers and those who hold office are strongly advised to reconsider defaulting to "tradition" without question if they have any lingering concerns about further marginalizing women and children culturally, politically, or economically. It is hoped all readers will push for more inclusion.

Through interaction, *Naat'áanii* were serious contenders for power in their relationship with colonial actors and not mere victims of colonization. From a nonhistorical point of view, the consequence of this interaction likely destroyed or at least delegitimized the *Naat'áanii* system of leadership. Following this logic may help to explain the "modernization" of Navajo Nation. Mahoney, a development scholar, has explored the process of economic development in Latin America (2010). One pattern that emerges from Mahoney's research, which has not been systematically applied to Navajo Nation, is the extent to which an Indigenous elite emerged that did more to serve colonial actors (such as the United States) than to serve an Indigenous constituency. A provocative way to look at contemporary Navajo institutions involves path dependency (Collier and Collier 1991).

The extent to which shocks sufficiently dislodged the *Naat'áanii* system are linked to the way scholars find Navajo institutions today. System shocks led to a period of policy fluctuation. Elite Navajo factions that successfully worked to lock in their own interests tended to be the most successful at monopolizing access to resources. This monopolization is inherently antithetical to egalitarian access to the Four Sacred Elements. (In fact, there are no latent or manifest ties between modern Navajo institutions and the Four Sacred Elements.) Post-1922 periods of policy stasis in Navajo institutions can be tied to the emergence of a Navajo elite.[2] It is no accident that this elite group emerged at the same time that finite extractable resources were attracting colonial actors and private corporations. An underutilized analysis tool in Indian Country generally is selectorate theory. The application of this theory involves investigating the impact of "foreign aid" on donor and recipient nations. When applied to Navajo Nation today, it is possible to identify a donor (e.g., the United States), donor leaders (e.g., U.S. elected officials), and a donor constituency (e.g., U.S. finite-resource customers). Recipient analysis (e.g., analyzing Navajo leaders and the Navajo constituency) also plays a role.

Collectively, the United States, a large winning coalition country, must disperse foreign aid based on an expected benefit in terms of public goods. Hence, treaty obligations and current federal funding to Navajo Nation must be critically reexamined as foreign aid from the United States. By using this international political and economic lens, scholars could reassess the impact of U.S. foreign aid on both Navajo leaders and Navajo constituents. Again, this type of analysis could be carried out with all Native nations. Selectorate theory forecasts that the United States would only deliver foreign aid in exchange for a policy concession from Navajo Nation that would benefit U.S. leaders and the U.S. constituency in the form of public goods, such as cheap finite resources. According to selectorate theory, for most of Navajo Nation's modern era, it would be called a small winning coalition nation. This means that a very small number of Navajo elites, fewer than one thousand, would needed to obtain a policy concession. A policy concession is any policy that delivers public goods to the United States while ignoring the best interest of the Navajo constituency. For Navajo Nation, the policy concession is typically the sale of finite resources to U.S. corporations for less than fair market prices and with nonexistent public and worker safety. The finite resources are then extracted and sold for a profit to U.S. constituents. Selectorate theory, then, forecasts that Navajo elites would be rewarded with access to foreign aid. Navajo elites then use their foreign aid to maintain their dynasties by rewarding members of their winning coalition. The big loser in all of this is the Navajo constituency (Denny and Lerma forthcoming).

When average Navajo citizens complain that the Navajo government ignores their interests, this analysis supports their contention. Navajo Nation's institutional structure is no accident. Scholars might call the era beginning in 1923 and continuing into the present the "modernization" of Navajo governance. The word *modern* should be thought of as a clearly dichotomous school of thought meant to denigrate the past as "savage" and "superstitious." In other words, U.S. policymakers, in conjunction with a Navajo elite, have tremendously benefited from a modernization movement that inherently devalues the notion of maintaining good and proper relations with the Four Sacred Elements. So long as the youth of Navajo Nation, who are organizing for change, fail to recognize the inherent bias against their grassroots advocacy, and so long as the Navajo constituency fails to push for a contemporary shock to their institutional chains, there will be no impact on the future of Navajo governance modernization. And given the role that the recently emergent Navajo elite play in their own institution building, this period might best be called the Navajo self-termination era.

4.2. MODERN CONCEPTS OF NAVAJO GOVERNANCE— SELF-TERMINATION ERA

So far the discussion here has been restricted to the functionality of Diné governance as it relates to the overt maintenance of good relations with the Four Sacred Elements. These concepts are based on a scant primary and secondary record, supplemented by a description of Diné philosophy furnished by Denny and Yazzie. However, as the patterns in Diné philosophy suggest, it is also beneficial to look at how some events may not have been foreseen by the Diné. Alternatively, perhaps Diné leaders did foresee the events, but what they saw could have been so catastrophic that it might not have been possible to utilize the Diné process to properly plan for the coming chaos. Perhaps this was the case when it came to the treaty of 1861, *Hwéeldi* (the Long Walk), the Carson campaign, and the treaty of 1868. For now, readers are invited to critically examine how these disruptive events impacted traditional institutions of Diné governance. These political and economic shocks likely dislodged traditional Diné institutions, creating a vacuum to be filled by non-Diné interests (Collier and Collier 1991). The causal impacts these events have had on traditional Diné institutions are discussed in detail in Chapter 6.

The four aforementioned events are possibly the most disruptive events that prevented the Diné from maintaining a proper distance and nearness toward the Four Sacred Elements. This "interruption" allowed for a power vacuum to settle into *Diné Bikéyah*, or Navajoland. As discussed in Chapter 2, by the 1920s, it appears that designated leaders ignored, were prevented from acknowledging, or were unaware of the importance of maintaining good relations with the Four Sacred Elements. It was not until natural resource conglomerates took notice that any individual was capable of securing control of the power vacuum left in the wake of the loss of the *Naat'áanii* system (Bailey and Bailey 1999, 35–36). Again, individuals can only monopolize access to the Four Sacred Elements if leaders who are concerned with this issue are sufficiently removed from power. Monopolization can also only occur if traditional Diné institutions have been sufficiently dislodged and replaced with institutions that promote monopoly.

4.2.1. Business Council of 1923

The ability to see function and dysfunction comes by understanding and linking intention and action. An even more complicated view is to consider what is missing. Readers are encouraged to consider how path dependency may have factored into the post-1923 governance institutions (Collier and Collier 1991). It should be obvious that neither knowledge holders nor scholars will see mention of the Four Sacred Elements in modern institutions. Additionally, the loss of the *Naat'áanii* system could be considered a political shock in which a vacuum was filled with a Navajo elite, supported by the U.S. government and energy interests. This shock theory is merely an assumption, and the focus now will turn exclusively to the absence of the Four Sacred Elements. Again, this approach puts scholars in an interesting bind of searching for the nonexistence of Diné philosophical traits (Ragin and Becker 1992).

The missing link from 1923 until the 1990s was a lack of manifest or latent consideration of the Four Sacred Elements. For the purpose of clarification, let us assume that the contemporary era of Diné governance dates back to 1923. The discovery of oil in Navajo Nation during the early 1920s was a major factor in the formation of a Business Council in 1922 (Wilkins 1987, 48). Hence, scholars may wish to apply path-dependency thinking to the discovery of oil as an economic shock that dislodged the stasis in the post-Long Walk period and replaced it with the 1922 council. As path dependency suggests, the shock of oil discovery led to policy fluctuation until about 1938 (Collier and Collier 1991). By using a path-dependency lens, it is clear that one of the greatest disservices that can be bestowed upon the citizens of Navajo Nation is to misrepresent the functionality of their contemporary governmental institutions. Expressing and depicting all of the forms that contemporary Diné governance took may be overwhelming. However, the concept-building process will highlight how things went wrong. Three-level views of contemporary Diné governance can work as a diagnostic tool that highlights problems that need to be addressed.

In many ways, this section requires a search for the absences of life, or *'Iiná*, and wisdom, or *Sạ'*. Recall that knowledge holders believe leaders are required to think and breathe life into institutions in a fashion that is similar to how the Holy Ones once thought the universe into being. Thoughts, again, are the output of a good and long-lived life, whereas wisdom is equated with action.

Consider Figure 4.2 and its depiction of the first Navajo Tribal Council of 1922. One of the most flagrant features of Figure 4.2 is the top-heavy structure of the council. The emphasis on administration is a good indication that very little connected the Navajo Tribal Council of 1922 with the interests of the Diné constituency. This was the clearest break with pre-Long Walk and post-Long Walk leadership tenets. Primary and secondary resources are scant regarding the Navajo Tribal Council of 1922 (Wilkins 1987, 48). Such vagueness is usually an indication that there is a problem with the concept itself, which makes it susceptible to conceptual stretching (Sartori 1970).

First, there was the distribution of royalties. This condition can be linked back to the change in policy that the U.S. government implemented, which enforced a revenue distribution mechanism across all of Diné Country and did not focus on the regions as it had before 1922 (Wilkins 1987, 49). Why this change? In superficial terms, the essence of redistributing royalties in any agreement must take into account a finite set of resources. That being the case, redistribution inherently must remove "surplus" resources and transfer them into the hands of non-Diné interests. Simply put, if there are fewer Diné individuals to be paid a royalty, the "surplus" can be delivered to non-Diné interests such as corporations. Second, if fewer Diné knew about the leases and signed off on them, it would make lease processing easier for non-Diné interests, who could also pay a lower rate for extraction.

Figure 4.2 reflects the inherent bias in several ways. The vague secondary-level condition of distributing oil revenues contained unstated underlying conditions (i.e., a conceptual stretch) (Sartori 1970). The primary and secondary resources on the Business Council document the

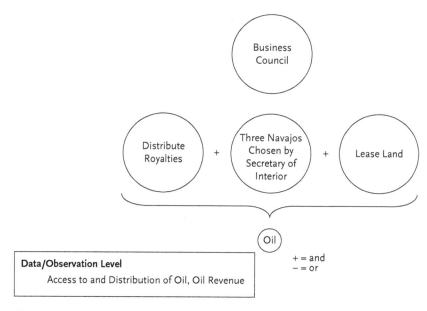

Figure 4.2: Three-Level View—Concept of 1922 Tribal Council

existence of resource extraction corporations (Wilkins 1987, 48–49). The Business Council, therefore, was not easily pinned to a clearly established agenda, thus making the council subject to conceptual stretching. In other words, individual administrators were free to inject their own judgment and, as many critics suspect, their own self-interest into how royalties were to be distributed.

The secondary-level condition of "the three Navajos" appointed by the U.S. Secretary of the Interior had its own problems with vagueness. For example, the necessary qualifications for being one of the three Navajos were unclear, there was no clear set of limits established for their actions, and there was no mention of accountability. There are various other ambiguities as well, which must have left such an arrangement under a cloud of suspicion.

The third secondary-level condition, involving land leasing, did not take much into account. Concept-building analysis leaves little doubt that the Business Council of 1922 was a rubber-stamp mechanism meant to ensure the vitality of parties interested in royalties related to oil on the Navajo reservation. The biggest concern with the three-level view of the Business Council is the absence of conditions and data/observation-level traits that would ordinarily be found in governance institutions. Again, this is more evidence that vague terms were present, which subjected the institution to being stretched. For example, there were no allowances for

Diné healthcare and education. Diné governing mechanisms continued to evolve, but the changes that followed were not a noteworthy improvement.

On January 3, 1923, the Business Council was modified and tasked with assembling a committee to create a Navajo Tribal Council (Wilkins 1987, 51). Using the concept-building method as a critique guide, the main problems with the modifications involved two basic-level conditions stacked on top of one another and a vaguely constructed data indicator. Figure 4.3 contains the three-level view of the modifications model. The main focus of the modifications, in comparison with the three-level view of the Business Council, involves the secondary-level conditions. In the absence of other information, it seems that the modifications of January 3, 1923, were the result of hasty work. Evidence in the primary and secondary literature points to self-interest. There is evidence that the January 3, 1923, model was hastily assembled because the Business Council model was not accepted as a legitimate body fit to represent the Diné (Wilkins 1987, 51).

Second, a three-level view of the January 3 model contains evidence of both careful and sloppy planning. Note that the secondary-level conditions are carefully constructed. The majority of the secondary-level conditions were under the scrutiny of some branch of the U.S. government. Delegates and alternate delegates were removable by the U.S. Secretary of the Interior. Also, the Navajo Tribal Council could only meet when the Commissioner of Indian Affairs was present.

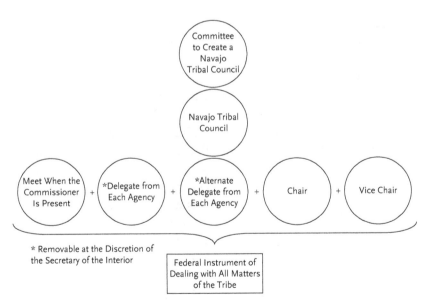

Figure 4.3: Three-Level View—Concept of Tribal Council Modifications of January 3, 1923

Less apparent is the connection that a chair and vice chair of the Navajo Tribal Council might have had with U.S. interests. Regardless, if a Navajo Tribal Council was to have functioned in service of the Diné, the collection of secondary conditions must be more deeply scrutinized. The most obvious problems could have involved conflicts of interest.

A holdover from the Business Council model is the vague and ambiguous language used in the data/observation level. When a goal for a council is a "Federal Instrument of Dealing with All Matters of the Tribe," it becomes much easier to table items, especially if the secondary-level conditions are weighted in favor of U.S. interests. Again, these institutional changes were devoid of Diné philosophy. More modifications followed.

4.2.2. Navajo Nation (Tribal) Council (1923–1938)

On January 24, 1923, a Navajo Tribal Council was formed (Wilkins 1987, 49). The day before, the Commissioner of Indian Affairs authorized federal regulations to create the council entitled "Regulations Related to the Navajo Tribe of Indians." On April 24, 1923, the federal regulations were amended, and the members making up the first Navajo Tribal Council were elected. Again, this was the beginning of an era in Navajo governance institutions better understood as a post-oil discovery shock that led to the policy fluctuation era (Collier and Collier 1991). Perhaps it is more accurate to state that the January 3 body was modified into the January 24 model. Figure 4.4 is a three-level view of the January 24 governing body. The January 24 model is still problematic, but it was the best model used thus far by the Diné since traditional Diné governance was in place—at least from the standpoint of concept-building criteria. The basic level is properly tied to the secondary-level conditions. These conditions all seem to have maintained a similar level of generality. The main issue is the continued weight that U.S. interests attempted to maintain within the Navajo Tribal Council. Some U.S. interests were systematically removed, as indicated by the asterisks, from the model. The first significant change came in 1933 when the secondary-level conditions "federal representative be present at council meetings" and "convene at the liberty of the commissioner" were revoked as necessary conditions (Wilkins 1987, 49). Nonetheless, the main problem involves the data/observation level, which had nothing to do with maintaining good relations with the Four Sacred Elements.

The vagueness of language still remained in the January 24 document, a problem that could have led to power domination by elites within the

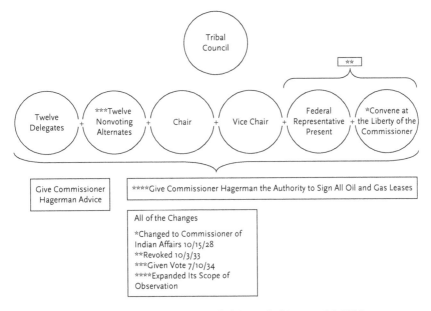

Figure 4.4: Three-Level View—Concept of Tribal Council of January 24, 1923

Navajo Tribal Council. However, the January 24 council was less likely to represent U.S. interests because the secondary-level conditions less overtly represented U.S. interests (Lukes 2005). Diné citizens hijacked their own Tribal Council based on several modifications that took place after its 1923 introduction. Over time, the data/observation level expanded to take on a form of Diné governance rather than merely serving as an advisory board to the U.S. Commissioner of Indian Affairs. Perhaps the January 24 model and its modifications would have remained in place had it not been for the Indian Reorganization Act (IRA).

The U.S. interest in pushing tribal governments into the envelope of a U.S. constitutional model of government contributed to Navajo Nation creating a Tribal Constitutional Assembly in 1938 (Wilkins 1987, 52). As was customary, U.S. interests were involved with Diné governance, creating a hierarchical model in tandem with some Navajo individuals. This is evident in the three-level view of the Tribal Constitutional Assembly in Figure 4.5. Another shock (cultural) occurred, and it involved livestock reduction. This shock probably led to a split within this latest iteration of the Tribal Council. While it is unclear which factions believed what, it is likely that factions that wished to prevent future livestock reductions were either unhappy with the latest version of the council or wanted to retain the current council. Regardless of the reason, the

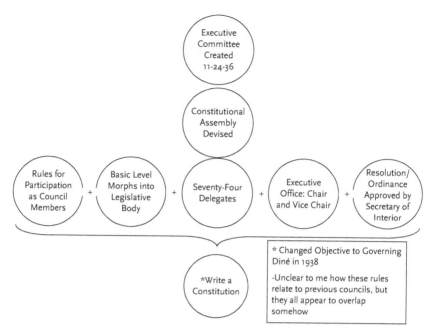

Figure 4.5: Three-Level View—Concept of Tribal Constitutional Assembly of 1938

shock probably contributed to the creation of the Tribal Constitutional Assembly (Wilkins 1987, 51–52). The constitutional assembly failed to successfully install a Navajo-approved constitution. Once again, a look at the secondary-level conditions point to U.S. interest. The most overt presence of U.S. interest was the approval requirement: resolutions could not take effect unless the U.S. Secretary of the Interior approved them. Less overt, but still questionable, was the secondary-level condition that involved rules for participation as a council member.

From a functional point of view, the basic-level condition of "constitutional assembly" floated down into the secondary-level conditions and became a U.S.-*approved* legislative body. Finally, a look at the data/observation level indicates that the constitutional assembly made a good start. However, shifting conditions created problems, and vagueness reappeared. We know that the original intent of the constitutional assembly was to write a constitution. But when that object was not fulfilled, a much broader scope of governing Diné Country was introduced by virtue of the Navajo Tribal Council voting itself into office (Wilkins 1987, 52). Ill-defined objectives allowed secondary-level actors to dominate the legislature (Lukes 2005). Left unclear in all of these changes is the impact that each of the various councils have on governance today.

4.2.3. Navajo Nation, 1938–1989 and 1989–2009

From about 1938 through 1989, the general framework for Navajo Nation governance largely remained the same. The period of fluctuation from about 1923 until 1938 led to an institutional stasis that was dislodged by the riots in Window Rock in 1989 (Collier and Collier 1991; Wilkins 2013). Hence, there was a constant in the form of institutional stasis that continued to not mention adherence to good relations with the Four Sacred Elements. The post-1938 stasis involved a Navajo Council with a chair and vice chair. There were limited checks on the power of the executive, and this issue would emerge later, in 1989. Navajo institutional stasis might have begun in 1938 when Jacob Morgan was elected chair (Wilkins 2013, 23). From that time until about 1959, Navajo Nation continuously reelected the same group of individuals to serve as chair and vice chair, which further not only demonstrates an institutional stasis but also provides evidence of a Navajo elite. The capacity of that Navajo Tribal Council remains questionable. A three-level analysis further drives the point home that post crisis (shock) institution building was ineffective in ensuring that Navajo sovereignty was fully secured or exercised. Simultaneously, there was (again) no mention of the Four Sacred Elements.

It is worth noting that archival research could certainly bolster understanding of the 1938–1989 era of contemporary Navajo governance. The following concept-building process can help guide Navajo historians in their research. Figure 4.6 is an attempt at a two-level view of the 1938–1989 Navajo Tribal Council. That council was composed of seventy-four delegates. The seventy-four-delegate body was later expanded to

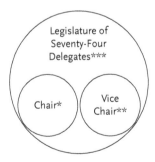

Legislature of
Seventy-Four
Delegates***

Chair*

Vice
Chair**

* Chair Split into Two Positions after 1989 Incident: President and Speaker of the House
** Vice Chair Relabeled as Vice President after 1989 Incident
*** Thirteen Delegates Added in 1976 Due to Reapportionment Requirements

Figure 4.6: Navajo Tribal Council—1938–1989, with Minor Modifications

eighty-eight in 1976 due to reapportionment requirements (Wilkins 2013, 130). From this group of delegates came the council's chairman and vice chairman (Wilkins 1987, 52). The secondary documents suggest that this body, which originated as a constitutional assembly, was likely concerned about the policies of the IRA, established in 1934, and livestock reduction. Prior to the IRA and livestock reduction, the Navajo political economy had become as powerful as it had ever been since interaction began with colonial actors (Bailey and Bailey 1999, 126). Following the IRA and livestock reduction, the Navajo political economy was decimated. This situation warrants further exploration. It is unclear how the reduction era benefited the U.S. economy. It could be that parts of the U.S. economy, in the states that bordered Navajo Nation, were being bolstered. Eliminating the Navajo political economy as a competitor could have further embedded Navajo individuals into the border-town economies. These impacts could have persisted into our contemporary era. For the analysis here, it is worth noting a lack of attention to this issue by the Navajo Tribal Council. While there may have been concerns that appear in archival databases, it is unclear if and how delegates of this era worked to prevent future U.S. policies from continuing to destroy the Navajo political economy. Hence, the concept-building process has illuminated gaping holes in current research. Other Native nations have successfully used their Western institutions to maintain and expand their sovereignty. Future research on Navajo Nation could explore how and where the post-1938 council attempted to maintain or expand sovereignty and where it failed.

The next interesting change came in 1959. The introduction of Navajo Nation's court systems may not have caused a shock, but it changed institutional stasis. The executive branch was also reorganized during this time (Austin 2009; Wilkins 2013, 25). These seemingly minor changes are reflected in Figure 4.7. The three-branch form of government is probably the most familiar form of governance to scholars of the U.S. political system. It is noteworthy that there was an attempt to introduce a "Supreme Judicial" body in 1978, but this branch was later eliminated, in 1985. Many questioned the validity of this judicial body (Wilkins 1987, 98). It should be clear that each of the necessary conditions in Figure 4.7 can certainly be expanded as standalone concepts with conditions under them. Readers should look to Austin for a comprehensive discussion of Navajo Nation's judicial branch history, philosophy, and case-law research (2009). The history of the executive and legislative branches is also subject to further concept-building analysis based on Wilkins (2013). The concept-building process discussed here can, again, be a guide for future research. Possible research questions might be the following: What committees were

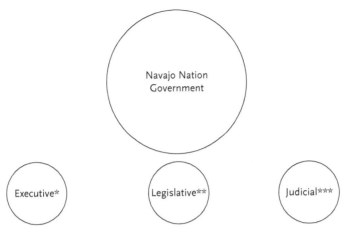

* Split from Chair and Vice Chair after 1989
** Expanded from Seventy-Four to Eighty-Eight
*** Added in 1959. See Austin 2009. Not Clear What Role 1978 Supreme Judicial Council
Played. Abolished in 1985.

Figure 4.7: Navajo Tribal Government—1959–1989

created between 1959 and 1989 within the council and within the executive branch? What other events in the evolution of the Navajo government can be referenced but may not be considered shocks to Navajo institutions?

In 1962, the Navajo Tribal Code was published, which led scholars to presume that Navajo governance is a constitution by council resolution because there is no adopted written constitution. Factions within Navajo Nation attempted and failed to employ a written constitution in 1937, 1953, and 1968. Scholars might consider these attempts as unsuccessful because there was no shock to existing institutions. If a shock had occurred, a window of opportunity would have emerged in the vacuum of the hypothetical shock. That vacuum could have been filled by a constitution. In 1987, Peter MacDonald was elected to an unprecedented fourth term as council chairman. His chairmanship is quite controversial.

The MacDonald chairmanship represents another shock to Navajo political institutions. Balanced and objective comprehensive accounts of the controversies surrounding the MacDonald era have yet to be produced and deserve research attention. Sadly, it is beyond the scope of this book to give the era the attention it deserves. The facts corroborate that in early 1989 MacDonald lost support from the majority of the Navajo Tribal Council. On February 16, 1989, he resigned but withdrew his resignation the next day. The council then voted to place MacDonald on administrative leave. MacDonald refused to acknowledge the leave order. A standoff ensued and turned violent, leading to the Window Rock riots of 1989, in which two individuals lost their lives and several others were injured. This "shock" to Navajo political institutions created a vacuum by dislodging the chair system as a legitimate form of government. The vacuum was filled with the Title II amendments of 1989. In 1990, the chair position was split into two positions: (1) president of Navajo Nation and (2) Speaker of the Navajo Nation Council. (See Figure 4.7.) This institutional shock, then, created a three-branch government with executive, legislative, and judicial branches (Wilkins 2013, 29–31). These institutional changes created and locked in another stasis period that lasted until approximately 2009.

From about 2007 until 2009, various branches of Navajo Nation faced increasing pressure from various factions. Perhaps unfairly, some elected officials have been accused of various misdeeds. While some of the accusations appear to be valid, others seem motivated by infighting and continued factionalism. President Joe Shirley, in what may be questioned as a move to expand the reach of the executive branch, rallied support from the public to diminish the power of the Navajo Nation legislature. There appear to have been two key events, which might also be considered shocks to Navajo political institutions, that contributed to the public's turn against the Navajo Nation Council: delegate rings and a trip to Hawaii.

In 2007, Shirley successfully capitalized on reports that the Navajo Nation Council spent $50,000 on delegate rings (Fonseca 2007). Later that year, a trip to Hawaii for the National Indian Education Association's annual meeting was also exploited for political gain (Landry 2007). President Shirley argued for reducing the number of delegate positions on the council and advocated for presidential budgetary line-item veto authority (Navajo Nation Government 2008). A public referendum held on December 15, 2009, approved both of these measures (Yazzie, Shirley, and Grant 2010). This latest shock to the Navajo political system created more institutional change. Figure 4.8 depicts the current twenty-four-member Navajo Nation Council. This analysis will examine not only the benefits but also the pitfalls of this current iteration of Navajo governance institutions. The basic level is the council with twenty-four delegates. Presumably, each of the twenty-four delegates is designated to chair or otherwise participate in some of the six committees within the council. The distribution of delegates across the various committees and subcommittees deserves scrutiny beyond what can be offered here. Committees that are dominated by certain interests are subject to special-interest-based decision making and could be the key to future strategies to put power into the hands of the Navajo constituency.

The public is correct to be concerned about the concentration of power in the hands of fewer and fewer representatives. For whatever reason, however, it seems the groups receiving the most scrutiny are the groups that

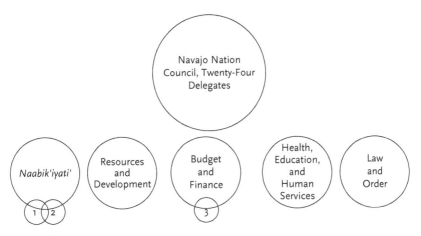

1 Gaming Task Force Subcommittee
2 Government Reform Subcommittee
3 Budget and Finance Subcommittee Preserving External Funds

Figure 4.8: Navajo Nation Council—Post-Reduction Committees Set Up

advocate for decentralized institutions. For example, Diné Policy Institute's research on the *Naach'id*, a traditional form of governance that Western scholars might liken to a "Navajo Confederacy," is seemingly dismissed as an inappropriate combination of state (Navajo) authority and religion (Fundamental Laws of the Diné). For traditional knowledge holders, this compartmentalization is absurd. Perhaps those who adhere to worldviews independent of *Nitsáhákees, Nahat'á, 'Iiná*, and *Sih Hasin* are suspicious of a religious dogma intent on cheating them out of their voice in Navajo governance. Comparatively speaking, the very nature of European politics and distrust of leaders is alive and well today, and for good reason. Sadly, it must be acknowledged that even Diné philosophy, like any philosophy, can be abused and misused by those who seek to enrich themselves and not lead their people ethically.

Contemporary Diné governance is an interactive process, as it was prior to interaction with colonial actors. Although "interests" may have changed, they have always been a part of Diné governance. If the institutional perspective is useful, it is useful because the structures of domestic and international relations are going to limit the activity of leaders. This assumption can be a benefit to the Diné by painting their leaders into a corner regarding policymaking. (However, traditional norms of Diné governance may be inconsistent with "forcing" leaders to behave ethically.) The leap that must be made now is accepting the possibility that traditional Diné governance may be worked into contemporary Diné institutions in such a way that they promote the well-being of the Diné citizenry. It seems overtly clear that if all contemporary Navajo citizens have proper relations with the Four Sacred Elements, they will be living in compliance with directives from the Holy Ones. Of course, the reality in Navajo Nation today is much different. For example, Navajo elders and the young are the most vulnerable populations and have limited access to things like fire in the winter if roads are too muddy or icy for driving. These limited access points are compounded if others (young adults) neglect their *ké* responsibility to their elders and their children. Still, this discussion helps us understand how institutions can work to keep leaders honest. It also is a blueprint for how some can push the institutions further into the area of traditional Diné governance. If there is an actively operating form of traditional philosophy of leadership now, it is likely found in the local community.

4.3. CRITICALLY RETHINKING DINÉ NATION REBUILDING— ATTEMPTING A RETURN TO BALANCE

The experiences of Navajo nation building tend to not follow the usual pattern of other Indigenous nations. Navajo Nation has always been an anomaly in terms of its trends in economic, demographic, and political growth (Bailey and Bailey 1999; Henson 2008, 115). Researchers interested in Navajo nation building may be most interested in describing the current situation or in further exploring the efficacy of traditional institutions. For example, Navajo economic development has been discussed in terms of sheep herding, the impact of informal flea markets, and its overall impact on neighboring states (Jorgensen 2007, 37–38; Henson 2008, 121–122). Complicating matters, Navajo Nation boundaries cross three U.S. state boundaries, which makes intergovernmental interaction strategies a necessary condition of any Navajo nation building (Jorgensen 2007, 254; Henson 2008, 73, 76). State jurisdiction issues have yielded interesting tax-exemption challenges (Henson 2008, 43). One interesting event in Navajo nation building was the passage of the Local Governance Act in 2001, which vested more control over policymaking in the hands of local municipalities (Jorgensen 2007, 169). A great deal of current research, relatively speaking, involves Navajo Nation courts.

Court systems in Navajo Nation have also been integrated with traditional teachings, which loosely translate into English as "peacemaking" (Nielsen and Zion 2005; Austin 2007, 2009; Jorgensen 2007, 124–126; Henson 2008, 47–50, 122–123, 127). Currently, Navajo Nation has utilized its governing powers to integrate traditional healing practices into dealing with alcohol and substance abuse by its citizens (Jorgensen

2007, 239). Finally, as is mentioned in detail elsewhere, there continues to be a push for the Fundamental Laws to have a role in contemporary Navajo Nation government (Jorgensen 2007, 126–128, 95, 62–63). Environmental issues also remain relevant as Navajo Nation attempts to resolve pollution and other toxic waste issues while doing a better job of managing its natural resources (Henson 2008, 162, 164, 178, 180, 184). All of these nation-building discussions, however, lack clear focus, and refocusing them on maintaining good relations with the Four Sacred Elements may make them more relevant to contemporary challenges.

All the while, Navajo Nation has not only borrowed from European philosophical thought but also worked diligently to retain what has worked from its own endogenous philosophy of leadership (Champagne 2007, 104; Lemont 2006, 43–44). The collective incremental nation-building changes to Navajo Nation governance have all been conducted under a government that has no written constitution. Perhaps this supports the argument that a nation need not have a written constitution for it to be relatively effective. As such, the collective concerns that may be relevant to Navajo citizens cannot be easily addressed by looking at the more broadly contextualized research on nation building. Still, even the majority of research about current and future Navajo Nation policy remains less than ideal.

The history of Navajo Nation governance is detailed elsewhere (Chapter 3) and follows the development from stories on leadership to war and trade interaction with colonial actors, to the early reservation period, and to the business councils that eventually evolved into the current Navajo Nation government (Kraker 2008; Bailey and Bailey 1999; Benally 2006; Bighorse, Bighorse, and Bennett 1990; Brugge and Correll 1971; Deloria and DeMallie 1999; Denetdale 2009; Wilkins 1987, 2002a, 2003; Navajo Nation Council 2002). Scholars may add here that each of these periods chipped away at the communitywide ability to maintain good relations with the Four Sacred Elements. While the history of Navajo governance has been and remains dynamic, so are the problems, issues, and concerns being raised by scholars of contemporary Navajo governance. The basic norms of social science inquiry require that scholars first describe the history accurately and then move forward to determine meaningful explanations for how and why things occurred as they have (King, Keohane, and Verba 1994). Accurate descriptive research on Navajo governance first began appearing in the late 1980s and early 1990s (Wilkins 1987, 2003). Later, explanations for how and why democratic institutions may or may not have taken hold in Navajo Nation yielded some insight into how and why certain modifications to Navajo Nation governance have been enacted since 1989 (Wilkins 2002a).

The research about Navajo Nation governance can be comprehensively dealt with briefly because not much exists. None of the research specifically addresses managing good relations with the Four Sacred Elements, but some of the research implies notions of healing and protection. What follows is an overview of the research by various authors in alphabetical order.

Justice Raymond D. Austin, retired from the Navajo Nation Supreme Court, provides a brief history of the Navajo Nation Court (Austin 2009, 1–36) and a wealth of information on Navajo philosophy. His research includes a description of the Fundamental Laws (37–52); *Hózhǫ́*, or peace, harmony, and balance (53–82); *K'é*, or Navajo kinship unity via positive values (83–136); and *K'éí*, or descent, clanship, and kinship (137–198). Austin's research appears to primarily involve description, and he leans toward future explanatory considerations as he addresses how the Navajo example may assist Indigenous populations throughout the world in dealing with globalization issues (xix).

Many others involved with the Navajo Nation Court, either as scholars or as practitioners, only add to the descriptive resources on the subject (Nielsen and Zion 2005). Possibly the most comprehensive work on Navajo history is that of Bailey and Bailey (1999); they describe the many facets of Navajo history from their own perspective. Bailey and Bailey use time as their organizing tool, which does not easily lend itself to Navajo nation-building purposes but remains a nice resource. Their work is especially useful for looking at Diné reservation history from 1868 to 1934 (25–104).

In a fashion similar to Austin, other researchers have argued that the governance practices of Navajo Nation can be helpful to other Native nations. For example, Lee (2006) argues that Navajo Indigenous identity may have salience for other Native nations dealing with identity and citizenry issues. Lee (2007) describes Navajo notions of nationalism and their relevance to a future Navajo Nation identity. He seems to equate a general definition of nationalism with Navajo nationalism, which, if carefully scrutinized, may end up becoming another example of conceptual stretching (Sartori 1970, 2007, 59).

Describing Navajo nationhood in terms of Navajo Creation Accounts may be a good way of encouraging a sense of pride, but calling such pride "nationalism" may backfire, as these sentiments may not be consistent with definitions of colonial-state nationalism (Lee 2007, 61–62). Still,

Lee is bringing up some very important questions about utilizing the past to inform the future of Navajo nation building, primarily drawing upon Navajo philosophical ideas. Lee's insights are most relevant to reconciling traditional and contemporary Navajo institutions when he discusses the manner in which traditional Navajo teachings addressed the same issues that contemporary nations must address (2008). Here, the challenges of Navajo assertions of independence from the United States are framed in terms of an inability of many individuals to reconcile Navajo philosophy with contemporary challenges of living in the United States (101). Hence, what may be considered non-Navajo influences (e.g., drugs, alcohol, and domestic violence) have leaked into individual Navajo lives because these individuals cannot apply Navajo philosophy as a solution to the problems they are facing. This may result from not understanding Diné philosophy or because individual Navajos fail to see how their Native philosophy can alleviate such problems (102).

All of these authors rely upon the same scholar for historical reference— David Wilkins. Any research on Navajo nation building must include his work. When Wilkins was an instructor at Navajo Community College, he decided to write a book about Navajo governance because he was frustrated by the lack of research on Navajo governance up to that time (Wilkins 1987). He would later turn his research into a more comprehensive study of Navajo Nation's historical and political developments (2003). Simultaneously, Wilkins remains somewhat skeptical about contemporary Navajo governance because it lacks the basic constitutive parts of democracy (2002a).

Although the work of all the scholars mentioned here has allowed current research on Navajo nation building to continue within a generally accurate historical context, the most ambitious effort to specifically address Navajo nation building remains the work of the Diné Policy Institute (DPI) and its report on Navajo constitutional reform (Yazzie et al. 2008).

The constitutional reform project was drafted in response to a long history of debate regarding the past Navajo constitution and the current Navajo constitution (Wilkins 2003). The report by Yazzie et al. (2008) considers constitutional philosophy (2–21), separation of powers strategies (22–32), and judicial oversight (33–39) The most innovative portion of the report involves proposals for future changes (40–70). Four models for change are arranged in general orientation to a specific goal. Model 1 addresses an improvement in the efficiency of the current system without much regard for other considerations (42–44). Model 2 addresses the conflict between the current centralized Navajo government and the Navajo philosophy of leadership, which was, generally, based on decentralized models and local autonomy. Hence, the suggestion here is to utilize a decentralized philosophy of governance and integrate it with a bicameral legislative body (45–53). Model 3 further explores decentralization of the current Navajo government and specifically focuses on the executive branch, eliminating a single president and replacing that person with an eleven-member panel tasked with basing its decisions more overtly on traditional and customary Diné laws (53–60). Model 4 is dialectical and cyclical in an effort to fully integrate Diné thinking into a contemporary and functional government. It is based on the assumption that Diné thinking can saliently address contemporary issues (60–70). The impact and salience of Diné thinking is more directly addressed in my Chapter 1 as it relates to maintaining proper distance and nearness toward the Four Sacred Elements.

4.3.1. Contemporary Tension between Diné Philosophy and Governing Institutions

DPI staffers learned a good lesson about the tensions between Diné philosophy and contemporary Navajo institutions. The tensions across "disciplines" are probably clearest in the constitutional document (Yazzie et al. 2008). The DPI experience in writing about Navajo constitutionalism highlighted what might be seen as a microcosm of what could be going on across the entire Navajo Nation. Some staffers and governors carry themselves in an adversarial manner. This adversarial approach can significantly silence others. In this way, there may be a default position that has been exploited by individuals with a nontraditional perspective. If they articulate their positions vociferously, they silence their critics, and thus, they are more likely to get their way in terms of policy development.

In many ways, the biggest communication breakdown might be misunderstanding. Certainly, there are voices that are vehemently against any integration of traditional Diné philosophy, and knowledge holders who were raised with Diné philosophy have been subjected to attacks from their adversaries. Most knowledge holders do not insist on pushing their worldview on those unwilling or unable to understand them. As a consequence, some individuals who are ignorant of Diné philosophy may be misunderstood by knowledge holders as being hostile toward Diné philosophy. Simultaneously, there may be a lack of patience or even a feeling of inferiority among those ignorant of Diné philosophy when they approach knowledge holders with questions. As a result, interaction between knowledge holders, the young, and those with Western education may, by default, lean away from truly engaging Diné philosophy. This outcome may be quite convenient for policymakers when their top priority is self-interest. DPI's next major project could be an interesting miniature case study of this process.

The background for DPI's Restructuring Project began around 2007. On July 10, 2007, it was reported that the Navajo Nation Council allocated $50,000 for the purchase of delegate rings. Many in the public decried this as an abuse of Navajo Nation's budget (Fonseca 2007). Then, on November 28, 2007, many in the public and in the news media began to cry foul about a large delegation of Navajo elected officials and staffers attending the National Indian Education Association's annual meeting in Honolulu, Hawaii (Landry 2007). Whether these expenditures were legitimate is not going to be settled here. What is noteworthy is that President Shirley used these events as a springboard to expand the powers of the presidency in two ways: he argued that the council should be reduced and that the executive branch should have budgetary line-item veto authority.

Under the guise that the Navajo Nation Council was abusing its spending authority and was simply too large, Shirley launched his campaign to reduce the council and obtain executive branch line-item veto authority (Navajo Nation Government 2008). Shirley argued that the council in reduced form would return to its original purpose of making policy and that the reduction would reduce costs. Shirley also cited a September 5, 2000, referendum in which 70 percent of the voters approved the reduction, stipulating that eighty-eight delegates should be reduced to twenty-four. The 2000 initiative ultimately failed because the language was worded in such a way that all 110 chapters of Navajo Nation would have had to produce an affirmative council reduction vote greater than 50 percent.

Shirley argued that this approval percentage would be impossible to achieve. This argument deserves some attention. The fact that achieving 51 percent or more votes in 110 chapters across Navajo Nation appears to be a very Diné-oriented way of turning away from *Naat'áanii* en masse. While this process may not be expedient for the ambitions of President Shirley, it could be that had his platform been adversarial enough, no advocates for a decentralized form of governing would have offered their objections. Regardless, nine years later, on December 15, 2009, both a reduction in the size of the council and the line-item veto power were approved by Navajo voters (Yazzie, Shirley, and Grant 2010). Reducing the size of the Navajo Nation Council appeared to have been carried out with no forethought about the consequences. How exactly would twenty-four individuals realistically carry out the work of eighty-eight people?

The Navajo Nation Supreme Court ordered that the twenty-second session of the Navajo Nation Council make the restructuring process the top priority of its session (Navajo Nation Supreme Court 2010). Again, there was little direction on how this process would actually occur. Around April or May of 2010, DPI was asked to assist the Navajo Nation Council. The staff of DPI was excited by the prospect of working in service to Navajo Nation. During this time, Robert Yazzie and Avery Denny were on the DPI staff. Mr. Yazzie had to settle down the rest of the DPI staff, as most staffers, perhaps all, were vehemently against the reduction vote. In a world outside of Navajo Nation, there is probably no individual who would think it is a good idea to reduce a legislature by sixty-four members, or 73 percent. It is a good guess that if individual Navajos were asked in the abstract if reducing the U.S. Congress by 73 percent was a good idea, many would say no. Yazzie, in a pep talk to DPI staffers, said that the reduction was a done deal and that DPI was needed to help Navajo Nation weather this shock.

The labor of the restructuring process seems to have been informally divided up based on individual staffer self-selection. Staffers appeared to work on those areas in which they were most interested. Some DPI staffers seemed more interested in the policy side of the research while others were more interested in the Diné philosophy side of the discussion. Amber Crotty was the mediator on the policy side, made up of Moroni Benally and Andrew Curley, while Yazzie and Denny worked on the philosophy side. As a consequence, the resulting restructuring document has a few transition issues (Yazzie et al. 2011). These transition issues may be a product of miscommunication due to disciplinary divides.

DPI can confidently claim credit for changing the scope of a Native nation government and steering it toward a traditional method of governance. It is unlikely that this has ever happened before, or at least not since the late 1930s, when some nations attempted to codify traditional knowledge within their IRA-era constitutions. Avery Denny later stated that the Diné philosophy contained in the restructuring document is based on the Lightning Way Ceremony. Robert Yazzie would later explain during DPI staff meetings that the elders discussed a method of Naa Bik'í Yáti', or "talking things" out. Yazzie, reflecting the thoughts of several knowledge holders, remarked that a Naat'áanii was responsible for riding a horse out to the people to discuss important matters. He also mentioned how even the process of riding the horse required a "nudging" or "finesse" to ensure that the horse would cooperate with the rider so that they both would arrive at their destination safely. This analogy was linked to the work of a Naat'áanii using the Naa Bik'í Yáti' process to guide the people through tough times to arrive at a destination that was best for all involved. This "theoretical" approach, a discussion of how the Navajo Nation Council *should* behave, became a very real opportunity to fill the postshock policy fluctuation period with ideas about the future policy stasis period. Still, many of the tenets outlined by the elders were not adopted verbatim.

The contemporary debate between how things should be and how things are carried out is not limited to mainstream governance around the world. Rather, Navajo Nation is now having these same debates when Diné knowledge holders discuss how things should be and the elected officials dismiss some of those teachings for more "practical" purposes. Again, researchers must confront the possibility that vociferous challenges to Diné philosophy perspectives may be a ploy to silence knowledge holders and allow a Western version of top-down, concentrated power to prevail. The philosophy behind *Naa Bik'í Yáti'* involves a great deal of tangentially related issues discussed throughout this book. For example, a true leader should legitimize the voice of the people, carry out planning in order to avoid conditions that drift away from *Sa'ah Naagh'áí Bik'eh Hózhóón* (such as being too close to or too far from the Four Sacred Elements), listen to the needs of the people, be accountable to the people, and exercise fairness in policy-making decisions (Yazzie et al. 2011, 8).

The Restructuring Report also delves into aspects of Diné philosophy that are further developed here. For example, managing relations with the six identified monsters was first articulated by Yazzie et al. (2011, 9). My Chapter 1 takes these discussions further. The Restructuring Report contains a figure of the six monsters that were allowed to live in order to encourage humans to strive for a good and long life (9). The discussion of the monsters directly contributed to further research by Denny and Lerma (2017). Readers should review Chapter 2's Figure 2.2 on maintaining a balance between *Hózhǫ́ǫ́jí* and *Hashkéjí* thought. The restructuring discussion, although incomplete, directly influenced the main theme of this book: managing proper relations with the Four Sacred Elements. While the restructuring document took a more negative turn (monsters), this book attempts to build on that research on monsters and make it more positive by focusing on aspects that contribute to a long, wisdom-filled life. A leader working toward a potentially unpopular but necessary direction to maintain balance within *Sa'ah Naagh'áí Bik'eh Hózhóón* is the most critical key to governing from a Diné point of view. Admittedly, this is a tough process to maintain. As a result, many of the recommendations contained in the Restructuring Report were necessarily watered down by the council. A council constructed of a group that does not proportionally represent its people cannot be a legitimate governance body. There is no council composed of 51 percent women. There is no council in which children are present. As Denny has stated repeatedly, Navajo age and wisdom are not necessarily based on chronological age. Children can be far more learned than some adults who currently hold office.

The post-reduction shock and the eliciting of information from DPI resulted in a watering down of the recommendations for a whole host of reasons beyond the scope of this discussion. For example, Denny's teachings that the prerequisite for a leader should be his or her ability to govern at home successfully is one such teaching that many in the Navajo Nation Council cannot live up to now.

When the Restructuring Report was publicly disseminated, members of the Navajo Nation Council continued to seek the advice of Yazzie and Denny through meetings and public discussions. It is unclear if debates occurred and, if so, between whom, as the work of the council went on behind closed doors. Regardless, there were times when some DPI staffers became frustrated by advocates for a Western-style concentration of power in the hands of fewer delegates. Even some DPI staffers deserve some blame for not seizing many opportunities that emerged during the consultation process. As often occurs in many capitals around the world, impromptu meetings between DPI staffers and sitting heads of state opened even more possibilities for the further integration of Diné philosophy into existing institutions. What emerged from the discussions, writings, and continued consultations was the next round of Title II amendments.

Sometime in 2011, the Navajo Nation Council issued amendments to Title II of the Navajo Nation Code (N.N.C. Title II 101–835). Within this document are contained some tenets of the Restructuring Report. For the purposes of this discussion, only those areas involving traditional Diné philosophy will be explored. By defining *Nitsáhákees, Nahat'á, 'Iiná,* and *Sih Hasin* in the amendments, the council attempted to incorporate these ideas (N.N.C. §§ 110). Yet the biggest openly verifiable impact that DPI has had on the future of the Navajo people was the introduction of the *Naa Bik'í Yáti'*. Coming from a former staffer and current ally of DPI, the following may appear self-serving. Yet in deference to many others at DPI, including Denny and Yazzie, all members and contributors to DPI should be honored for their dedication to what can, at times, be a thankless job.

DPI is now a part of the history of Navajo governance, and DPI staffers deserve the utmost credit for attempting to save Navajo Nation from self-colonization. According to Dana Eldridge, a former DPI staffer, DPI is an apparatus in which young Diné and Indigenous individuals seek guidance from elders, and elders seek to guide. While there can be divisions within the DPI family, there is also humility and a lack of fear when the obvious occurs: When an individual does not know an answer, that person should not pretend he or she knows an answer. He or she should instead seek guidance from those who may have the answers. Admitting ignorance may be DPI's most valuable asset. There remain questions about the "literacy" of current and future delegates regarding Diné philosophy. Some DPI staffers are of the opinion that current and future research using Diné philosophy to craft policy has not gone far enough because too many "loopholes" are left behind to be exploited by unscrupulous policymakers.

One of the biggest objections from many outside of both the council and DPI is that there cannot be an integration of religion and governance. As previously stated, neat boxes for religion and governance do not work. It seems Western religions teach the practice of selling ideas with any language necessary. This does not mean that Diné philosophy cannot also be exploited by some for personal gain. Knowledge holders would simply add that if Diné philosophy is abused, humans will not have it for very long: The knowledge will take care of itself. So long as some humans are cognizant and respectful of Diné philosophy, it will live on. This is the resiliency of Diné philosophy, and it can be observed.

CHAPTER 5

Dibé Nitsaa (Mount Hesperus)

Regenerating Concepts of Diné Governance

Figure 5.1 represents the push by some policymakers to plan a future with Diné philosophy as a foundation. This move to refound Diné government within Diné philosophy is very clear when one considers that many of these policy strategies have had varying levels of success. They have, at times, been diluted into meaninglessness, created confusion among those unfamiliar with or closed-minded toward Diné thinking, or been ignored when it was in the interest of some policymakers.

When the day has concluded and the sun is setting, humans enter a regenerative state. So long as individuals continue to think, plan, and live, they will need a space for regeneration and/or reflection. This book explores Diné philosophy as it pertains to leadership. Thinking about how things should or ought to be is key to this thinking stage and represents the first part of this book. Next comes an exploration of how plans were carried out in the past and later disrupted by colonial actors through the monopolization of the Four Sacred Elements. By the time the subject turns to living concepts of governance, two clear trajectories have to be explored: (1) how things should be according to Diné philosophy and (2) how things are according to Western ideas about governance. If colonialism had been successful, there would be nothing to regenerate. Navajo Nation would be just another subunit of the global political economy. Individuals would be praised for climbing to the top and amassing access to the Four Sacred Elements for themselves and for their nuclear families. Knowledge holders might protest such selfishness and bring up *K'é*, reminding those who

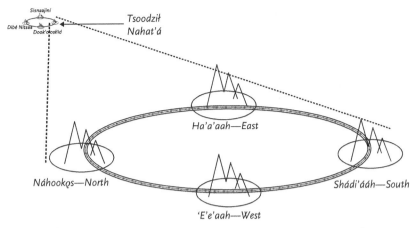

1. *Sisnaajiní*—Thinking about Plans for Tomorrow—How Will Diné Thinking Address Contemporary Issues?
2. *Tsoodził*—Planning the Plans—Navajo Nation Council Resolution
3. *Dook'o'ooslííd*—Living with Plans—Fundamental Law in Supreme Court Opinions
4. *Dibé Nitsaa*—Regenerating Plans—A Philosophy of Regeneration for Tomorrow

Figure 5.1: Planning Diné Thinking in the Twentieth Century

are selfish to not act as though they do not have relatives (Austin 2009, 153). Most people today seem to remember the benefit of clan relations, yet fewer discuss or live up to the obligations personally owed to clan relatives. If people worried about their obligations and allowed life's benefits to take care of themselves, there would be no need to discuss the two trajectories in the modern Navajo government.

Without a time for regeneration, there cannot be a continuous cycle of a long and wisdom-filled life. What some might call stubbornly clinging to the past others might say is the resiliency of Diné philosophy. Many in Diné society were raised with certain values. These values make them who they are today. Without the regenerative quality of Diné philosophy, there would be no way to talk about traditional approaches to governing in a contemporary setting. In the mid- to late 1980s, community members in and around Tsaile, Lukachukai, and Round Rock began writing down their take on *Diné Nitsáhákees*, or "Navajo thinking," which has been referenced throughout this book as Diné philosophy. As has been mentioned before, there is no monolithic standard of Diné philosophy. Regional distinctions exist, and there is no disrespect meant by focusing on one or another version of Diné philosophy. The varying philosophies can happily coexist. Still, it is debatable whether the regional foundation of Diné philosophy relied on here can be exclusively traced to the early 1990s emergence of Diné philosophy in contemporary institutions of governance. What is indisputable, however, is that the regeneration process has already begun, and the only thing that can stop this process is other factions within Navajo society that feel threatened by their ancestors' way of knowing.

5.1. CONTEMPORARY ROLE OF TRADITIONAL DINÉ GOVERNANCE

Recently, there has been a turn back toward traditional Diné philosophy as a basis for contemporary governance. Still, many traditional members of the community may find this movement less than satisfying. The reason for this dissatisfaction is that there are questions about the knowledge contemporary elected officials have about Diné philosophy. Hence, this is the difference between talking about traditional knowledge and applying traditional knowledge to contemporary issues. In fact, there is no mention of the Four Sacred Elements and the role they could play in contemporary governance. Admittedly, bridging the gap between discussion and practice is going to prove very difficult. One can find traditional governance discussions in many of the contemporary governance institutions of the Diné. The Fundamental Laws of the Diné are one source of these traditional discussions. A concerted effort emerged in the 1990s to incorporate the Fundamental Laws into various aspects of contemporary Diné governance. At the urging of the Speaker of the Navajo Nation Council, Edward T. Begay, research was conducted on the Fundamental Laws (Wilkins 2013, 32). The heads of all three branches of the Navajo government signed a Statement of Fundamental Priorities.

The Statement of Fundamental Priorities concluded that the key to securing the sovereignty of Navajo Nation was to integrate the Fundamental Laws into all branches of the Navajo Nation government (Bobroff 2004–2005). This effort has been successful in establishing the Fundamental Laws as one form of governing guidelines that are accepted as legitimate not only domestically (within Navajo Nation) but also internationally (beyond the borders of Navajo Nation). While it is beyond the scope of this discussion to detail every facet of the reintegration of the Fundamental Laws into the various branches of Diné government, we can review some of the recent interactions. Still, as has been detailed in Chapter 4, the emergent Navajo elite might shun any changes that would threaten their monopoly. Hence, "talking about" the Fundamental Laws might be okay if it secures the status quo. We can also highlight how each example might better accomplish the integration of Diné philosophy into contemporary practice by focusing on the Four Sacred Elements.

The Navajo Nation Council passed resolution CN-69-02 entitled *Diné Bi Beehaz'áanii Bitsé Siléí*, loosely translated in English as "The Foundation of the Diné, Diné Law, and Diné Government." This resolution officially recognized four aspects of the Diné Fundamental Laws: Traditional Law, Customary Law, Natural Law, and Common Law. CN-69-02 points out that these Fundamental Laws are the basis for the Diné way of life and explains how these laws need to be included in contemporary Diné government:

> It is the duty of the Nation's leadership to preserve, protect, and enhance the Diné Life Way and sovereignty of the people and their government; the Nation's leaders have always lived by these fundamental laws, but the Navajo Nation Council has not acknowledged and recognized such fundamental laws in the Navajo Nation Code. (Navajo Nation Council 2002)

Given the problem identified by the amendment, the next step was to officially recognize the Fundamental Laws of the Diné. Section 8 of the resolution calls for the branches of Diné government to "learn, practice, and educate the Diné on the values and principles of these laws" (Navajo Nation Council 2002). In section 9, the council acknowledges that much more work is needed and that merely recognizing the Fundamental Laws is not enough (Navajo Nation Council 2002). They must be integrated into contemporary governance, which is not a realistic goal for the council to undertake in isolation. But the path toward integration can be facilitated if we examine how the Navajo Nation Council might help encourage a good and proper relationship between the Nation's leadership, its citizens, and the Four Sacred Elements.

It is important to revert back to the discussion about how institutions may work to constrain future leaders' policy implementations. Can contemporary Diné institutions prevent future individual leaders from violating norms regarding the Four Sacred Elements? The institutions of the Diné, like those of all governments, have a life of their own. Individuals merely adapt their choices to maintain their interests as their identity is impacted by the interaction of their government with other international actors. Non-Diné governments put Diné citizens' relationship with the Four Sacred Elements at risk when Diné leaders thoughtlessly adopt contemporary political and economic practices. This is especially true when Navajo Nation Council policy specifically aims to monopolize access to any of the Four Sacred Elements. From a Diné philosophical point of view, monopolizing access to the Four Sacred Elements not only is inconsistent with Diné philosophy but could also be considered a contemporary diminishment of Diné sovereignty. Consequently, future policymakers should consider how contemporary institutional constraints can work well to guide the behavior of leaders when they are based on the virtues of the Fundamental Laws. The necessary conditions for using contemporary Navajo institutions to maintain a proper relationship with the Four Sacred Elements are present right now.

5.1.1. Institutions of Traditional Diné Governance: Ałch'į' Sila

As has been previously argued, institutional leadership constraint is one way of ensuring that traditional Diné values remain at the forefront of policymaking decisions. Admittedly, it is antithetical to Diné values to consider imposing rules of conduct involving cultural norms on a contemporary governance institution. Yet it is not clear that an alternative to such a practice exists. The notion that European philosophical thought is out of sync with Diné values is not lost on this researcher. But just as has been demonstrated in other sections, the ability to fine-tune methodological approaches is the key to resolving conflicting ideas regarding governance and institutions today. The most fundamental mix-up might be that not all of the current leaders share the same ideals about relations with the Four Sacred Elements. This very basic idea has the consequence of shifting the policy agenda priority list to a point where very little can be accomplished. Reviewing how contemporary governments might work independent of philosophy might help refocus attention back to the Four Sacred Elements.

In the spirit of fine-tuning, the most closely related explanation for the survival of traditional Diné institutions involves the theory that these institutions have a life of their own. While the idea that Diné knowledge will take care of itself is certainly held by many knowledge holders, this portion of the discussion will rely on non-Diné perspectives to make the same point.[1] This institutional life is based on the interaction of identity, choices, and interests, which all collaborate to exhibit governance behavior. Diné identity (arising from Diné philosophy) allows some policy choices but not others. Navajo policymakers should not make choices that monopolize access to the Four Sacred Elements. It is in the interest of all Diné citizens to have a good relationship with the Four Sacred Elements. Consequently, all Navajo policy should likewise maintain good relations with the Four Sacred Elements.

Keeping these caveats in mind, we can explore the notion of Ałch'į' Sila. Ałch'į' Sila is a good way of creating institutions in contemporary Diné governance that are capable of surviving the self-interest of future leaders who may not be willing to live up to traditional Naat'áanii norms. In other words, if the behavior of future leaders can be guided along institutional boundaries set forth by Ałch'į' Sila, they will be one step closer to realizing how traditional Diné governance remains salient today and tomorrow.

It is not possible to properly translate Ałch'į' Sila into English. Rather, some examples can illustrate the complementary attributes of Ałch'į' Sila. There are many areas that can be explained through Ałch'į' Sila. One such area, which is discussed throughout this book, is the Four Sacred Elements. A narrower example of Ałch'į' Sila is the balance between healing and protection when it comes to fire. It should be clear by now that too much fire will burn down a house and too little fire will prevent humans from cooking and heating a house. The relationship with fire is constantly changing, and change requires humans to be diligent in managing their relationship toward fire. This is the idea of maintenance of a proper distance or nearness to fire. Again, this process is applicable to all the other Sacred Elements as well, including water, air, and pollen. Humans are required to protect themselves from being too far away and to heal themselves so they may be far enough away. Simultaneously, humans must also protect themselves from being too close and to heal themselves so they may remain properly distanced. These complementary halves are the essence of Ałch'į' Sila, and they are also present in recognizable aspects of nature.

Consider the Diné notion of male and female rain. Generally, rain is called níłtsá. But in the Navajo language, there are at least two types of rain based on seasonal changes and the characteristics of the rain. From late July to early September, monsoons impact the weather pattern on Navajo land. The elevation, proximity to warm water near the equator in the Pacific Ocean, and high and low pressure patterns allow humidity to rise when compared to nonmonsoon times. The result is a muggy feeling during this time of year. During this time, the elements work together to create thunder, lightning, and heavy but brief rain downpours. The Diné call this kind of rain níłtsá bika', or male rain. The characteristics of male rain are associated with masculine characteristics—namely, violence, loudness, and suddenness. But there also exists a gentler, more subtle downpour that is associated with the winter months. This female rain, or níłtsá bi'ááó, is said to characterize the demeanor of women since it is quiet, gentle, and subtle. The distinction is made not to rank the two types of rain, but to identify them. Both rains are necessary for the survival of the Diné; this was especially true before interaction with non-Native people (Cody 2009). In the Hajinéí era, the Diné could not live with only one type of rain. The two rains complemented each other and made the Diné complete. Male and female rain are one example of Ałch'į' Sila. There are many other examples of Ałch'į' Sila, and some are relevant to governance.

Lessons regarding the proper way to rely on *Ałch'į' Sila* as a guide for successful leadership had always been a part of *Hajinéí*-era Diné governance. For this discussion, *Ałch'į' Sila* can be seen at work in terms of healing and protection to maintain a good relationship with the Four Sacred Elements. The impact *Ałch'į' Sila* has on contemporary leaders is debatable, diverse, and difficult to observe. But that some of the leaders still rely on *Ałch'į' Sila* to guide their decisions today attests to how it could be a great foundation for a contemporary institutional construct—one that future leaders can utilize for the best interest of the Diné. Constructivists argue that institutions survive because they are shaped by the culture of the people who created them based on their identity, their interests, and their policy choices that result in a particular group behavior (Hopf 2002). Again, maintaining good relations with the Four Sacred Elements is central to Diné philosophy and Diné identity, which shaped Diné policy choices during and after the *Hajinéí* era. A general depiction of how *Ałch'į' Sila* may have been used to govern in the past is provided in Figure 5.2. That the set-theory configuration represented in Figure 5.2 does not reflect Diné cultural norms is okay for the moment. Tables and figures only represent a blank template that can be filled with various aspects of traditional Diné prescriptions for leadership, such as *Ałch'į' Sila*. Two configurations offered in Figure 5.2 lend themselves to a consideration of how the identity of the contemporary Diné is not static.

The idea of *Ałch'į' Sila*, in theory, may be a *Hajinéí*-era philosophy free of European influence, but such an assumption seems unlikely. Those wishing to assume the "contact-free" approach may do so and rely on Figure 5.2 as their configuration of choice, because the assumption in that figure is that a pure Diné identity is free of European influence. Hence, if the

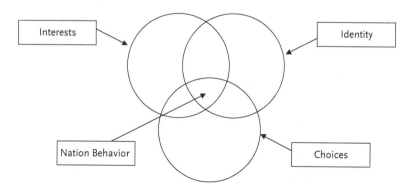

Figure 5.2: Set-Theory Approach to Social Constructivism as Adapted from Hopf 1998. This figure depicts a *normative* balance among all three factors that make up nation behavior.

identity is pure Diné, then the impact of a pure identity can be assumed to directly affect the interests, choices, and behaviors of the Diné government. There are many legitimate reasons to come at this research from such an approach. Yet for the purposes of this discussion, recalling traditional Diné governance for contemporary benefit, it is safer to assume that the Diné identity has been impacted by European contact. Thus, Figure 5.3 may be more appropriate for planning future Diné policy.

Note that in Figure 5.3 identity has an overarching impact on interests, choices, and nation behavior. The reason for this assumption is that identities have shifted in Diné Country. Various philosophies have impacted governance decision making today. Evidence of this is vast and widespread. For example, there are at least three faiths in Diné Country, with some overlapping: the Native American Church, Christianity, and the traditional Diné religion. Also, there is a diversity of political beliefs regarding Diné governance; these beliefs can be researched independent of the writing here (Wilkins 2002b, 2003). Thus, the observable evidence for political, cultural, and economic identity cannot be the only source for crafting interests, choices, and nation behavior. At the same time, *Ałch'į' Sila* cannot realistically be considered a thought process free of European or other non-Diné thought. Using Figure 5.3 makes it possible to take all of the above qualifications into account. With philosophical diversity in mind, returning to basic tenets about how governing should take place is key. Again, all

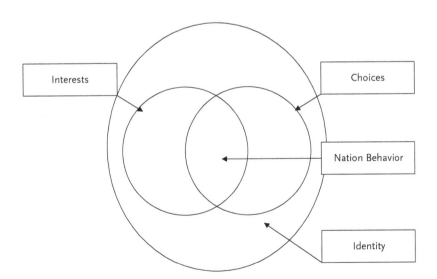

Figure 5.3: Alternative Configuration of Subset Relationships Shaping Nation Behavior. The key difference here is that identity has a complete, overarching impact on all other governance factors.

humans currently have a relationship with fire, water, air, and pollen. In the end, and regardless of their political, cultural, or economic orientation, the Diné should be the final arbiters of how they wish to govern themselves and be governed. If *Ałch'į' Sila* can be used to achieve governance ends, so be it.

Keeping these ideas in mind, we can move on to a closer look at *Ałch'į' Sila*. What follows is only my interpretation of how the idea works. It will need to be fine-tuned to its environment in the same way that a musical instrument is tuned to its accompanying environment of sound. In other words, *Ałch'į' Sila* concepts must be tuned to maintain good relations with the Four Sacred Elements.

It might be wise to consider *Ałch'į' Sila*, along with its component parts, in relation to its independent level of generality. Level-of-generality issues, in terms of research methods, have been explored in depth elsewhere (Sartori 1970). Table 5.1 is a collection of the various components that are relevant to contemporary Diné governance. Within *Sa'ah Naaghái Bik'eh Hózhóón* is the process of Diné thinking articulated in Chapter 1. The components within *Sa'ah Naaghái Bik'eh Hózhóón* are as follows: *Nitsáhákees, Nahat'á, 'Iiná,* and *Sih Hasin*.

Components of *Ałch'į' Sila* must be understood in relation to one another and in terms of their level of generality. Table 5.1 indicates that the higher up on the ladder of generality, the more abstract the idea is and the more a diverse set of numerous ideas are potentially nested within it. These ideas are rearticulated in set-theory form in Figure 5.4, with some accompanying cautionary qualifications. Here it is enough to understand the relationship that these ideas have with one another in terms of level of generality.

Note how *Ałch'į' Sila* and *K'é* are the most general components. *K'é* may be more general than *Ałch'į' Sila*, because it is within the foundations of *K'é* that one will find some of the aspects of *Ałch'į' Sila*. This might seem counterintuitive. The research is attempting not only to determine a relative

Table 5.1. COMPONENTS OF TRADITIONAL DINÉ GOVERNANCE
RELEVANT TO CONTEMPORARY DINÉ ISSUES

Within *Ałch'į' Sila*	Within *Sa'ah Naaghái Bik'eh Hózhóón*
K'é	*Nitsáhákees*
Sa'ah Naaghái Bik'eh Hózhóón	*Nahat'á*
Hózhǫ́ǫ́jí	*'Iiná*
Hashkéjí	*Sih Hasin*
	Manage *Kǫ', Tó, Niłchí, Tadidiin*

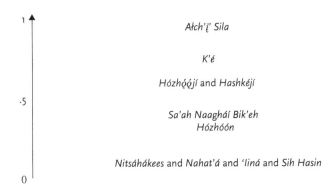

1

Ałch'į' Sila

K'é

Hózhǫ́ǫ́jí and Hashkéjí

·5

Sa'ah Naaghái Bik'eh
Hózhóón

Nitsáhákees and Nahat'á and 'Iiná and Sih Hasin

0

Figure 5.4: Components of *Ałch'į' Sila* with Relative Levels of Generality, from Sartori 1970. "1" equals "most general" and "0" equals "most specific".

idea of generality but, specifically, to focus on the relationships between various Diné protocols. *K'é*, in general, is a governing body that impacts many beings, including *bilá ashdla*, or the five-fingered people. Concern with the aspect of *K'é* related to the responsibilities of the five-fingered people implies that *K'é* is only slightly broader than *Ałch'į' Sila*. In other words, *Ałch'į' Sila* does not encompass all that has been or ever will be in relation to *K'é*.

The other factors are less complicated, relatively speaking. Once the above assumptions are made, the other components seem to arrange themselves. *Hózhǫ́ǫ́jí* and *Hashkéjí* are another example of *Ałch'į' Sila*. This idea is similarly associated with maintaining proper distance and nearness toward the Four Sacred Elements. Thus, *Hózhǫ́ǫ́jí* and *Hashkéjí* are less abstract than *Ałch'į' Sila*. As for *Sa'ah Naagh'ái Bik'eh Hózhóón*, it may simultaneously be both more abstract than *Nitsáhákees, Nahat'á, 'Iiná,* and *Sih Hasin* and less abstract than *Hózhǫ́ǫ́jí* and *Hashkéjí*. The reason for this assumption is that, as detailed in Figure 5.7 (page 151), it lies within the overlapping (gray) area between *Hózhǫ́ǫ́jí* and *Hashkéjí* that scholars may find the best use for the principles contained within *Sa'ah Naagh'ái Bik'eh Hózhóón*.

The purpose of life is to be on earth for a long time in order to gain and distribute wisdom. The purpose of *Sa'ah Naagh'ái Bik'eh Hózhóón* is to assist with this process. The pursuit of a good and long life requires both healing (*Hózhǫ́ǫ́jí*) and protection (*Hashkéjí*). Hence, a person can go beyond the confines of *Sa'ah Naagh'ái Bik'eh Hózhóón*. This expanse beyond *Sa'ah Naagh'ái Bik'eh Hózhóón* is outside of the scope of living a good long life. Put another way, it is possible to misuse any of the Four Sacred Elements, but individuals are strongly advised to avoid abuses. Many believe that none of these considerations are taken seriously by contemporary policymakers, which results in the environmental contamination of water and air. Again, the purpose of this discussion is to demonstrate how a very abstract idea can come down to a data point on the earth, such as water and air quality.

It is important to ensure that ideas are properly oriented. It is easy to verbally express ideas without much guidance regarding the true relationship these ideas have with one another. The challenge is to connect abstract thought to the Four Sacred Elements. Going further, the lessons from set theory highlight the manner in which implicitly nested ideas seldom have their true relationships fully explored and articulated. Figuring out the relative generalities within *Ałch'į' Sila* also serves to avoid confusion by providing a level of transparency not available in English descriptions of the relationships. This effort is in line with the effort to keep the process "tunable" to its environment and, thus, invites community feedback. Figure 5.5, a set theory representation of *Ałch'į' Sila*, keeps in mind the relational generalities first expressed in Figure 5.4.

Figure 5.4 displays the level of generality among the various ideas discussed here. Figure 5.4 depicts a subset relationship at work. Figure 5.5 might be more confusing if it were not for the work first laid out in Figure 5.4. *K'é* is a superset of *Ałch'į' Sila*. All of the five-fingered peoples' instructions regarding *Ałch'į' Sila* are articulated within *K'é*. *Ałch'į' Sila*, then, is a superset of *Hózhǫ́ǫ́jí* and *Hashkéjí*. This means the teachings regarding the proper handling of *Hózhǫ́ǫ́jí* and *Hashkéjí* issues can be found within

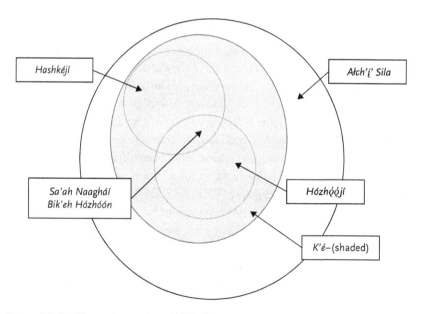

Figure 5.5: Set-Theory Approach to *Ałch'į' Sila*

notions of *Ałch'į' Sila*. All of these lessons impact how humans maintain proper relations with the Four Sacred Elements.

Be aware, however, that *Ałch'į' Sila* is not the only source of instructions. It is simply noted that there is an isolated relationship across these aspects of Diné philosophy to one another. The relationships expressed here are not exhaustive. Thus, *Sa'ah Naagh'áí Bik'eh Hózhóón* as an aspect of Diné philosophy will be used to solve problems when the gray area between *Hózhóójí* and *Hashkéjí* is encountered. These ideas all relate to maintaining proper distance and nearness toward the Four Sacred Elements. Within *Sa'ah Naagh'áí Bik'eh Hózhóón* can be located the notion of *Diné Bitsáhákees*, or Diné thinking. With the issues of relative levels of abstraction given attention—not settled forevermore—those interested may look at these components of Diné thinking in a fashion that allows them to have a voice in a contemporary setting.

If the above assumptions hold, scholars may better understand the way in which these aspects of Diné thinking could potentially play a role in contemporary governance. Specifically, focus may center on the Four Sacred Elements in an attempt to utilize the notion of how identity, interests, and choices can have a substantial impact on nation behavior. Exploring identity, interests, and choices may uncover new ways for traditional aspects of Diné thinking reengage with Navajo Nation's current and future direction. The institutional structures are traditional aspects of Diné thinking. Since they already exist, it makes sense to use them in a contemporaneous context. This approach may alleviate problems of legitimacy. Although it is difficult to have a starting place, since it is likely that issues can arise in almost any place within the model, let us start at *Sa'ah Naagh'áí Bik'eh Hózhóón*, where decision making regarding policies is located. Readers may wish to skip ahead and look at Figure 5.7 (page 151). Notice that *Sa'ah Naagh'áí Bik'eh Hózhóón* lies within the gray area between *Hózhóójí* and *Hashkéjí*. The gray area will still play a role after elaborating on *Sa'ah Naagh'áí Bik'eh Hózhóón*.

The exploded view of *Sa'ah Naagh'áí Bik'eh Hózhóón* in Figure 5.6 illustrates Diné thinking, or *bitsáhákees*. (For a detailed description of Diné thinking, refer back to the discussion of Diné philosophy in Chapter 1.) Essentially, this is the same thinking linked to the philosophy of the Sacred Mountains and *hooghans*. For this discussion, it is only necessary to acknowledge the relationship between *Sa'ah Naagh'áí Bik'eh Hózhóón* and Diné thinking. This is a cycle within a cycle, or a nested model. By thinking about maintaining proper distance and nearness toward the Four Sacred Elements, an individual can begin to appreciate the situation. Then, that

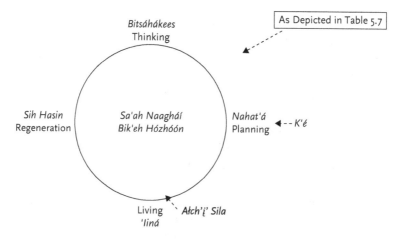

Figure 5.6: Exploded View of *Sa'ah Naagh'ái Bik'eh Hózhóón* and Diné Thinking

individual can plan a strategy to either get closer to or further from the Four Sacred Elements and then apply the proposed solution to the real world. The person then observes the world and reflects upon the solution. It's important to remember that solutions require regeneration. If the solution is successful, a person cannot rest assured indefinitely, because the elements will continue to move. These movements require constant conciliation with the Four Sacred Elements. This example of problem solving is only one very narrow aspect contained within a very broad idea called *Sa'ah Naagh'ái Bik'eh Hózhóón*. The discussion can now back away from the problem-solving process to better understand why the problem-solving process is necessary in the first place.

By pulling away from the close-up image of *Sa'ah Naagh'ái Bik'eh Hózhóón*, the idea of *Hózhǫ́ǫ́jí* and *Hashkéjí*, or moving toward harmony (healing) and away from disharmony (protection), comes into focus. In Western thinking, something positive is typically thought of as a polar opposite of something negative. Yet there does exist within Western thought the ability to negate that which is positive in order to transform it into a negative and vice versa. In other words, identifying all of the attributes that make up positive ideas can theoretically negate all of those attributes to create the polar opposite of that positive idea. This is the process of converting a positive into a negative. The reverse of the process changes a negative into a positive. Understanding this idea of converting one polar opposite into another provides the context for discussions of *Hózhǫ́ǫ́jí* and *Hashkéjí*. An extended account of *Hózhǫ́ǫ́jí* and *Hashkéjí* in relation to the Navajo Nation court system explains one application (Nielsen and Zion 2005).

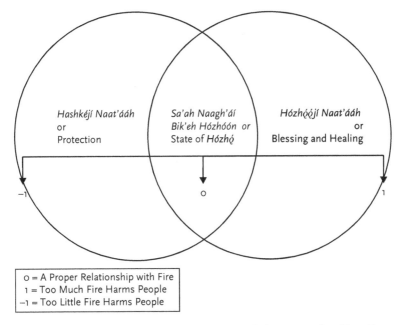

Figure 5.7: Concept Continuum of Any of the Four Sacred Elements, Such as *Kó*, or Fire, and How It Relates to *Sa'ah Naagh'áí Bik'eh Hózhóón*

Robert Yazzie discusses how justices within the Navajo peacemaker court had the task of taking the Fundamental Laws of the Diné and applying them to contemporary issues that Diné individuals faced (Nielsen and Zion 2005, 42–58). Figure 5.7 may more clearly illustrate how to apply Fundamental Laws to contemporary issues. The idea is to move individuals toward *Hózhóójí*, or the beauty way, to begin healing. When a person moves toward *Hózhóójí*, that person also moves away from *Hashkéjí*. Yet each of these moves requires a different approach since the normative goal is to maintain balance between *Hózhóójí* and *Hashkéjí*. A drift toward *Hashkéjí* (toward *Hózhóójí*) could require a protective *or* healing approach to return toward balance. But this does not mean that life can simply be lived in a state of *Hózhó* at all times. Yazzie states that the condition of *Hashkéjí* is a consequence of the individual falling out of balance (Nielsen and Zion 2005, 42–58). Further exploring Figure 5.7 may better illustrate this point.

Figure 5.7 illustrates how a drift away from a balance between *Hózhóójí* and *Hashkéjí* is not a good thing for the individual. (Note how *Hózhóójí* and *Hashkéjí* can overlap. This is considered to be a balanced state.) Maintaining the balance is predicated on an assumption that life is constantly moving all around an individual. (This movement has been thoroughly described in relation to the Four Sacred Elements.) Hence, the individual has the responsibility to respond to constant change. It is not advised that individuals attempt to capture balance in a static, non-living arrangement. Both healing and protection processes are required to maintain the balance and prevent the emergence of *Anáhóót'i'* (Austin 2009, 62). *Anáhóót'i'* might be characterized as the process of an individual drifting outside of the overlapping conditions of *Hashkéjí* and *Hózhóójí*, or balance. It is the job of a justice of the peacemaker court to act as a guide for those who are out of balance (Nielsen and Zion 2005). These sentiments are echoed by former Navajo Supreme Court Justice Raymond Austin. He added the idea of *Hóxzhǫ*. Austin states that moving away from balance in any direction (see Figure 5.7 on page 151, which is also included in Chapter 2) means that individuals will find themselves in a state of *Hóxzhǫ* (Austin 2009). Austin's comments on *Hóxzhǫ* may represent a direction of travel for an individual. *Anáhóót'i'* is a disruption of balance (*Hóxzhǫ*) created by the presence of a disruptor, such as the monsters discussed in Chapter 1 (Austin 2009, 62). When tied to the Four Sacred Elements, fire could be creating imbalance. As a result, individuals may need to protect themselves from exposure. After protection is secured, healing may commence. Still, it is too simplistic to state that one is "good" and one is "bad."

One of the interesting attributes of set theory is the way in which gray areas are made clearer. In Figure 5.6, for example, the logic behind the gray area is that problem solvers can be clear about the way things go well and the way things go badly. These are the extreme positions that exist in the world. There is not a lot of debate regarding some aspects of *Hózhóójí* and *Hashkéjí*. Some things are clearly *Hózhóójí*, such as having water to drink. Some things are clearly *Hashkéjí*, such as having too much snow, which can put life at risk. The areas with little debate, in theory, can be located in the extreme areas indicated by 1 and −1 in Figure 5.7. Note how some areas are clearly separate from their polar opposite. In other words, the entire set of plausible phenomena associated with *Hózhóójí* can be found within the circle labeled "*Hózhóójí*." Some aspects of *Hózhóójí* that do not go near *Hashkéjí* are the areas that are not debated. Most medicine people (*Hataałii*) agree on some aspects that are clearly *Hózhóójí* and other aspects that are clearly *Hashkéjí*. The more interesting events occur in the gray area between *Hózhóójí* and *Hashkéjí*. One might say that this is the place where real life occurs. As Yazzie puts it, "People are supposed to strive for *Hózhǫ*, but a human will never attain *Hózhǫ* in this lifetime" (Yazzie 2009).

It is important here to revisit another aspect of Diné philosophy (elaborated upon in Chapter 1) regarding the way in which the world should be encountered:

Sistsiji Hózhǫ́, or beauty in front of me
Shikishli Hózhǫ́, or beauty behind me
Shiyaagi Hózhǫ́, or beauty beneath me (Mother Earth)
Shik'igi Hózhǫ́, or beauty from above me (Father Sky)
Shinaadę́ę́ Na Tso Hózhǫ́, or beauty all around (across the horizon)
Shizéé'dee Hózhǫ́, or speaking one's thoughts with beauty
Nanita Sa'ah Naaghai
Nanita Bikeh Hozhoon
Hózhǫ́ Nahasdlii
Hózhǫ́ Nahasdlii
Hózhǫ́ Nahasdlii
Hózhǫ́ Nahasdlii

The above affirmation is asking that the *Diyin Dine'é* (creator) guide an individual's daily encounters with the Sacred Elements. The assumption is that during a day, a person will necessarily encounter aspects of life that are clearly *Hózhǫ́ójí* and *Hashkéjí*. The best way to encounter aspects of life that are *Hashkéjí* is to have enough *Hózhǫ́ójí* within to balance out the *Hashkéjí* that is encountered. People must protect themselves from harm and heal themselves afterward. This process, again, helps avoid a drift toward *Hóxzhǫ*. The affirmation is asking for guidance with the encounters that a person experiences during the day. Failure to abide by these guidelines invites the *Hóxzhǫ* condition. Although it may seem vague, the daily affirmation is based on the assumption that life is the gray area between *Hózhǫ́ójí* and *Hashkéjí*. For example, water appears unthreatening, but, obviously, it can take life away. The affirmation acknowledges that the way to deal with *Hóxzhǫ* is not to eliminate it but to balance it out with healing or protection depending on the specifics of the condition itself. And while this is true for individuals, it is also true for governance decision making that will affect communities and beyond.

Future approaches to Diné governance may wish to fall back on the philosophy of the Diné involving the gray area between *Hózhǫ́ójí* and *Hashkéjí*. This is especially true if people take the Four Sacred Elements seriously. It should be intuitively apparent that political problems are all about the interaction between positive and negative events. Threats to relations with the Four Sacred Elements are key. More accurately, all political concerns involve a matter of collective healing for the people or a need to be collectively protective of the people. Threats the community as a whole faces to its relations with the Four Sacred Elements require healing for restoration to occur. Hence, the manner in which "issues" (events that need to be addressed for the sake of the community) are discussed and solutions offered may be served well by notions within *Ałch'į' Sila*. Do events require healing? Do they require protection? That is why Diné thinking appears within the gray area of *Hózhǫ́ójí* and *Hashkéjí*, which is within the gray area of *Sa'ah Naagh'áí Bik'eh Hózhóón*. These interrelated areas of philosophy are not really separable and must work in concert toward goals of healing or protection. It's a matter of magnification. Focusing on one area (abstraction) does not dismiss or ignore another area of magnification (concreteness).

A *Naat'áanii* may be an individual best able to handle communitywide decisions by taking into account *Hózhǫ́ójí* (healing) and *Hashkéjí* (protection). *Naat'áanii* are selected and acknowledged as legitimate leaders if they can handle everyday community problems. These problems should intrinsically address maintenance of a communitywide appropriate relationship with the Four Sacred Elements. The notion of life in the gray area of *Hózhǫ́ójí* and *Hashkéjí* puts a challenge in the hands of a *Naat'áanii*. When a decision is made, the solution is implemented. The community then watches closely to see whether the result of the decision has negative and/or positive consequences. Did decisions properly lead to a healing and, thus, *Hózhǫ́*? If not, perhaps the decisions deliberately led to protection and, again, toward *Hózhǫ́*? In other words, making decisions about relating to the Four Sacred Elements requires balancing within the gray area of *Hózhǫ́ójí* and *Hashkéjí*. Put another way, healing or protection is required to offset the imbalance depending on the situation. Good *Naat'áanii* will have spent their lifetimes learning how to accomplish this. Communities will oversee the results.

Community oversight is depicted by the presence of *K'é*, or the set of connections that individuals and families have to one another as well as their perception of relations with the Four Sacred Elements. Assuming the issue is resolved, *K'é* may then focus on other aspects of their institutions, which may include other issues. In political terms, this is akin to community feedback to elected officials. In Diné philosophy, it is the traditional way in which problems were brought to the *Naat'áanii*. But balance between *Hózhǫ́ójí* and *Hashkéjí* is a delicate process requiring constant maintenance, just like humans must maintain a proper distance and nearness toward the Four Sacred Elements. Surprises or a lack of maintenance allow imbalance to set in, which leads to an *Anáhóót'i'* condition. In other words, only careless individuals allow fire to get out of control. Thus, it is more likely that the issue will be reintroduced to the *Naat'áanii* for continued monitoring. The issue being readdressed is not necessarily a failure but could merely be a continued maintenance of the balance between *Hózhǫ́ǫ́jí* and *Hashkéjí*. Maintenance supplements the regeneration process. The issues may change, but the institutions of *Ałch'į' Sila* remain difficult to remove. Thus, although today's issues may seem daunting, there should be confidence in the fact that *Ałch'į' Sila* can even be discussed at all.

5.1.2. Local Governance Institutions

Future governance modifications must work to close the gap that has emerged between local governance and national governance. The details of how the gap emerged are contained in Chapter 2. Briefly, U.S. corporations discovered natural resources on Navajo Nation land. In an effort to create a rubber-stamp committee to sign off on land leases, a hierarchical version of what is today the Diné national government was formed. At least two aspects of the early government are key to understanding the gap that exists today between local and national governance. First, the rubber-stamp committee was handpicked by U.S. corporate interests to serve the interests of resource extraction corporations. Second, the idea of consolidated national governance is not consistent with Diné norms prior to the 1920s. In sum, none of these trends are consistent with maintaining a good relationship with the Four Sacred Elements. The details of these events can be located in many works but specifically in Wilkins (1987, 2002a, 2003). This notion of closing the gap between local and national governance assumes that governance should be bottom-up and all-inclusive as well as guided by Diné cultural norms. This might mean that only certain learned people are capable of leading, in the same way that *Naat'áanii* might be selected and recognized. So what institutional guidelines might lead to more integration of local governance institutions (chapter houses) into national governance institutions?

While it is beyond the scope of this discussion to outline every way in which the gap between local and national governance can be closed, scholars can look at the reasons why European institutions survive and look for ideas that may apply to understanding the survival of Diné institutions. Figure 5.2 can assist in exploring a dynamic picture of contemporary Diné governance. Diné identity, in general and specifically in terms of governance, has been impacted by interaction with colonial actors. The details of the identity impact can be found in Chapter 2. Briefly, colonial interaction put the Diné communitywide relationship with the Four Sacred Elements in serious jeopardy. As is shown in Figure 5.2, adopting (or being force-fed) European philosophical thought should have impacted Diné identity, which in turn impacted choices that the various *Naat'áanii* made. Simultaneously, other interests were shaped because new issues needed attention—especially those pertaining to trade and warfare.

These factors all led to changes in the behavior of Diné governance, as explained in discussions about treaty making in Chapter 2. After *Hwéeldi*, or the Long Walk, the same can be said of the agency formation, which is also detailed in Chapter 2. A trend toward national hierarchical consolidation for all Indigenous tribes via federal policies of reorganization, termination, and relocation also contributed to a national/local divide (Getches, Wilkinson, and Williams 2005). Yet the survival of Diné thinking is expressed as a condition of Peoplehood (Holm, Pearson, and Chavis 2003). Briefly, only those aspects of Peoplehood visible to federal policies were significantly impacted, and these were at the national level. This explains why the aspects of Diné philosophy discussed in this chapter survive. The resultant situation is not necessarily good or bad. Recall, however, how institutions are difficult to erase—whether they are European or Diné. Thus, incorporating chapter houses into national governance is an exercise that lends itself to *Ałch'į' Sila*, so long as a positive relationship with the Four Sacred Elements is clearly an aspiration.

Based on the number of chapter houses in existence today, the process will necessarily require 110 separate attempts to reconcile the disruption between local and national governance. Again, this could take the form of reconciling the focus of 110 different communities on their relationship with the Four Sacred Elements. One of the main issues involved includes creating greater efficacy in implementing national policies at the local level. Still, opposition at the national level to incorporating more local governance policies and procedures can be expected as institutional opposition. This is evident today in the current push for so called "regionalization" of the chapters (Curly and Parish 2016). The push to consolidate power in Window Rock is basically a monopolization of policymaking that, nearly without exception, impacts one or more of the Four Sacred Elements. The key to gaining more integration and eliminating hierarchy could work in at least two ways: First, there is a legitimacy issue that *Ałch'į' Sila* need not demonstrate. It has always worked out well and has stood the test of time. European-style governance in Diné Country lacks this legitimacy. Second, understanding the root of opposition may give those with an interest in integrating local and national governance an advantage when it comes to achieving their goals.

Questioning the legitimacy of European institutions in Diné national governance is the second key to integrating local and national governance. The simplest way of questioning legitimacy is to simply ask if the current national government truly has maintained a proper relationship with the Four Sacred Elements. Using the process of *Ałch'į' Sila* as a mechanism for determining unambiguous actions to undermine specific European institutions of governance may work very well. Data clearly point to negative impacts of European institutions on at least water and air quality, which indicates both *Anáhóót'i'* and *Hózhǫ*. Thus, the aspiration is to find local leaders who are in line with concepts of traditional Diné leadership: the *Naat'áanii*. This is a search for priorities in which the Four Sacred Elements set the stage for all other concerns.

5.1.3. Domestic *Naat'áanii* Revisited

In this section, the discussion will briefly return to concept building as a tool for building future institutions of Diné governance that focus on maintaining good relations with the Four Sacred Elements. Recall that concept building was used heavily to describe traditional institutions of Diné governance in Chapter 3. Concept building was also used to describe post-1922 Navajo governing institutions. Concept building, as applied to traditional approaches to Diné governance, has explained how legitimacy was built into the institution itself. Evidence of legitimacy is largely tied to a history of maintaining good relations with the Four Sacred Elements. Therefore, it is worth revisiting some findings from Chapter 3 here.

It seems self-evident that Diné knowledge holders, who tend to be elders both in age and in their ability to demonstrate the application of Diné wisdom, would agree that they wish contemporary Diné institutions to reflect traditional Diné values. They believe that contemporary leaders using contemporary institutions have not performed well in maintaining proper distance and nearness toward the Four Sacred Elements. Some have cited recent problems (e.g., hanta virus and riots in Window Rock) as evidence of the drift away from Diné values. What follows are "rough draft" concepts of contemporary Diné institutions that do not exist in the real world. All concepts need fine-tuning to ensure that they work properly to maintain good relations with the Four Sacred Elements. Concept building, for example, will allow a group to come together and openly critique my work. Criticisms do not entail outright rejection so much as they acknowledge the need for further fine-tuning for the concept to be relevant today. Again, another key assumption is that traditional Diné institutions are actually relevant and applicable to contemporary issues. There is no denying that all humans need fire, clean water, clean air, and pollen.

Revisiting the domestic *Naat'áanii* now should further illuminate the need for traditional Diné thinking to take a foundational role in contemporary Diné governance. Figure 5.8 links traditional thinking with contemporary salience. It is certainly open to criticism and can be improved.

Here, it would be most legitimate to start from the concept of Diné *Naat'áanii* and build from there. Some of the traits of *Naat'áanii* are useful for today, including regional agenda setting, being a good speaker, and the like. The most work will need to be invested in creating the list of responsibilities. This area will require a major initiative to garner feedback from the Diné constituency. Perhaps the initial focus should be on the Four Sacred Elements. Some research suggests that any kind of Native nation building requires a clear set of responsibilities delineated after careful deliberation (Jorgenson 2007). Still, policymakers in the Navajo Nation and other Indigenous nations are strongly discouraged from taking a Bureau of Indian Affairs approach to this task; they should not simply draft a series of "job descriptions." A concept-building approach with a three-level view to developing a living job description is key for several reasons. It allows for fine-tuning, creates an environment that fosters equity and equality, and perhaps inspires the young to participate in the future of their own Native nation governance. The laundry list of responsibilities that have not been explicitly addressed in post-1922 institutions can be a starting point for a set of data/observation-level criteria in which individual Diné citizens take responsibility for their own neighbors and, in the process, themselves. Data levels should closely monitor relationships with the Four Sacred Elements.

Each of the potential data indicators must be directly tied to community needs and the Four Sacred Elements. This could be a reinterpretation of *K'é*, or the embedding of not only a benefit from the community but also, and probably most importantly, an obligation to the community via Navajo clan ties. The clan links from the community as a whole to individuals responsible for specific needs, such as energy policy or water policy, can be directly tied to a domestic *Naat'áanii*. Then, domestic *Naat'áanii* would be responsible to the various branches of the centralized Navajo government in a manner similar to a confederacy. In this way, what has previously been assumed to be an outdated method of leadership (traditional Diné methods) may be quite salient today, because without basic access to fire, water, air, and pollen humans cannot live.

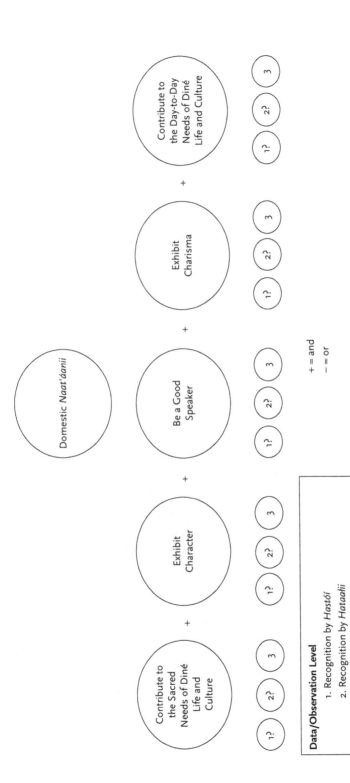

Figure 5.8: Three-Level View—Concept of Proposed Domestic *Naat'áanii*

Again, it is very noteworthy that a history of interaction with colonial actors has forced *all* Native nations to surrender their international relations or diplomacy mechanisms in exchange for certain guarantees outlined in almost five hundred treaties (Deloria and DeMallie 1999). Navajo Nation is no different, and this occurrence needs much more attention in any future research on Native and Navajo Nation governance. It is overtly clear that the question of the United States' trust responsibility to Navajo Nation and all Native nations is under scrutiny. But again, the trust-responsibility issues are often raised through domestic U.S. institutions and rarely as a matter of international relations. (One exception is the Trail of Broken Treaties movement of the late 1960s and early 1970s.) Citizens of Navajo Nation, policymakers, and members of the Diné Policy Institute, or DPI, and the advisory circle must further evaluate the premises offered here. All of these institutional discussions can have very real impacts for Navajo Nation in a rapidly globalizing world.

It seems consistent to rely on a traditional Diné notion of having specialists set agendas during times of crises as was done when the *Naach'id* was operational in the mid-1870s. Building up institutions that support an international *Naat'áanii* would be key to ensuring that Diné interests are represented beyond the realm of the Six Sacred Mountains. Our globalized world requires an international focus on threats to maintaining good relations with the Four Sacred Elements. International *Naat'áanii* would be responsible for acting as diplomats with representatives of New Mexico, Arizona, Utah, and the United States. The reason for taking an international approach involves the interests of the United States contradicting, or at least not being consistent with, the interests of Navajo Nation. This is especially true in terms of the political economy. Still, the key to ensuring that these types of institutional reconstructions have salience is to embed them within the traditional Diné aspects of *K'é* so that a genuine notion of responsibility resonates through all levels of Navajo Nation and its post-1922 adoption of a Western-style governance hierarchy. In many ways, the manner in which Navajo chapter houses were created reflects the preexisting Diné notions of *K'é*. In other words, perhaps the solution to retraditionalizing Diné government is to merely recognize what is already hiding in plain sight.

Chapter house governance has been likened to eliminating the Navajo words for leaders and replacing them with Western terms such as *president* and *vice president*. Yet the underlying network of connections based on *K'é* may still be intact. (It is beyond the scope of this discussion to prove or disprove this claim, but it deserves further study.) Perhaps the emergence of the chapter house system in Navajo Nation in the early twentieth century is an example of conceptual stretching (Sartori 1970; Goertz 2006). It appears that the network of *K'é* was either misunderstood or underestimated by non-Diné policymakers and changed to an English word (chapter house), while none or very few of the underlying networks were disturbed. Similar arguments have been made about economic development in Latin America today. There is a link between colonial actors who were able to co-opt or destroy Indigenous political economy networks and contemporary economic growth. Colonial actors who could not destroy or co-opt Indigenous political economies have experienced stagnant economic growth since colonization began (Mahoney 2010).

These conclusions could also be at work in regions of Navajo Nation today, but they have yet to be fully explored. Regardless, the prospects for economic development of Navajo Nation today may never be fully realized unless further discussions take place about the concept of the international *Naat'áanii*. None of these discussions have to date referenced good relations with the Four Sacred Elements. Still, interested parties should reserve judgment until recent research on Navajo nation building is further explored.

5.2. INCONVENIENT PHILOSOPHY—BREATHING LIFE INTO AN ABANDONED *HOOGHAN*

The double-edged sword that is "modern" Navajo governance is not a simple story. Many policy outcomes come from the convoluted interaction of colonial actors and Navajo elites. How do Navajo citizens negotiate their best interests when there are so many barriers to meaningful policy formation? What keeps the citizens of Navajo Nation motivated to push back against Navajo self-termination? Perhaps it is the "inconvenient" philosophy at the local level that might serve as a foundation for grassroots reclamation of Diné sovereignty. Many Navajo elites have misguided their constituency into mistakenly believing that simply eliminating representation in central Navajo governance is the same thing as reclamation. In fact, eliminating institutional access to central Navajo institutions is the antithesis of reclamation. It's simply a concentration of power in the hands of fewer individuals. Those interested in local governance cannot refuse to participate and expect the central government to "go away." A lifeway home has been abandoned, and the Navajo community must be willing to breathe life back into its own philosophy of leadership, or things will get ever more concentrated in the hands of fewer Navajo elites.

Avery Denny once advised that people must be willing to think and breathe life into institutions of Diné philosophy. He discussed this as a lesson from the Holy Ones, who are credited with thinking the universe into existence. Just as the Holy Ones thought the universe into being, so can humans breathe decentralized institutions into relevancy. If the traditional homeland of the Diné is a giant *hooghan* with Sacred Mountains as various posts, doorways, and chimneys, then the people are ultimately capable of breathing these abandoned institutions into the realm of the living if they so choose. Reclaiming Diné sovereignty, then, is a process of reoccupying the *hooghan*-mountain model abandoned by Navajo elites in the early twentieth century. What follows is a description of local governing bodies that should be utilized to reclaim Diné governance and sovereignty. This process of reclamation may wish to explore strategic pursuit of policy preferences that exploit future shocks to modern Navajo institutions. Successfully recapturing modern Navajo institutions may require creating several contingency plans in anticipation of a shock. The extent to which advocates for local governance lock in their preferences for decentralized governing institutions likely depends on a grassroots push for change when a future shock dislodges the current policy stasis in Navajo Nation.

5.2.1. Incorporating Local (Chapter House) Governance

Future governance modifications must work to close the gap that has emerged between local governance and national governance. This chapter has summarized how the various versions of the modern Navajo Nation were structured hierarchically. It seems obvious that hierarchy can only work to create more distance from the Four Sacred Elements, and this is not a good condition.

Consolidated national governance is not consistent with Diné norms prior to the 1920s. Closing the gap between local and national governance implies an assumption: governance should be bottom-up and all-inclusive while guided by Diné cultural norms. This might mean that only certain learned people are capable of leading in the same way that *Naat'áanii* might lead. Perhaps only those who are familiar with the Four Sacred Elements and how to maintain proper relations should be the key advisors consulting *Naat'áanii* on how to lead effectively. What institutional guides might lead to more integration of local (chapter house) governance into national governance institutions?

It is beyond the scope of this work to outline every way in which the gap between local and national governance can be closed. Still, researchers can examine factors that led to changes in the behavior of Navajo Nation as a national unit, as is detailed in the discussion on treaty making in Section 2.2. The formation of the Navajo regional agencies in the aftermath of the Long Walk is one step in consolidating power away from the local community and into the hands of centralized governing institutions. Nationally, this same impact was experienced by many Indigenous nations during federal policy eras involving reorganization, termination, and relocation policies (Getches, Wilkinson, and Williams 2005). I argue that Diné philosophy of governance survives today because of it's nesting in ceremony, language, place, and sacred history (Holm, Pearson, and Chavis 2003). Federal policy, being myopic in nature, could only successfully attack the most visible portions of Dine Peoplehood. The portions of Diné philosophy that survive today were always hiding in plain sight unrecognized by colonial actors. The same is also true of the Four Sacred Elements. Hence, we see a pattern of monopolization of the Four Sacred Elements involving water first and pollen second. The earlier discussion of Navajo institutions explains how such aspects of Diné philosophy survive today. And while all of the factors discussed above have also impacted local Diné governance, the level of impact appears to have been more severe at the national level. Put another way, the rural communities appear to still respect relations with the Four Sacred Elements, while national centers of power in Window Rock have exhibited more evidence that they are indifferent to or okay with monopolizing access to the Four Sacred Elements (Crawford 2011; Navajo Nation 2013).

Some of the main issues involved include creating greater efficacy at the local level to incorporate what goes on at the national level. Transparency and accountability about maintaining proper relations with the Four Sacred Elements is simply not manifestly or latently discussed as an important issue—and perhaps transparency and accountability should be the highest priority. Still, the opposition at the national level to incorporating more local governance is an institutional opposition. The key to gaining more integration and eliminating hierarchy could work in at least two ways. First, there is a legitimacy issue that traditional approaches need not demonstrate. These approaches have always worked out well and have stood the test of time. European-style governance in Diné Country lacks this legitimacy. Second, understanding the actual root of opposition may give those with an interest in integrating local and national governance an advantage when it comes to achieving their goals.

There can be no discussion about reintroducing traditional norms of Diné governance until there is a serious questioning of the contemporary practices used today. Using traditional processes as a mechanism for determining specific actions to European institutions of governance may work very well. Thus, the Diné can search for their aspirations in the form of local leaders who govern based on concepts of traditional Diné leadership: the *Naat'áanii* (headmen).

5.2.2. Concept of Domestic *Naat'áanii*

A typical and well-reasoned response to research dealing with Indigenous peoples is its relevancy to the people the research purports to serve. Criticism of academic research that does not serve the Indigenous communities it studies was famously articulated by Vine Deloria (1988). This section is offered as an attempt to move away from pure theory and into the realm of policy application. What impact can traditional Diné governance have on contemporary Diné issues? That depends on how seriously policymakers take their relationship with the Four Sacred Elements.

There are many ways to provide evidence of legitimacy in governance institutions. The intent here is to directly point to the wants of the elders within the Navajo homeland, or *Diné Bikéyah*. For example, many Diné (though may be not a majority) are fearful of the drift away from traditional Diné governance in contemporary times. Some elders blame the shift away from traditional teachings for the development of the hanta virus in the early 1990s (Wilkins 2002a). In Western terms, returning to traditional Diné values is tantamount to ensuring governmental legitimacy because it makes contemporary Diné governance culturally relevant. Bringing contemporary governance in line with traditional teachings can be accomplished by using concept building, which can be modified to accommodate differing applications to obtain and maintain harmony within their respective environments. Maintaining focus on the Four Sacred Elements may mitigate claims that traditional teachings are not relevant to today's world: all humans require fire, water, air, and pollen.

Consider a three-level view of a domestic *Naat'áanii* (Figure 5.8). Based on the traditional concept of *Hózhǫ́ǫ́jí Naat'áanii*, a domestic *Naat'áanii* today would be a replica of the traditional *Naat'áanii*. All of the secondary-level conditions that make up a traditional *Naat'áanii* are present in the proposed contemporary domestic *Naat'áanii*. The only difference between a traditional *Naat'áanii* and today's domestic *Naat'áanii* would be the list of responsibilities that go along with being a contemporary domestic *Naat'áanii*.

There are also two asterisks next to two conditions: sacred needs (which could be based on the Four Sacred Elements) and day-to-day needs. These conditions *must* be addressed by the Diné constituency. They could opt to address these conditions themselves or possibly assign the decision-making responsibility to knowledge holders. Another angle on the open questions involves data indicators with question marks. Whether to depend on *Hastói* or *Hataałii* for *Naat'áanii* legitimacy is another serious question that only the people can answer. Finally, this area of research deserves much more attention in the future. The best advice that can be offered now is as follows: when the responsibilities point back to maintaining good relations with the Four Sacred Elements, this will indicate that Diné philosophical thought is once again a high priority.

A list of responsibilities must be articulated and added as a necessary condition to the concept of a contemporary domestic *Naat'áanii*. Alternatively, the list of responsibilities may be expressed under the standalone necessary condition entitled "Contribute to the Day-to-Day Needs of Diné Life and Culture." The main idea is to revive the specialization quality of traditional Diné governance by respecting the experience and knowledge of a *Naat'áanii* (Figure 3.2) or peace *Naat'áanii* (Figure 3.4). Specialists involved with the upkeep of contemporary Diné governance must be identified and placed in the position of domestic *Naat'áanii*. Their main goal would be to ensure that the internal matters of the Diné are handled appropriately and without caving in to special interests. Here is a potential list of responsibilities of a contemporary domestic *Naat'áanii*:

- Law enforcement
- Education
- Healthcare
- Housing
- Roadways
- Environmental preservation and maintenance
- Energy
- Fiscal budget

It is important to note that the contemporary domestic *Naat'áanii* would have direct ties to the community, and each category of responsibilities listed above would have a direct impact on the local populations. Thus, each community would have a direct link to its domestic *Naat'áanii*. Simultaneously, the domestic *Naat'áanii* would have a direct link to the national branches of Diné governance. Ideally, contemporary community issues would be brought to the domestic *Naat'áanii*.

5.2.3. Concept of International *Naat'áanii*

Focusing only on domestic issues within *Diné Bikéyah* would replicate mistakes made by past colonial-style governments. There also needs to be a focus on international issues. The international *Naat'áanii* is an entirely new concept in Diné contemporary governance. It would need serious revision from traditional concepts to have any impact on improving contemporary Diné governance. Perhaps a good starting point is Figure 5.8. The basic level of the domestic *Naat'áanii* can be changed to "international *Naat'áanii*." The daily needs can reflect the international needs of the people, and the sacred needs would need more serious discussion. In general, the main focus would involve ways of protecting Navajo Nation from external threats to proper relations with the Four Sacred Elements. Still, resolving or healing processes are also required to correct past imbalances. Future research can include developing the responsibilities needed to carry out the function of an international *Naat'áanii*. These responsibilities must be clearly articulated, with levels of generality consistent across responsibilities, and they must be clearly distinguished from the responsibilities of the domestic *Naat'áanii*.

The main objective in making the distinction between domestic and international *Naat'áanii* is to retain the tradition of appointing separate specialists for times of war and for times of peace. More specifically, both healing and protection processes will be key to governing in the future before ecological disaster places all inhabitants of the earth at the point of no return. An international *Naat'áanii* concept could promote the use of specialists with a vested interest in promoting the needs of Diné citizens at an international level. Namely, these *Naat'áanii* should probably focus on maintaining good relations with the Four Sacred Elements. Specifically, international *Naat'áanii* could be in the best position to maintain and expand Diné sovereignty. In many ways, ensuring proper relations with the Four Sacred Elements may be the most Diné-specific way of defining Diné sovereignty (1 N.N.C. §§ 201–206). Some possible responsibilities might include interacting with foreign entities such as the state of New Mexico, the state of Arizona, the state of Utah, and the U.S. government and establishing free-trade agreements with other countries in the Americas that are governed by Indigenous values. Nation-states such as Nunavut and Bolivia are potential trade partners, especially if their leaders are beholden to their Indigenous populations. Further research is necessary to discover what can be traded and how loyal the political leaders of these nations are to their Indigenous citizens. However domestic and international *Naat'áanii* are ultimately conceptualized, there must be a clear strategy to integrate the current Diné governance institutions and the two new institutions proposed here.

In the *Hajinéí* era, the *Naach'id* dealt with issues that affected a larger regional setting than an individual *Naat'áanii* could be expected to grapple with alone. Therefore, this mechanism for dealing with regional issues in pre-colonial actor interaction times can be revisited to deal with global issues today. This can be a starting point for establishing a potential international or domestic *Naach'id*. Many of the same issues addressed in Figure 5.8, including discussion about the role of respected elders, or *Hastóí*, as well as medicine people, or *Hataałii*, have yet to be comprehensively discussed in the twenty-first century. There would likely be a need to meet more often than was traditionally the case. Again, specific *Naat'áanii* associated with healing and protection would set agendas when they reviewed and advised the people about their nationwide relationship with the Four Sacred Elements.

Still, it is worth noting that a contemporary legislature currently exists and functions at the behest of what some might call the elite of Navajo Nation. With these caveats in mind, we can explore the interesting possibilities of a chapter house organizational structure.

The usurpation of local governing institutions by a national Diné level did more to represent the interests of the United States than it did to see that Diné citizens had their own interests met. Simply put, national Diné institutions seem to have little knowledge of or respect for a proper relationship with the Four Sacred Elements. The trend toward national consolidation was abruptly forced upon the Diné around the time that natural resources were recognized as profitably extractable by corporate interests. Consider how eleven international *Naat'áanii* from various regions and eleven domestic *Naat'áanii* from various regions could come together. The regions could be the five agencies in Diné Country, which could be broken down into local chapters. In the absence of in-depth site/location research, the following breakdown might be considered an example of a preliminary vertical integration strategy.

The five agencies could serve as intermediaries between local and national governance. If all five agencies split up the local chapters equally, then each agency's region could have twenty-two local chapters that represented various regions within the geographic area represented by the agency. Perhaps eleven local chapters could produce a domestic *Naat'áanii* and eleven chapters could produce an international *Naat'áanii*. Regional *Naat'áanii* could meet biannually, and in this way, they could bring local and regional concerns into a national meeting. One note of optimism is the way in which the chapters seem to nicely fit into a scheme of domestic and international *Naat'áanii*. Perhaps this breakdown is more than a mere mathematical coincidence.

There will be some readers who intuitively favor a Diné philosophical approach to governance reform. On the other hand, there will be some who will remain aligned with empiricism and will not be convinced—until there is observable evidence that will persuade them to consider another direction. Many scholars have debated whether Indigenous culture can survive in a contemporary world. Others have debated the relevance of Indigenous philosophy to contemporary times. This chapter has offered some evidence of the contemporary relevance of Diné philosophy. There has been little empirical evidence that links cultural mechanisms for survival with contemporary life in the aftermath of colonial activity. Chapter 6 will review how Diné philosophy can even exist today regardless of extreme duress.

CHAPTER 6

Dziłná'oodiłii (Doorway Mountain) and *Ch'óol'í'í* (Chimney Mountain)

Self-Generating Traditional Diné Institutions in the Face of Colonial Interaction

The doorway of the *hooghan* is the entry point for humans and the Four Sacred Elements. It faces east to greet the sunrise. People who are responsible by being cognizant of their relations with the Four Sacred Elements will understand that the early dawn brings the spark of ideas and knowledge. Knowledge, in its simplest form, means individuals will ask themselves if they are prepared for the day with enough firewood, water, and food. Monitoring air quality, on the other hand, is a matter for the chimney. Life is at the center of the *hooghan*, and the wood-burning stove in the *hooghan*'s center will breathe in life from the atmosphere surrounding Mother Earth and will exhale smoke into Father Sky. Songs and prayers can travel upward in the smoke as the living beings who occupy Mother Earth cooperate with one another in balance. Most imbalances will self-correct, requiring little, if any, human intervention. Within the *hooghan* is the heart of Diné philosophy, and its causal impacts on Mother Earth and Father Sky are observable. This chapter outlines these concrete observations. It may be the first time that "the sacred" in Diné philosophy has

Michael Lerma. 2014b. "Shocks to the Navajo (Diné) Political System: Resiliency of Traditional Diné institutions in the Face of Colonial Interaction (Contact to 1923)." *Indigenous Policy Journal* 25 (1): 1–20.

been tested using empirical data. If readers believe that Diné philosophy is sacred, this chapter demonstrates that Diné philosophy takes care of itself.

The institutional perspective describes characteristics of past and present Diné institutions. Diné institutions guide contemporary domestic and international interaction among Diné and non-Diné political actors. It was once the job of the *Naat'áanii* to look at domestic and international challenges to manage an appropriate relationship with the Four Sacred Elements. Examples of these challenges include corporate interests; local, county, and state interactions; federal interactions; and international interactions on Navajo Nation land. Thus, Diné institutions not only offer guidance but also prevent special interests from dominating the interaction process to varying degrees. Now that the *Naat'áanii* no longer have oversight over these challenges, special interests have successfully co-opted any contemporary interest in maintaining good relations with the Four Sacred Elements. This is not to say that Diné self-interest is nonexistent. Rather, at worst, institutions force actors to covertly cater to their self-interests; at best, they force actors to overtly and deliberately work hard to pursue the interests of Navajo Nation. (Readers should not assume that Navajo Nation possesses a singular interest, just as no one would legitimately assume this to be true of any other contemporary nation.) A Diné institution is any aspect of contemporary Diné governance that guides and constrains interactions between Diné actors and other Diné and non-Diné actors. It remains unclear today how contemporary Diné institutions address the Four Sacred Elements—if they do so at all. Thus, our attention should focus on the guidance/constraint mechanism (institutions) and events (as characterized by the culmination of interactions).

6.1. WHY INDIGENOUS INSTITUTIONS SURVIVE CATASTROPHIC EVENTS

Early American colonial history involved appropriation of Indigenous lands. "Cases and Materials on Federal Indian Law" references colonial events and outcomes (Getches, Wilkinson, and Williams 2005). Historians may be satisfied with an understanding of American domestic legal and public policy systems and their overt and covert attempts to subjugate Native nations (Getches, Wilkinson, and Williams 2005). However, normatively, the tools necessary for understanding and improving Indigenous governance must step away from the "official" policy of the colonizer. The "history" of Indian law and policy is not only a history: it is also a story of self-interested polities interacting with other actors and shaping Indigenous institutions to maximize the level of extraction of resources via exploitation. As Mahoney (2010) has pointed out, interaction is the key to colonial extraction via existing institutions and changing or destroying institutions that limit colonial extraction. Native nation rebuilding requires a similar approach to interaction. That Indigenous institutions have survived this long deserves some attention.

Native nations have been characterized as resilient because of their ability to withstand five hundred years of colonial activity. The concept of "Peoplehood" offers an explanation for this resiliency. It explains that four characteristics are needed to state definitively that a distinct people exists. These characteristics are place/territory, ceremonial cycle, language, and sacred history. No one aspect of Peoplehood is more important than another (Holm, Pearson, and Chavis 2003). When policy forms the basis for an attack (event) upon an Indigenous nation, that attack usually targets only some portions of the Peoplehood characteristics. These characteristics are generally the most visible aspects, such as the land and the ceremonies. Indigenous peoples may still be able to go into their homes and speak their language. They may also retell their sacred histories. Hence, the concept of Peoplehood theoretically explains why Indigenous cultures continue to exist today. Absent genocide, chances are that a people may be able to reflect on their own land and ceremonies if they continue to speak their language and take their sacred histories seriously. Peoplehood can explain how Diné institutions, including governance or leadership, survived colonial onslaughts.

The punctuated equilibrium model (PEM), as it has been applied to public policy research, explains how institutions are lost. Social science PEM applications include research on public policy formation and rivalries (Diehl and Goertz 2000). PEM can help us explore events (such as biological, public policy, or Indigenous institutional survival) most relevant to the current research.

PEM is characterized by two key framing mechanisms: "critical junctures" and "path dependency." Depicted in Figure 6.1, PEM assumes that a "shock" to the political system opens up an opportunity for several options to occur. The shock is more generally known as a critical juncture—a point in time in which several policy options become available in the aftermath of the political shock. Several paths can be chosen, but system investment in one path creates "sunk costs" or the allocation of resources into building an infrastructure in support of a single path. Hence, it becomes more difficult as time and resources are sunk into a single path to change to other paths. This phenomenon of path dependency explains why a system of governance can be unforgiving and inefficient or otherwise negative: there are too many invested powerful entities (individuals, corporations, and so forth) to allow a path to change (Collier and Collier 1991; Pierson 2004;

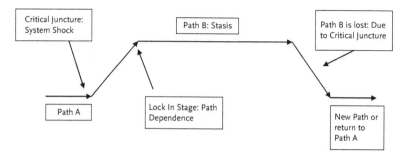

Figure 6.1: Diagram of PEM and Its Reliance on Critical Junctures and Path Dependancy

Mahoney 2003). Using PEM, it is now (hopefully) easier to explain the connection between the arrival of colonial actors and the emergence of contemporary Diné governance.

Contemporary Diné governance did not arrive by accident. Many would argue that it is the legacy of centuries of U.S. federal Indian policy (Getches, Wilkinson, and Williams 2005). From a Diné point of view, each U.S. policy era was specifically designed to further alienate the people from having a good and proper relationship with the Four Sacred Elements. Referring to Figure 6.1, it is now possible to consider Path A as a *Hajíneí*-era system of Diné governance (Deloria 2006; Holm, Pearson, and Chavis 2003). The critical juncture, or system shock, was, for example, a war, a treaty, or an act of removal. PEM offers a more systematic way of examining past and future critical junctures or windows of opportunity.

Studying past critical junctures may be promising when attempting to forecast future policy implementation strategies. For example, if policy language suggests that traditional Diné knowledge should guide future governance, the language must be deployed soon after a critical juncture occurs. In other words, a traditional knowledge path must be driven into the gap created by the political shock. Any path that is newly introduced must overcome its critics while producing quick gains early on. Second, the various alternative paths must be discredited to the point that people abandon them as quickly as possible. These two strategies would encourage more resource allocation toward traditional Diné governance. Perhaps pathways in the aftermath of a shock are more likely to be adopted if they prove to be easily adoptable by the public. Again, a focus on the Four Sacred Elements might meet this threshold. PEM explains why institutions (in general) survive and what it takes to dislodge institutional pathways. Peoplehood explains why some pathways go dormant only to potentially reemerge. Using the individual history of Diné governance events as a data set will further illuminate this theoretical framework.

6.2. TESTING DINÉ INSTITUTIONS

As stated earlier, Peoplehood explains why some Indigenous institutions survive, and PEM explains why some institutions (generally) do and do not survive. Together, they create a framework for reassessing the history of Diné governance. However, applying this framework requires some simplifying assumptions. First, traditional and contemporary Diné governance is expressed, at the very least, through institutions of governance. Second, interactions between the Diné and colonial actors are events. Third, some of those events are shocks to Diné institutions of governance. Finally, there are at least two outcomes to shocks: institutions survive (possibly modified) or institutions disappear. After testing the history of Diné governance with the Peoplehood and PEM framework, two aspects of Diné governance will become clearer:

1. Few Diné institutions were eliminated solely based on colonial activity.
2. Diné institutions that "appear" to have been eliminated may actually be suspended institutions. In other words, Diné institutions that seem to have disappeared may, in fact, remain dormant today because traditional Diné leaders decided to strategically obscure them.

The events, outcomes, and shock ratings are depicted in Table 6.1.

What is included and excluded from Table 6.1 remains debatable; not everyone will be satisfied with the current approach. Nonetheless, the period in which the greatest series of shocks to Diné institutions occurred was from the period of contact up until the formation of the Navajo Nation (Tribal) Council in 1923. Other shocks to the system certainly existed in the oral account era (Benally 2006), and shocks have taken place in the post-1922 era as well (Wilkins 2003). These other shocks are beyond the scope of this research and assuredly warrant future attention. The evidence does indicate that between 1583 and 1923 colonial attempts to destroy Diné institutions of governance largely failed.

Table 6.1 depicts events between the first non-Indigenous contact in 1583 and the formation of contemporary Navajo governance institutions in 1938. The list of events is more or less comprehensive. In other words, Table 6.1 lists events typically addressed by non-Navajo-oriented history texts. The list is supplemented with Diné accounts of their own history to elaborate on interactions with colonial actors. The outcome column depicts a brief interpretation of the event—strictly framed as Diné interpretation and impact experience. The outcome can be considered subjective because the following events are necessarily derivative of such interpretation.

Table 6.1. LIST OF EVENTS, OUTCOMES, AND RELATIVE SHOCK
SCALE RATINGS

	Event	Outcome	Shock Rating
1	Contact of 1583	None	.01
2	Treaty of 1706	Diné (and other tribes) work to drive out Spain.	.17
3	Treaty of 1786	Diné allow Spain to occupy New Mexico area.	.36
4	Treaty of 1805	Ceasefire due to 100 Diné killed in fighting	.23
5	Treaty of 1819	Ceasefire due to losses (Spanish and Diné)	.09
6	Mexico Declares Independence, 1821	None	.01
7	Treaty of 1822	Encourages European warfare	.05
8	Treaty of 1823	Encourages slave trade, political and economic interaction	.08
9	Treaty of 1824	Not known (lost to time)	.01
10	Treaty of 1835	Not known (lost to time)	.01
11	Treaty of 1839	Offsets the kidnapping of Diné women for a time	.12
12	Treaty of 1841	Ceasefire to recover from war, slave raids, etc.	.07
13	Treaty of 1841 II	Not known (lost to time)	.01
14	Treaty of 1841 III	Not known (lost to time)	.01
15	Treaty of 1844	Ends war, encourages free trade	.05
16	United States Takes Southwest	None	.01
17	Treaty of 1846	None	.01
18	Treaty of 1848	None	.01
19	Treaty of 1849	Aims to end war, slave raids, killing of *Naat'áanii*, and resentment	.14
20	Treaty of 1851	Redundant, 1849 treaty replayed with other Diné	.1
21	Treaty of 1855	Split approach (peace *Naat'áanii* sign the treaty; war *Naat'áanii* do not sign the treaty)	.32
22	Armistice of 1858	Ceasefire to prepare for peace negotiations, animals killed	.4
23	Treaty of 1858	Eastern boundary set; legal authority of the United States imposed east of the boundary.	.24
24	Treaty of 1861	War continues.	.65
25	*Hwéldi* 1864	Walk to Bosque Redondo	.77
26	1864–1868	Carson extermination at Canyon de Chelly: some Diné walk away from Bosque Redondo; others stay and starve. United States gives up on Bosque Redondo experiment and allows remaining Diné to walk home.	.74

Table 6.1. CONTINUED

	Event	Outcome	Shock Rating
27	Treaty of 1868	Diné homeland returned to Diné. Remaining people return home. *Naach'id* suspended indefinitely.	.61
28	Fall 1868	Blessing Way held at Window Rock. Domestic governance resumed and groups go in four directions—basis for contemporary agency system. Note lack of "protection-way" ceremony.	.3
29	Congressional Act of 1869	Treaty of 1868 generally acknowledged; assimilation period begins.	.28
30	1878–1884	Reservation expanded outside U.S. reservation boundaries listed in 1868 treaty.	.13
31	1878–1910 Indian Agent Appointments	"Traditional" leaders (*Naat'áanii*) age and are replaced by new leaders chosen by Bureau of Indian Affairs agents. New leaders chosen as outlined by U.S. federal Indian policy of assimilation.	.42
32	1884 Police Chief Appointment	Chee Dodge replaces Manuelito: bilingual mixed blood replaces legendary war leader.	.19
33	1901–1911 Agencies Formally Established	Four directions formally acknowledged and a fifth central agency set up.	.11
34	1921 Oil Discovered	Corporations take notice of Shiprock Agency when oil is discovered. They lease land on Navajo Nation, allowing for more corporate interaction with less oversight by the Navajos.	.32
35	1922 Business Council Formed	Distribution of revenue simplified so that fewer Navajos are needed to agree to leases on Navajo Nation land for the purpose of extracting oil. Corporations allowed easier access to oil deposits for less than fair market value.	.41
36	1/3/1923 Business Council Modifications	Navajos take more control over land leases for purposes of oil extraction. U.S. government approval forced into the model.	.3
37	1/24/1923 Business Council Modifications	Business Council expands scope of operation and becomes the Navajo Tribal Council—an overarching federal system of governance encompassing all five agencies.	.27
38	1933	Tribal Council revokes direct U.S. impact on its policy decisions (covert influence remains).	.23

(*continued*)

Table 6.1. CONTINUED

Event	Outcome	Shock Rating
39	1934 Indian Reorganization Act	Ends allotment and encourages the Navajo tribe to write a constitution similar to the U.S. model—Navajos resist	.15
40	1938 Tribal Constitutional Assembly	Members of Tribal Council create an assembly to write a constitution. They fail to write a constitution and instead vote themselves into power, becoming the Tribal Council. Provisions about approval from the U.S. Secretary of the Interior and other overt attempts by the United States to exert power over the Navajo tribe are rejected. Covert influence remains at work.	.24

So what is the impact of events on Diné institutions? Table 6.1 shows a relative shock rating experienced by the Diné after an event occurred. A rating of 0 indicates that there was no impact, but it does establish the boundary for impact. On the opposite extreme, a shock rating of 1 denotes the greatest possible shock and impact surrounding an event. Such an event may be so impactful that it eliminates the group. Alternatively, a shock rating of 1 may indicate a transformation to such a degree that the group no longer can be considered the same group it was before the event. (An example might be a tribe forced to seek refuge with another tribe and be adopted as a separate clan). Including an event that ranks as a 1 should be considered a red flag that indicates there is more to the story. Rankings of 1 may also indicate that all of the other events along the continuum need calibration. Events that are ranked at the extremes are considered "ideal types" (Collier and Collier 1991; Goertz 2006; Ragin 2008; Sartori 1970). See Figure 6.2 for a visual depiction of the shock continuum.[1]

Figure 6.2 shows a spectrum of events that have impacted Diné institutions. The poles have been established by reordering the events in Table 6.1 along a continuum. Any event ranked 0 is not relevant to Diné institutions. Any event ranked 1 is so fantastic that it is improbable—if not impossible—that it ever occurred (since Diné institutions survive). The scale of shock is subjective in that the shock is based on Diné perception of the event. Each event is assigned a number in the order of time in which the event occurred. In this way, all of the events can be placed on the continuum.

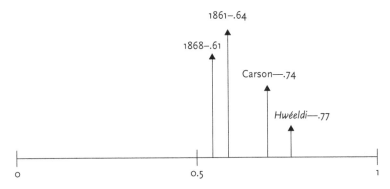

Figure 6.2: Visual Depiction of Shock Spectrum of Events/Severity of Shock

The most outstanding events have had the most impact and warrant a starting point. The most impactful event from Figure 6.2 is the Long Walk, or *Hwéldi*. Yet even this event is not a 1 on the scale of impact.[2] Presuming the Long Walk was the most shocking event in the history of Diné institutions, the event may rank .77. On the other end of the spectrum are events with minimal impact. Some events are simply not well understood. Missing information is treated as having little or no impact. These events have been assigned a rating of .01. The history of such occurrences seems to manifest little, if any, coercive impact on the Diné. Low-ranking events may be worth reconsideration to see how relevant they really are to the Diné. In other words, these events probably mattered much more to colonial actors than they did to anyone else.[3]

Figure 6.3 is a collection of descriptive statistics based on Diné historical events. There are a number of events recorded by non-Navajo historians that had little to no impact on Diné institutions. It is worth noting that only two events get a ranking above .6, and only four events go beyond .5. The majority of the events are in the left or low-impact end of Figure 6.3.

The bar on the far left represents ten events that had very little impact on the Diné. The bar second to the left represents the treaty of 1822 and the treaty of 1844. The next bar represents the treaty of 1841. Next is the treaty of 1823, the treaty of 1819, the treaty of 1841, the emergence of the agency system, the treaty of 1839, the collective expansion of the reservation via executive orders, and the treaty of 1849.

Continuing with the single events, and about one-third of the way between least impactful and mid-impactful events, is the passage of the Indian Reorganization Act of 1934. Next is the appointment of Chee Dodge, the treaty of 1805, and the The January 3, 1923, Business Council modifications rank next. Two events, the treaty of 1855 and the oil discovery of 1921, follow. The treaty of 1786 comes next. Slightly more shocking is the

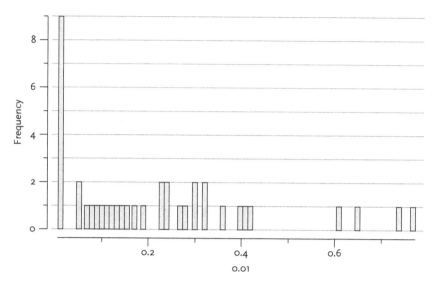

Figure 6.3: Descriptive Statistics: Impact of Key Events in Diné History

armistice of 1858. These events are followed by the formation of the 1922 Business Council and the replacement of the pre-1868 leaders. Note the gap in the graph here, which possibly indicates a shock-level tipping point. The four most shocking events are the treaty of 1868, the treaty of 1861, the Carson campaign, and the Long Walk. The data warrant further contemplation of the four most shocking events.

Table 6.2 shows the distribution of event frequency and the relative shock value of the individual events. There are a total of forty events. The

Table 6.2. DISTRIBUTION OF EVENT FREQUENCY AND RELATIVE SHOCK VALUE (WHERE 0 REPRESENTS VIRTUALLY NO IMPACT AND 1 REPRESENTS EXTREME IMPACT TO THE POINT OF DORMANCY OR ANNIHILATION)

Event Frequency	Lower Shock Range	Upper Shock Range
15	.0	.09
8	.1	.19
6	.2	.29
4	.3	.39
3	.4	.49
0	.5	.59
2	.6	.69
2	.7	.79
0	.8	1.0

Table 6.3. TWO-BY-TWO TABLE OF INSTITUTIONAL
IMPACT OF EVENTS ON DINÉ GOVERNANCE

Shock Level	Institutions Survive	Institutions Go Dormant/Cease
Shock less than .59	37	0
Shock more than .6	4	1

distribution of events based on relative shock to Diné institutions is in line with what the concept of Peoplehood forecasts. The majority of events, although qualitatively horrific, had little impact on the viability of Diné institutions in general.

Table 6.3 depicts how events impacted Diné institutions. The first column (far left) indicates the relative levels of shock to Diné institutions of governance. The second column represents the survival of institutions. The third column represents Diné institutions that stopped operating. Based on the historical record, there is only one instance of a Diné institution halting. According to most accounts, the *Naach'id* was last held prior to the Long Walk (Austin 2007; Wilkins 1987). There are no other events that indicate a Diné institution ceased to operate. This is the first hard evidence that colonial attacks on Diné culture have failed. But this is not to say that Diné institutions have not been modified. This preliminary conclusion can be pursued further with even more interesting interpretations.

That only one event in Diné history produced the outcome of an institution ceasing to operate is a clue that there are certain conditions that result in such outcomes. The conditions that lead to the loss of Diné institutions follow:

A. Forced removal
B. Active warfare
C. Impact on a nation's political economy
D. Ineffective treaty/reservation confinement (commitment problems)

Explicit definitions help to explain these four conditions. *Forced removal* (A) is defined as overt attempts by a colonial actor to remove an Indigenous people from their traditional homelands. An example of forced removal involves the colonial actor designating a relocation area and forcing Indigenous peoples to march to the relocation area. *Hwéldi* is the forced-removal event for the Diné.

Active warfare (B) is defined as an overt military campaign by a colonial actor against an Indigenous nation. An example of active warfare involves the occupation of land belonging to, or adjacent to, Indigenous peoples' homelands for the purpose of extinguishing aboriginal title (Getches, Wilkinson, and Williams 2005, 69). The Kit Carson campaign against the Diné is one example of an active war event.

Impact on a nation's political economy (C) is defined as overt maneuvers by a colonial actor to cut off Indigenous peoples' access to food and products. Contemporary scholars might call such activity an embargo. Carson's campaign into *Tsé yí*, or Canyon de Chelly, involved a "scorched earth" policy of burning cornfields and *hooghans* to impact (destroy) the Diné political economy.

Commitment problems (D) are defined as the inability or unwillingness of colonial actors to honor treaty obligations. An example of commitment problems involves the inability of the United States to prevent settler encroachments on Indian lands. Another example involves the maldistribution of rations to families most friendly to colonial actor interests. The United States constantly instigated conflict with the Diné or, alternatively, was not capable of preventing conflicts of a personal nature from spilling over into warfare. The United States also was not capable of committing to various treaties signed with the Diné, as is evidenced by the failure of the U.S. Congress to ratify seven of nine international treaties with the Diné.

These are the four factors that led to *Naach'id* loss. The outcome, ceased institutional operation, may be represented by X. Hence, the following equation:

$$A + B + C + D = X$$

By negating even one of the conditions from A through D, Diné institutional resilience is more likely—in other words, the action will not stop a Diné institution from operating. For example, consider the events that rank at .6 or higher on the scale of shock. These four events are the treaty of 1861, the Long Walk, the 1864–1868 Carson expedition in *Tsé yí*, and the treaty of 1868. The events share some of the conditions that culminate in the stoppage of a Diné institution. No other events exhibit conditions A through D. Forty events are depicted in Table 6.4, a truth table of all historically recorded Diné events from initial non-Indigenous contact to 1923. Each event is analyzed for the presence or absence of the four conditions listed above.

Table 6.4. TRUTH TABLE OF EVENTS AND CONDITIONS

Event	Condition A Removal	Condition B War	Condition C Economy	Condition D No Commitment	Outcome X Dormancy
1	No	No	No	No	No
2	No	Yes	No	Yes	No
3	No	No	Yes	Yes	No
4	No	Yes	No	Yes	No
5	No	Yes	Yes	Yes	No
6	No	Yes	Yes	No	No
7	No	Yes	No	Yes	No
8	No	Yes	Yes	Yes	No
9	No Data	Lost			
10	No Data	Lost			
11	No	Yes	Yes	Yes	No
12	No	Yes	Yes	Yes	No
13	No Data	Lost			
14	No Data	Lost			
15	No	Yes	Yes	Yes	No
16	No	No	No	No	No
17	No	No	No	No	No
18	No	No	No	No	No
19	No	Yes	Yes	Yes	No
20	No	Yes	Yes	Yes	No
21	No	Yes	Yes	Yes	No
22	No	Yes	Yes	Yes	No
23	Yes	Yes	Yes	No	No
24	**No**	**Yes**	**Yes**	**Yes**	**No**
25	**Yes**	**Yes**	**Yes**	**Yes**	**Yes**
26	**Yes**	**Yes**	**Yes**	**No**	**No**
27	**No**	**No**	**No**	**No**	**No**
28	No	No	No	No	No
29	No	No	No	No	No
30	No	No	Yes	No	No
31	No	No	Yes	No	No
32	No	No	No	No	No
33	No	No	No	No	No
34	No	No	Yes	No	No
35	No	No	No	No	No
36	No	No	Yes	No	No
37	No	No	Yes	No	No
38	No	No	No	No	No
39	No	No	No	No	No
40	No	No	Yes	No	No

Table 6.5. TRUTH TABLE WITH EVENT SHOCK OF .6 OR HIGHER

Event	Condition A Removal	Condition B War	Condition C Economy	Condition D No Commitment	Outcome X Dormancy
24	No	Yes	Yes	Yes	No
25	Yes	Yes	Yes	Yes	Yes
26	Yes	Yes	Yes	No	No
27	No	No	No	No	No

The most impactful events are highlighted in Table 6.4. Removing less relevant events yields a more manageable view. A logical limiter involves focus on events with a .6 level of shock or higher. Table 6.5 represents events with .6 shock levels and higher. For both Tables 6.4 and 6.5, the first column represents the events (for Table 6.5, only events with shock values of more than .6). The subsequent columns from left to right are conditions present in the given events. By negating one of the conditions, the resultant loss of an institution is prevented. Examination of the four events in question, in order of chronology, is warranted. The 1861 treaty lacked the forced removal condition (A). When the Diné were within their Sacred Mountain boundaries, they had no reason to give up the *Naach'id*. The Long Walk event did contain all four conditions, leading to the suspension of the *Naach'id*. The Carson campaign lacked the necessary enforcement of prior treaty guidelines (D). And the treaty of 1868 event lacked three conditions: forced removal (A), active warfare (B), and destruction of political economy (C). However, the treaty of 1868 was signed after the last known *Naach'id* took place in 1859 (Austin 2009).

Table 6.6 is a two-by-two table of causal conditions and outcomes. The conditions are based on a threshold rating of event shocks equal to .6 or higher. An event rating greater than .6 is a necessary condition for

Table 6.6. TWO-BY-TWO TABLE OF CONDITIONS AND OUTCOMES FOR EVENTS WITH A SHOCK RATING OF .6 OR HIGHER

Type of Outcome	Number of Conditions Absent (No Shock)	Number of Conditions Present (Shock)
Outcome Present	3	1
Outcome Absent	0	0

stopping a Diné institution. There are no losses of institutions below a rating of .6. Yet even if the rating level is sufficiently high, it is not enough to prevent an institution from operating. All four causal conditions must be present. What this table suggests is that events must be sufficiently shocking to the cultural system before the conditions necessary to eliminate an institution come into play. Even when the shock value is high enough, all four conditions must be met or the institution will continue.

6.3. CONSEQUENCES OF SURVIVING COLONIALISM

Several causal mechanisms are at work in Diné governance history. Taking into account five hundred years of colonial activity, there is a recipe that leads to Diné institutional dormancy. The relationship between events and impacts on institutions is quite drastic and clear. Figure 6.4 depicts a reexpression of the causal relationship using set theory.

Set theory is a method used to better understand the relationship between outcomes and causal conditions. These connections may remain

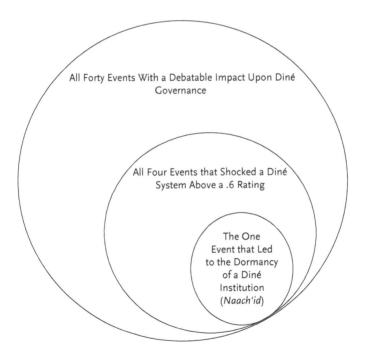

All Forty Events With a Debatable Impact Upon Diné Governance

All Four Events that Shocked a Diné System Above a .6 Rating

The One Event that Led to the Dormancy of a Diné Institution (*Naach'id*)

Figure 6.4: Causal Mechanism Leading to Dormancy in Diné Institutions of Governance

obscured by allowing our histories or our other linguistic efforts to take charge of understanding the relationships. Of the forty events mentioned by mainstream Diné history, only four can be logically traced to a threat to Diné institutions of governance. Of the four events, only one event can be traced to the dormancy of a Diné institution of governance, the *Naach'id*.

The most interesting result of the analysis thus far is the rarity of events that resulted in the dormancy of a Diné institution of governance between the time of first contact with non-Indigenous peoples and 1923. But the research can be taken even further. A part of the family of methodological approaches mentioned earlier includes fuzzy set analysis (Ragin 2008). The rare characteristics of the events and outcomes can be calculated to provide evidence that the events are in fact rare, thus demonstrating that colonial activity is futile when it comes to destroying institutions of Diné governance. Fuzzy set methodology holds that a "recipe" can be illuminated further. Hence, the previously identified four conditions must all be present for an institution of Diné governance to go dormant. These conditions (removal, war, economic impact, and commitment problems) were only present one time in the known history of colonial interaction with the Diné.

Looking at the percentage of all the events in which all four conditions existed proves the rarity of Diné institutional dormancy. By taking the truth table (Table 6.4) and converting the "yes" answers into 1 and the "no" answers into 0, consistency and coverage of the four conditions and their relationship to the outcome of institutional dormancy can be tested. The level of coverage is only .04, or 4 percent. Hence, 96 percent of the time there was no outcome that indicated that an institution had been forced into dormancy. Dormancy is the most extreme outcome that can be measured.

6.4. SURVIVING AND HIDING IN PLAIN SIGHT

The evidence here incontrovertibly demonstrates that the relationship between colonial activity up to and including acts of genocide has failed to eliminate the majority of *Hajinéí*-era Diné institutions of governance between first non-Indigenous contact and 1923. Traditional Diné institutions of governance still exist today even if they are in a dormant state. The role of the Four Sacred Elements in contemporary Diné governance, then, is largely unaddressed. Yet hope exists that even in the face of all documented colonial activity, there may be contemporary interest in fire, clean water, clean air, and pollen. Even though one Diné institution seems to remain in dormancy, the necessary conditions for creating more dormancy have not been exercised since 1864. The theoretical explanation for dormancy and the potential for revival are complex and dynamic, yet they hold up. These explanations may be expanded to address other histories of colonial impact on Native nation interaction-era institutions of governance and leadership.

The test of institutions is designed to demonstrate how past historical research has merely retold the official story from the perspective of several colonial actors, including the U.S. government. While this fact is neither new nor groundbreaking, what is unique is that the research has not been "reinterpreted," nor has new archival research come to light that impacts the entire picture. Rather, the mainstream evidence, supplemented by oral accounts, forces researchers to reexamine the "main events" that have been handed down by past historians. Citizens of Navajo Nation need to understand how powerful and resilient their traditional institutions of governance were and are. They may need reminding that, once upon a time, their priorities were quite salient so long as they were addressed in terms of maintaining a good and proper relationship with the Four Sacred Elements. Such powerful evidence supporting the strength and resiliency of traditional institutions of Diné governance should remove doubts about the ability of those same institutions to serve the citizens of Navajo Nation today.

CHAPTER 7

Atsa (Eagle) and *Ma'ii Tso* (Wolf)

Search from Above, Search from the Earth

There are some additional issues and considerations that the Diné leadership may encounter domestically, within Diné Country, and internationally, outside the borders of Diné Country. For example, there is the issue of change. Many people consider change a scary proposition. When change does visit a people, they usually fear that the changes may create consequences far more troubling than the conditions that came before or the problems they were meant to solve. It is understandable that change is feared by the Diné, given their recent history. Changes in the last five hundred years have resulted in many tragedies for the Diné, including acts of genocide and ethnic cleansing. However, the joke is on the colonizers, because the Diné continue to exist. Yet this may not be true in the near future unless there are overt efforts to refocus on the Four Sacred Elements.

Ultimately, a decision must be made regarding the future of Diné Country. Are Diné citizens willing to change their governance structures toward the direction of Diné philosophy? For example, how much do they value their relationship with the Four Sacred Elements? The Diné are in the best position to evaluate proposals for reform based on traditional Diné governance. Such reforms may not be so much a change as a return to traditional Diné values. That being said, one must also consider the reaction to change in Diné governance structures by those outside Diné Country. Many actors interact with Diné Country, which is surrounded by the United States. Diné Country surrounds Hopi Country, and it interacts with various colonial actors and multinational corporations. While some of these relationships started out as acts of aggression and war, they have evolved over time to a point of veiled aggression at their worst and interdependence at their best. In a globalizing world, it is necessary to consider how domestic Diné governance changes will affect the relationships Diné Country has made with foreign entities. Specifically, should the Diné begin to reassert their interests toward the Four Sacred Elements, this might be perceived as a threat to the dominant society and other entities, such as states, international organizations, multinational corporations, and other Native nations. The idea that Diné Country is reverting back to its traditional governance roots might not sit well with those unfamiliar with Diné cultural norms. Such issues of unfamiliarity are resolvable by using the concept-building method.

Concept building is a method of organizing information to avoid vagueness. Vague language can be used to justify actions not originally intended. Concept-building methods can be used to lock Diné cultural values into whatever type of governance Diné citizens choose to utilize. Concept building can also be used to lock in the salience of the Four Sacred Elements if people are inclined to do so. The beauty of Diné governance structures, based on concept-building methods, is that concepts can be rearticulated in plain, adjective-rich English. Perhaps this is the next step after concepts have been fine-tuned. Concept-building methods are new to academia, and as such, they are not well known outside academic circles. In fact, very little has been published on the subject (Goertz 2006; Goertz and Mazur 2008). It is possible to use the concept-building method to supplement any syntax-style language. So long as English syntax refers to concepts by their basic-level names, it should be possible to lock in all of the underlying concept's secondary and data-indicator-level traits so that future Diné citizens can derive benefits for their children and grandchildren. For example, an international *Naat'áanii* need not be called by that name. By replacing the basic-level name holder with a more easily understood term (such as legislator), the outside world is less likely to uncover the reassertion of sovereignty within Diné Country.

Consider that most international actors who adhere to the international relations theory of realism might be concerned that Diné Country governance structures are reasserting international sovereignty. Meanwhile, international actors who consider themselves liberal or socially progressive are more likely to support Diné Country's reassertion of international sovereignty (Hopf 1998, 2002; Morgenthau 1948; Waltz 1979). Here is a key place to look for and take advantage of opportunities to create new international norms. New norms will be supported by liberal nations, and "functional creep" will allow a return to traditional concepts and behavior on the part of Navajo Nation. The real key is to keep the secondary and data-indicator-level traits intact. I believe that those concerned with returning Diné Country to traditionally inspired Diné governance principles have good reasons to be optimistic so long as the data point to the Four Sacred Elements.

7.1. WHY TRADITIONAL DINÉ INSTITUTIONS ARE NOT GOING AWAY

I trust that I have incontrovertibly demonstrated in Chapter 6 that the relationship between colonial activity up to and including acts of geno-cide has failed to eliminate the majority of *Hajínéí*-era Diné institutions of governance. The topic of Diné philosophy as a foundation for governance would not be possible if that philosophy was eliminated or lost. Remnants of the philosophy remain as an institutional reference and in terms of the Four Sacred Elements. It is also possible to conclude, albeit cautiously, that those philosophical traits that appear "lost" may in fact remain embedded within the Sacred Mountains and within the *hooghans* of individuals who remain silent today. Evidence for the way in which such philosophy may still exist has been tied to Peoplehood, and it gives me hope that there will be a time when a traditionally inspired approach to contemporary Diné governance can reemerge.

At least one obstacle remains: the fact that history books assert assumptions that are not questioned openly. I hope the research here assists with this barrier of "history." Further research on the history of Diné interaction is certainly warranted, and Navajo Nation archives can be consulted.

7.2. *DZIŁNÁ'OODIŁII* AND *CH'ÓOL'Í'Í*—DOORWAY AND CHIMNEY

The Peoplehood model expresses what I have interpreted as a set of four necessary conditions for a people to exist. Sacred history, ceremonial cycle, place/territory, and specific language are embedded in all people (Holm, Pearson, and Chavis 2003). I have deduced that if these necessary condi-tions are the key to sustaining a people, then it makes sense that colonial activity cannot thoroughly destroy all of these aspects unless there is an act of systematic extermination.

We understand now that the Diné were given many attributes by the *Diyin Dine'é* to sustain themselves. These attributes thrive in the form of land, ceremony, history, and language. We understand that the Diné have been attacked by many colonial actors through war, forced removal, and economic destruction. These encounters have put the maintenance of the proper distance and nearness to the Four Sacred Elements at risk. The Diné had no choice but to return to their *'Iiná hooghan* as they were instructed by the *Diyin Dine'é*. They went into their homes via *Dził̃ná'oodiłii*, or the entryway. There, the philosophy and *Dził̃ Łeezh* bundles remained dormant as chaos dominated outside their *hooghan*. Relations with the Four Sacred Elements were maintained as best they could be, given the severe limitations imposed by colonial actors. Many Diné lost their lives waiting for a time to emerge from their *'Iiná hooghan*. Much of the traditional Diné philosophy was lost to age, boarding schools, Christianization, and U.S. wars of colonization. Only now are some Diné leaders emerging via *Dził̃ná'oodiłii*, with *Dził̃ Łeezh* bundles to support them. They have priorities based on maintaining a good and proper Diné relationship with the Four Sacred Elements. *'Iiná hooghan* can sustain life, philosophy, and future generations if Diné leaders are capable of entering and exiting at the correct times. Future leaders must relearn how to gauge the needs of the people and their distance from, and nearness to, the Four Sacred Elements.

Before remaining within *'Iiná hooghan* became required, the basis for sustaining life was given to the Diné via *Ch'óol'í'í*, or the chimney. Specific language in the form of songs and prayers (*Nahagha*) was preserved by those capable of passing them on to their children during the dormancy stage of Diné history. *Diyin Dine'é* listened as the songs and prayers resonated within the bounds of the Sacred Mountains and out through the chimney. Discussions of managing good relations with the Four Sacred Elements by using healing and protection processes carried the people into the now. Perhaps questions were asked by the five-fingered earth-surface people as they stayed within their *'Iiná hooghans*. Perhaps the answers to their questions could only be transmitted through the chimney.

Dził̃ Łeezh bundles needed sustenance within *'Iiná hooghan* via the chimney. This meant that, in practical terms, food was prepared for the holders of bundles in the *'Iiná hooghan*, and exhaust smoke escaped via the chimney. Heat was provided by the forest during the cold winter months, and exhaust escaped via the chimney. The Four Sacred Elements (*K'ó, Tó, Niłchí, Tadidiin,* and *Nahaadzaan*) needed a way into *'Iiná hooghan* during times of siege. It can be deduced that these elements gained entry and exit via the doorway and chimney. When it was time to emerge after centuries of onslaught, many were no longer on the earth. However, all was and is not lost.

7.3. *ATSA*—LOOK FROM ABOVE

Stories of animal leaders elaborated upon their attempts to lead and their failures to properly govern. Perhaps these animals failed because they could not understand how to keep their proper distance and nearness toward the Four Sacred Elements. Perhaps these stories mean that leaders need animal traits from time to time. Maybe the failure of animals to properly lead means that no one animal trait on its own can be used to sustain Diné life. However, the traits of animals do come in handy during certain times. With this in mind, I asked Denny (2010) if there are certain animals that can assist the contemporary Diné to lead their nation. He answered that two animals may be able to help: the eagle, or *Atsa*, and the wolf, or *Ma'ii Tso*.

Atsa has a unique point of view that is unlike a human's vision. *Atsa* can remain in the air and closer to Father Sky. Perhaps *Atsa* can explain how to learn from Father Sky. *Atsa* may provide a proper vision of the Sacred Mountains, the forces outside the Sacred Mountains, and the internal struggles individuals face—a different vantage point from which to gauge human distance and nearness toward the Four Sacred Elements. *Atsa* can see that war harmed the Diné. *Atsa* could see the Long Walk, the campaign in Canyon de Chelly, and the return of some Diné from Bosque Redondo. *Atsa* could see when it was safe for the Diné who did not walk to Bosque Redondo to emerge from their *'Iiná hooghan*. *Atsa* could and does see those people and traits that are "lost" today within and beyond the Sacred Mountains. *Atsa* can see a clear path toward healing and protection as well as toward maintaining a proper relationship with the Four Sacred Elements.

7.4. *MA'II TSO*—LOOK FROM THE EARTH

Denny (2010) also explained that the traits of the wolf, or *Ma'ii Tso*, may be key to discovering a future path for Navajo Nation. According to Denny, the wolf has attributes that make it ideal for locating the lost. Perhaps there are forgotten paths to maintain good relations with the Four Sacred Elements. I assumed Denny not only meant lost people but also lost abilities that probably still remain hidden within the bounds of the Sacred Mountains. These abilities will again involve healing and protection pathways. He probably also meant that individuals who can assist beyond the bounds of the Sacred Mountains can also be located. He explained the process in terms of wolves being able to find humans. Denny said a human could be lost someplace in the vast land that is Navajo Nation. A wolf can howl to communicate the need to search for the lost person. Other wolves will hear the call and begin the search. The various wolves can collaborate in a number of ways. They will each search their domains for the missing person. As each wolf searches, each can announce the results of its search with howls that other wolves will hear.

Denny explained that, in this way, regions can be ruled out as possible places for locating the missing individual so that other areas can be searched. The search becomes more and more focused as this process continues. Eventually, a wolf will discover the missing person. Once discovered, the wolf will then announce the discovery to other wolves so that all will know the location of the missing person. Thus, all of the missing people, or philosophies, can be located with assistance from the wolf. Perhaps this method can be used to discover new (old) ways of maintaining good relations with the Four Sacred Elements. I took this story to mean that persons can also represent attributes that can lead to good policy. Problems can seem vast and perhaps insurmountable. Yet using the philosophy of the wolf or using what I have interpreted to be a ground-view orientation, we should be able to find many facets of Diné governance. In other words, all the answers are contained within the boundaries set forth by the Sacred Mountains. Thus, locating exactly what is needed can be accomplished. Answers may not be located easily or quickly. A slow and tedious result may only mean that a given set of individuals may not be capable of carrying such knowledge. Recall Justice Raymond Austin's statement: "If you were not meant to carry sacred knowledge, it will avoid you" (2009, 56). Perhaps Austin's wisdom is applicable to the lesson from the wolf.

We five-fingered earth-surface people have openings that we can use to interpret our environments. We can detect the information first within our homes. As adults, if we can sustain a home, children, and a spouse, we can possibly contribute beyond our homes to our communities. It is not a choice to contribute. It is an obligation to contribute if we are endowed with such abilities. This is why if an individual is not meant to carry an obligation, that person will not be able to hold certain knowledge. Long ago, all individuals seemed to understand this fact. People got up in the morning to plant and harvest because they understood they needed to provide for their families. The Four Sacred Elements provided all the tools to sustain life. When outside forces came within the Sacred Mountains, many people, songs, prayers, bundles, and perspectives were lost.

Today is the best time to look for the lost. *Atsa* can tell us what is coming around the corner, and we can take that hint into *Dibé Nitsaa* or *Sih Hasin hooghan* and reflect on our life today. Here we can utilize pollen for regeneration. We can then discover what is missing within *Sisnajiiní* or *Sodizin*

Hooghan. We can discover the spark needed to find what was lost. *Ma'ii Tso* can locate what we discover (rediscover) is lost during our time within *Sodizin Hooghan.* When we find what we have lost, we can begin to plan for today and tomorrow via *Naha'tá hooghan.* We can begin to implement our long-lost abilities. Our moisture may give sustenance to a long-dormant pollen particle. Then we can return home to *'Iiná hooghan* to ensure that we sustain ourselves and our families. Within *'Iiná hooghan* we can deal with negating the seven monsters the Hero Twins allowed to live. We can maintain our cleanliness, our appetites by eating and drinking, our subsistence via enough wealth, and our maturity. We can give breath to all that has been misplaced or forgotten. Through research we can reclaim what is dormant—our way of life.

Ni 'Iiná. T'áá ákódí.

AFTERWORD

Principles of Diné Leadership

ROBERT YAZZIE, CHIEF JUSTICE EMERITUS

When I first came to know Mike, it was not clear to me if he would be back to the reservation or if it would be just a summer job. In the end, I had to take his interest seriously because he kept asking questions about Navajo leadership. I think he learned a great deal listening in at the advisory circles and listening to me talk with others about Navajo leadership qualities. Ultimately, every chapter in this book is about Navajo leadership, past, present, and future. Some of the chapters are about how leaders should behave. Some of the chapters are about how leaders did behave. And some of the chapters are about how leaders misbehaved. No one is perfect, but having a good heart and a good mind will lead to good things. Those who wish to be leaders need to know a thing or two, on a personal level, in order to be good leaders. It is certainly important to pay attention to the institutions of leadership. However, one must not forget about the individual ethics of a good Navajo leader.

Some of my Navajo relatives understand Diné leadership in terms of the definition, qualities, challenges, and experiences of leadership of yesterday and today. For purposes of achieving a better government, I truly believe that our modern-day Diné leadership has all the capabilities to reestablish and incorporate the traditional principles of Navajo good governance from the past. I agree with Navajo knowledge holders that if we do not do this, we will suffer the consequences.

What is leadership? From our studies of and education about political systems, we know that there is a scale of differing patterns from absolute, authoritarian leadership to leadership that is only persuasive. Some leaders around the world exercise command with force, and others only persuade. I have come to realize that most forms of Western leadership are based on the notion of power to back up a command. Leadership in that respect usually means power, control, authority, or coercion. Traditional Diné leadership is not about power, control, or coercion but a recognition that "words are powerful" through influence and persuasion. My late grandfather Tom Becenti, a medicine man and practitioner in the enemy-way ceremony, once said in Navajo that persuasive leadership is based on compliance with the command or advice of a leader, such as a wise uncle or other relative, out of respect.

Exactly how do Navajos understand the meaning of the word *leadership*? Navajos in their traditional teachings tend to describe and explain the root meaning of words. *Naat'áanii*, which in essence means "a planner," comes from a word base "speaking." The word for planning is *nahat'á* and refers to "talking things out" to make a plan. The Navajo word for leader, *Naat'áanii*, arises from power as a speaker, and the word for planning, *nahat'á*, is about problem solving in discussing plans. My elder *Naat'áanii* always said that being a leader is about learning how to think, *nitsáhákees*, as well as how to use your thinking ability to plan, *nahat'á*. Those *Naat'áanii* used their thinking and planning as tools for leadership.

As Navajos we understand that traditional Navajo leadership possesses wisdom, with the ability to speak and create plans for successful outcomes; the results create respect that compels people to follow. Their words are something like law. What makes a leader a leader? How does one get the qualities of leadership and earn respect?

Hózhǫ́ǫ́jí Naat'áanii and *Hashkéjí Naat'áanii (hashkééjí naat'ááh)*, the concept of "peace chiefs" and "war chiefs," helps us to understand the Navajo leadership definition and qualities according to the early traditional style of leadership, *Naach'id*. *Naach'id* was last observed in 1859 near Chinle, Arizona. We only wish that more information were available to see how our traditional style of governance may have operated. By listening to Navajo knowledge holders on Navajo history, I learned and understand that two kinds of traditional leadership style, the *Hashkéjí Naat'áanii*, or war leaders, and the *Hózhǫ́ǫ́jí Naat'áanii*, or peace leaders, serve as key components of decision-making processes. The word *Hashkéjí* relates to decisions that are harsh, prompt, powerful, and aggressive. Remember what the Hero Twins said to their father the sun bearer. The Hero Twins worried that their acts in killing the *Yei'ii Tsoh* would be like killing their siblings. But the father sun bearer said that there is another angle. Since the *Yei'ii Tsoh* are taking life, it is required to protect the *Hózhǫ́ǫ́jí* way by eliminating the monsters. The speaking done for that quality is for war, so the ability to immediately evaluate a situation and speak to a plan of immediate and aggressive action is necessary. Individuals get a reputation of being successful warriors. The word *Hózhǫ́ǫ́jí* comes from the word root *Hózhǫ́*, or a state of being where everyone and everything are in their proper place, relating and functioning well with everything else to achieve a state of "harmony," or perfection. That style of speaking aims to achieve a "perfect state" that is wise and successful.

During my tenure as a justice and judge with the Navajo Nation Courts in the 1980s through the early 2000s, I worked with Justice Raymond D. Austin, author of *Navajo Courts and Navajo Common Law* (2009). I have much respect and admiration for his scholarly work. He maintains that *Hózhǫ́*, a perfect state of condition, is the duty of being a *Naat'áanii*, or leader. Where there is a *anáhóót'i'*, or a problem, the *Naat'áanii* has the obligation to engage himself or herself in *Diné bi nazhnit'ah*, that is, to think for the people to define the problem and identify the causes for the disruption of the state of *Hózhǫ́*.

It seems that individuals who want to be leaders do not appoint themselves. The status is earned. The Western notion of advancing one's own name for political office by election makes no sense from the Navajo perspective. "Election," in a traditional sense, is spontaneous and based on necessity. For example, plans for spring planting may be made over a winter fire, so there would be talk of when to plant, who could read the stars to know when that should done, and other matters that call for leadership guidance. So people talk about who would be the best person to guide the planting season. That is a way leaders were chosen.

I served as a Navajo Nation court judge, and later as a chief justice for the Navajo Nation Supreme Court, for nineteen years. As Navajo judges we are considered successors of the traditional *Hózhǫ́ǫ́jí Naat'áanii* (peace chief), because we are chosen for our individual qualities. Traits that make a difference in being a good Navajo leader include adherence to the duty of promoting harmony and order and treating people with fairness and humility. *Naat'áanii* of the past and today are looked upon as role models, and the respect for our decisions depends on our personal integrity. Humility is a personal value that prompts people to respect us judges for our decisions, and not for our position.

During my tenure as chief justice, my predecessor Tom Tso, Chief Justice Emeritus of the Navajo Nation Supreme Court, gave me very valuable advice. He said, "As a leader, *Diné joosanigo iishla*, in return, they will *dahoosą́ą́ dooleeł*." This means that you treat the people whom you lead with much care while exercising tremendous caution and compassion. It is ideal that the people will treat their leaders in the same manner. He meant that if I treat the people with gentleness and sincerity in my leadership, the people will treat me the same.

One of the traditional Navajo terms for a leader is "that person who is slightly higher than the others," and it reflects the view that leadership, and acceptance of its authority, comes from those who conduct themselves well. It comes from individuals who speak well, plan well, show success in community planning, or can "talk the goods" for the people. Humility is not simply "self-effacing" behavior, but behavior that is consistent with confident leadership and that is tempered with humility. Leadership is not for the self but for the people. The people are the source of the power.

What is the traditional Navajo process for planning and decision making for leaders? One way of achieving *Hózhǫ́* is by talking things out. The Navajo word *nahat'á*, meaning "to talk," is related to leadership because of the common Navajo expression that "words are powerful." Words of great Navajo leaders are powerful because they speak solution into reality. Navajos believe thoughts become action in words and that words create action or reality when they are spoken. Thinking becomes speech becomes action. That is a thought system in which thinking and intuition drive words and speaking. Speaking in groups is planning, and action is the result of thinking and planning. The Navajo word for leader, *Naat'áanii*, arises from power as a speaker, and the word for planning, *nahat'á*, is about problem solving in discussing plans.

Whenever I attended *Nidaa'* (enemy-way ceremony) in the summers, I remember seeing men ride their horses in the midst of numerous gatherings around camping grounds and speaking in loud voices for hours at a time. They would be talking about issues and concerns of life. Little did I realize that those men, as community leaders, were conducting *Naa Bik'í Ya'ati'*, or talking things out, by having "free discussion" with the public to clarify relationships, identify problems and disputes, and provide a method for planning and making decisions. *Naa Bik'í Ya'ati'*, or the talking-out process, requires that reciprocity be practiced to ensure there is equal and equitable treatment for the people. By this practice, people knew the mark of good leadership.

During my childhood, I always noticed that some but not all Navajo leaders were very nice, polite, and generous. My mother, aunties, and uncles constantly advised my brothers, sisters, and me to know how to treat people with dignity and respect. They would say that *k'é hwiindzin* is one of the sure practices of *K'é*. A *Naat'áanii* is always expected to "act as though all are your relatives." There is a Navajo saying that goes, "You act as though you have no relatives." This means an individual is forgetting about his or her obligations through *K'é*. A *Naat'áanii* is always expected to honor his or her obligations through *K'é*.

Talking things out with the people helps a leader to learn about the ideas, expectations, and recommendations of the community. For a leader, an important aspect of making effective decisions is being well informed on the issues and concerns of the people. To be informed is to know what the people want.

During my undergraduate years in college, I learned about qualities of leadership as related to notions of democracy. This includes discussion on how a good leader notifies others of things that he or she intends to do or things that need to get done. That is a form of notice. Once notice is given, there is an invitation to those who may be affected by a plan. This is due process. People who are impacted by pending plans are encouraged to participate in a positive effort. Alternatively, someone may wish to prevent plans from having an adverse impact on issues of import. There must be the right of participation. That right might not be exercised, but it must be offered. The next step is meaningful talk and planning, with everyone's voice mattering.

Being transparent, what is it? *Nahat'i' doo náńdáíní da* means you can't hide your plans. *Náahat'a iishjání óóázin. Nahat'a' doo nánídáíní da. Nahat'a* requires transparency, the free flow of information, and a duty to communicate and make known the issues at hand. Planning for action must be transparent (except for war-way planning) so that everyone who is affected can see what is going on and have an opportunity to have a say. Navajo tradition requires energy and goodwill when putting plans into action so that good intentions reflected in positive energy will produce a good result. The result is then analyzed to see if the plans were successful, so they can be used again or changed to fit circumstances.

As I mentioned before, harmony is *Hózhǫ́*. This ideal state and the cement that creates it and holds it together come from the practice of *K'é*. That word is law and speaks to the reality of relationships among people that arise from blood and clan relation and from living in communities. As always, the goal of a *Naat'áanii* or leader is to restore and maintain *Hózhǫ́* (harmony and balance) from disruptive conditions.

What are the challenges and experiences of leadership in Navajo Country? I clearly remember the crisis (turmoil) of the 1989 Navajo Nation government. It nearly put the whole Navajo Nation on its knees. The Navajo Nation Council sought to place then-chairman Peter MacDonald on administrative leave for being accused of bribery and kickbacks, among other serious criminal allegations. He refused to step down on grounds that the council lacked the legal basis to justify its action. The Navajo Nation

Supreme Court reviewed the matter on a certified question and ruled that under the traditional Navajo method of selecting leaders, people choose their *Naat'áaniis* based on trust and confidence. If a leader breaches that trust by wrongful acts, the people simply walk away. This practice was what justified the council action to remove Chairman MacDonald from office.

Our Navajo grandmothers have much aspiration to *Holsiil*, a Navajo word for "solidarity," which is another aspect of leadership. It involves a voluntary system of working together for the good of all. The word *Holsiil* speaks to common or mutual benefit and a collective effort to achieve that good. It prompts a form of persuasive leadership that is inclusive and promotes mutual benefit.

Our Navajo population is approximately three hundred thousand and growing. These people are extremely diverse in their views and opinions. It can be difficult to get them to buy into a certain course of action. No matter what, being positive and maintaining one's solid foundation with one's leadership goals help in more ways than one. At times the atmosphere toward leadership can be very negative. People are living a hard life, frustrated and overwhelmed with trying to make ends meet. Because there are no jobs, no money to pay rent, and no educational opportunities, and they suffer from domestic violence, people cannot help but feel that leadership is inefficient and ineffective. Do the principles of traditional Navajo governance have a role in this scenario?

The reality of leadership is that some people will dislike, disagree with, or oppose your leadership. Being a people pleaser is not an option. Doing so adversely impacts the best interest of the people. True leaders can't just please people and do what people want. How does this connect to the process of talking things out and consensus building?

Can the traditional Diné leadership of yesterday make a difference in today's world? The teachings of traditional leadership and good governance make a lot of sense. They teach how the need for leadership emerged in Diné Creation Accounts. Chaos, utter confusion, and disorder in the Diné journey through the four worlds gave rise to a desperate need for strong and effective leadership and governance. There were many mistakes, and thus struggles with hardship, chaos, and disharmony, caused by the people in the third world. This gave rise to the birth of monsters, which later took a toll on people's lives. The confrontation of the Hero Twins with the *Yei'ii Tsoh* (big monster) led to the killing of the monster. Before the confrontation, the Hero Twins' father, the sun, instructed his children to carefully study and observe the movement and behavior of the monster. Thinking before you make the attack is a value that advises leaders today to carefully study and observe the problem before taking any sort of action.

There is a Navajo paradigm based on the four directions reflected in the qualities mentioned above. It is in the maxim *Diné Banihaj'a*. This literally means moving your head around. But it really means you are using your mind to think around the issues or problems for your people. You are searching for a way to think about the problem. You could say it is like searching for the ideal answer. It also means you are planning for the people so they can live a long and wisdom-filled life. At the same time you are listening carefully. In this way, you are responsible for thinking for the people. There is *nazhint'a*, or "moving the head," meaning leadership through the head, that is, directing or motioning. You can put the two ideas of thinking for the people and moving your head around together in order to do the best job in leading your people. You are trying to do your best for your constituents. This process of "moving your head around" can be used for planning anything that is important to the people. Both war and peace chiefs used this approach. Many of the alternatives will be considered and the best strategy employed. Above all, it is important to remember that these are your relatives and you owe them your best efforts. You are not a leader all alone.

T'áá altso alk'éí daniidlị—we are all related to everyone and everything. This is a foundational principle for all forms of life. The life being is everything. We are all related to the Four Sacred Elements, the plant people, the people with hooves, the people with wings, and we have our own purpose. We make things happen together. We speak to one another, and we make life happen. We have *k'é*- or clan-based relationships. This means we have responsibilities and obligations to one another as relatives, be they water, plant people, people with stingers, people with wings, and people with five fingers. This is something a good leader should know about his or her people. The better a leader can maintain this relationship, the better a person can exercise his or her leadership responsibilities. Leaders must be tied into this network of relationships.

It is a mistake to think of leadership being based on power and on top-down authority. It is really a collective decision-making process that rewards good personal qualities that are reflected in success. We need to think about, and reject, authoritarian methods of planning and governance and instead acquire habits of persuasive leadership that prompt confidence and common support, so that good planning is done and wise decisions prompt action that benefits everyone.

NOTES

INTRODUCTION

1. Readers will notice I am utilizing the phrase "*Hajinéí* era." This refers to a place in time before recorded history when the Diné coexisted with other Indigenous nations. This time period might be generally understood as a gap between Navajo emergence at *Diné Tah* and contact with Spain.
2. While there is no static idea of precolonial identity or philosophy, it is worth noting that colonial interaction obviously impacted all Indigenous peoples, including Diné. "Colonial actor" refers to what would become European-based settler states that emerged and took root in the Western Hemisphere at the expense of Indigenous nations. I first used the phrase "colonial actor" to describe nearly all nations founded in the Western Hemisphere after the arrival of Europeans (Lerma 2014a).
3. "Colonial actor" is a phrase adopted to dispense with the specific names of contemporary states. The history of Navajo and colonial actor interaction may require a tedious explanation every time one colonial actor replaced another. Hence, rather than call the colonial actor Spain in one time period, Mexico in another, and the United States in a third, it seems easier to introduce the phrase "colonial actor" and consistently refer to all of these nations as colonial actors.
4. Some may wish to know more about the phrase *Dził Łeezh;* however, some knowledge holders believe more details are not appropriate for sharing in a book.
5. See Diné Bi Beenahaz'áanii (1 N.N.C. §§ 201–206), not so much for a comprehensive discussion about the Four Sacred Elements but for how they are merely mentioned by the Fundamental Laws of the Diné.
6. This information was furnished by Avery Denny, a cultural liaison working for the Diné Policy Institute at Diné College.

CHAPTER 1

1. Many of the faculty of Diné College, past and present, have discussed the "corn-stalk philosophy" approach to Diné knowledge. These individuals include the late Mike Mitchell, Wilson Aronilth Jr., Avery Denny, Lorene Legah, and Herbet Benally, among others.
2. *Nitsáhákees* and *bitsáhákees* are essentially the same word. The "ni" prefix indicates it is the thoughts of two or more people. The "bi" prefix indicates it is "your" thoughts, but it does not necessarily reference one's own thoughts.
3. As mentioned before, many aspects of *Dził Łeezh* are intentionally vague due to knowledge holder norms of sharing information. Details are not appropriate for sharing in book form.

4. Denny's premises must be true, but the outcome may or may not be true. Just as in other philosophies, it is important to defer to the knowledge holders in matters of inductive reasoning. In other words, we can only challenge the accuracy of the premises as a basis for challenging the conclusions drawn. Describing the premises of Diné knowledge must happen before debate and disagreement can occur. Critical research on Diné knowledge is future research for others to pursue.

CHAPTER 2

1. *Naach'id* is the Diné ceremony where war and peace leaders come together to make decisions based on the current problems at hand. More details are contained later in this chapter and elsewhere (Austin 2009, 11).
2. *Naayéé'ji Nahaghá* can be superficially understood in English as war ways using songs and ceremonial practices. Another word that has popped up is *Hashkéjí*. I will use the word *Hashkéjí* throughout this book. AnCita Benally uses the word *Naayéé'ji*. I will use her word choice when I cite her research. While the two words are not synonymous, for our purposes here, due in part to advice from Avery Denny and Robert Yazzie, I have decided to use the word *Hashkéjí*.
3. A *Kinaalda* is superficially understood in English as a coming-of-age ceremony.
4. See Jenkins and Schroeder (1974, 33–44) for a complete description of the economic problems faced by the New Mexican government, including details of lack of revenue to run the government, internal power struggles within the New Mexican government, and rumors of a subsequent full-fledged invasion by the United States.

CHAPTER 3

1. Readers may visit http://www.navajocourts.org/indexpeacemaking.htm for more information on Navajo peacemaking as it is currently carried out.
2. It is not the purpose of this chapter to retell the history of Diné governance. Instead, this section will outline several traditional Diné governance concepts using the concept-building method. Those interested in a brief history may revisit Chapter 2. Alternatively, information on traditional Diné governance can be located in the following references: Nielsen and Zion 2005; Wilkins 1987, 2002a, 2002b, 2003).
3. See Nielsen and Zion 2005.
4. See Holm in Deloria and Wildcat 2006, 48–49.

CHAPTER 4

1. Many will argue that Indigenous peoples are not people of color. This passage is only referring to Western philosophers who did not care to distinguish individuals across anything other than a binary between "white" and not white (Olson 2004).
2. Readers should be aware that I am using 1922 to signify events related to the discovery of oil on Navajo Nation leading the U.S. government to encourage the construction of the modern Navajo government (Wilkins 2013, 18). The first Navajo Tribal Council did not meet until July 1923 (Wilkins 2013, 19). Reference to a general "post-1922" government reflects a position that anything after 1922 was an attempt by the United States to heavily impact Navajo policy related to resource extraction.

CHAPTER 5

1. Do not assume that this section aims to verify what Diné knowledge already believes to be correct using a non-Diné point of view. Perhaps it is fitting to argue that Diné perspectives can be used to corroborate the applicability of social constructivism generally.

CHAPTER 6

1. Ideal types are perfect and, therefore, cannot exist in the real world. There is, however, room for the ideal type in normative theoretical research that discusses where policy should or ought to be 0 or where policy should not or ought not be 1. Of course, normative policy discussions as depicted here assume that policymakers want as little change as possible to Diné governance and that the elimination of Diné governance is not desired. An infinite range of possible shock values exist between the values of 0 and 1. Hence, events are ranked relative to one another and in between the values of 0 and 1. The above methodological approaches come from various sources and culminate here to best frame the Diné colonial experience (Goertz 2006; Ragin 1987, 2000, 2008; Ragin and Becker 1992; Ragin, Drass, and Davey 2006; Sartori 1970).

2. For an example of a 1 event involving non-Diné, there is evidence of California tribes that were victims of extermination at the hands of settlers. The European settlers encountered small bands of Indigenous men near the California coast, and the Indigenous men were killed in the initial battle. The Indigenous women and children remained in the village waiting for word from the men regarding the new arrivals. With no word from their men, the women and children either waited or realized that something horrible had happened and fled to other villages. Many were set upon by settlers and killed (Bordewich 1996; Trafzer and Hyer 1999; Heizer 1993). This type of event would rank as .95 since it catastrophically impacted the tribe and, by extension, its governance institutions. Since there never was an event like the one just described for the Diné as a whole, one cannot hastily rank the Long Walk as 1.

3. More information on calibrating concept-continuum scales can be found here (Ragin 2008).

REFERENCES

Alfred, Gerald R. 2009. *Peace, Power, Righteousness: An Indigenous Manifesto*. 2nd ed. Don Mills, ON; New York: Oxford University Press.

Austin, Raymond D. 2007. "Navajo Courts and Navajo Common Law." Diss., American Indian Studies, University of Arizona, Tucson.

Austin, Raymond Darrel. 2009. *Navajo Courts and Navajo Common Law: A Tradition of Tribal Self-Governance*. Minneapolis: University of Minnesota Press.

Bailey, Garrick Alan, and Roberta Glenn Bailey. 1999. *A History of the Navajos: The Reservation Years*. Santa Fe, NM: School of American Research Press.

Barker, Joanne. 2011. *Native Acts: Law, Recognition, and Cultural Authenticity*. Durham, NC: Duke University Press.

Begay, David, and Nancy C. Maryboy. 1998. "Nanitá Są́ąh Naaghái Nanitá Bikèh Hózhóón." Diss., California Institute of Integral Studies, San Francisco.

Benally, AnCita. 2006. "Diné Binahat'a', Navajo Government." PhD Diss., Arizona State University, Phoenix.

Bighorse, Tiana, Gus Bighorse, and Noël Bennett. 1990. *Bighorse the Warrior*. Tucson: University of Arizona Press.

Blackhawk, Ned. 2006. *Violence over the Land: Indians and Empires in the Early American West*. Cambridge, MA: Harvard University Press.

Blue, Martha. 1988. *The Witch Purge of 1878: Oral and Documentary History in the Early Navajo Reservation Years*. Tsaile: Navajo Community College Press.

Bobroff, Kenneth. 2004–2005. "Diné Bi Beenahaz'aanii: Codifying Indigenous Consuetudinary Law in the 21st Century." *Tribal Law Journal* 5 (4).

Bordewich, Fergus M. 1996. *Killing the White Man's Indian: Reinventing of Native Americans at the End of the Twentieth Century*. New York: Doubleday.

Brady, H., and D. Collier, eds. 2004. *Rethinking Social Inquiry: Diverse Tools, Shared Standards, Data-Set Observations versus Causal-Process Observations: The 2000 U.S. Presidential Election*. New York: Rowman & Littlefield.

Brugge, David M., and J. Lee Correll. 1971. *The Story of the Navajo Treaties*. Navajo Historical Publications. Documentary Series no. 1. Window Rock, AZ: Research Section, Navajo Parks and Recreation Dept., Navajo Tribe.

Bueno De Mesquita, Bruce. 2009. *Principles of International Politics*. Washington, DC: CQ Press.

Cajete, Gregory. 2000. *Native Science: Natural Laws of Interdependence*. Santa Fe, NM: Clearlight Publishing.

Champagne, Duane. 2007. *Social Change and Cultural Continuity among Native Nations*. Lanham, MD: Altamira Press.

Cody, Herman. 2009. Class Lecture, Tucson, Arizona.

Collier, Ruth Berins, and David Collier. 1991. *Shaping the Political Arena: Critical Junctures, the Labor Movement, and Regime Dynamics in Latin America.* Princeton, NJ: Princeton University Press.

Cornell, Stephen, and Joseph P. Kalt. 2000. "Where's the Glue? Institutional and Cultural Foundations of American Indian Economic Development." *Journal of Socio-Economics* 29:443–470.

Coulthard, Glen Sean. 2014. *Red Skin, White Masks: Rejecting the Colonial Politics of Recognition.* Indigenous Americas. Coulthard, MN: University of Minnesota Press.

Crawford, Amanda J. 2011. "A Bond Offering from the Navajo Nation." *Bloomberg Business Week Magazine*, Phoenix, AZ, November 10.

Curly, Andrew and Parrish, Michael. 2016. Local Governance and Reform: *A Conceptual Critique of Regionalization and the Title 26 Taskforce.* Diné Policy Institute.

Deloria, Vine, Jr. 1973. *God Is Red.* New York: Grosset & Dunlap.

Deloria, Vine, Jr. 1974. *Behind the Trail of Broken Treaties: An Indian Declaration of Independence.* Austin: University of Texas Press.

Deloria, Vine, Jr. 1979. *The Metaphysics of Modern Existence.* San Francisco: Harper & Row.

Deloria, Vine, Jr. 1988. *Custer Died for Your Sins: An Indian Manifesto.* Norman: University of Oklahoma Press.

Deloria, Vine, Jr. 1997. *Red Earth, White Lies: Native Americans and the Myth of Scientific Fact.* Golden, CO: Fulcrum Publishing.

Deloria, Vine, Jr. 2006. *The World We Used To Live In: Remembering the Powers of the Medicine Men.* Golden, CO: Fulcrum Publishing.

Deloria, Vine, Jr., and Raymond J. DeMallie. 1999. *Documents of American Indian Diplomacy: Treaties, Agreements, and Conventions, 1775–1979.* Vol. 1, *Legal History of North America.* Norman: University of Oklahoma Press.

Deloria, V., Jr., and D. R. Wildcat. 2006. *Destroying Dogma: Vine Deloria, Jr. and His Influence on American Society.* Golden, CO: Fulcrum Publishing.

Deloria, Vine, Jr., and David E. Wilkins. 1999. *Tribes, Treaties, and Constitutional Tribulations.* Austin: University of Texas Press.

Denetdale, Jennifer. 2006a. "Chairmen, Presidents, and Princesses: The Navajo Nation, Gender, and the Politics of Tradition." *Wicazo Sa Review* 21 (1):9–28.

Denetdale, Jennifer. 2006b. "Securing Navajo National Boundaries: War, Patriotism, Tradition, and the Diné Marriage Act of 2005." *Wicazo Sa Review* 24 (2):131–148.

Denetdale, Jennifer. 2009. *The Long Walk: The Forced Navajo Exile.* New York, NY: Chelsea House Publishers.

Denny, Avery. 2010. Ongoing consultation. Tsaile, AZ: Diné Policy Institute.

Denny, Avery. 2011. "Keshjee—The Diné' Shoegame Story." Lecture, Flagstaff.

Denny, Avery, and Michael Lerma. 2017. "Diné Principles of Good Governance." In *Navajo Sovereignty Understandings and Visions of the Diné People* edited by Lloyd Lee. Tucson: University of Arizona Press.

Diehl, Paul F., and Gary Goertz. 2000. *War and Peace in International Rivalry.* Ann Arbor: University of Michigan Press.

Diné College, ed. 2008. *Diné College Catalog 2008–2009.*

Eldridge, Dana, James McKenzie, Robyn Jackson, Avery Denny, Robert Yazzie, Amber K. Crotty, and Crystalyne Curley. 2014. *Diné Food Sovereignty: A Report on the Navajo Nation Food System and the Case to Rebuild a Self-Sufficient Food System for the Diné People.* Tsaile, AZ: Diné Policy Institute.

Farella, John. 1984. *The Main Stalk: A Synthesis of Navajo Philosophy*. Tucson: University of Arizona Press.

Fonseca, Felicia. 2007. "Navajo Council Approves $50,000 for Delegate Rings." *Albuquerque Journal*, Albuquerque, NM, July 10.

Foster, Lynn V. 1997. *A Brief History of Mexico*. New York: Facts on File.

Getches, David H., Charles F. Wilkinson, and Robert A. Williams. 1998. *Cases and Materials on Federal Indian Law*. 4th ed. St. Paul, MN: West Group.

Getches, David H., Charles F. Wilkinson, and Robert A. Williams. 2005. *Cases and Materials on Federal Indian Law*. 5th ed. American Casebook Series. St. Paul, MN: Thomson/West.

Getches, David H., Charles Wilkinson, Robert A. Williams, and Matthew L. M. Fletcher. 2011. *Cases and Materials on Federal Indian Law*. 6th ed. St. Paul, MN: West.

Global Security. 2009. *Fort Wingate Army Depot*.

Goertz, Gary. 2006. *Social Science Concepts: A User's Guide*. Princeton, NJ: Princeton University Press.

Goertz, Gary, and Amy Mazur. 2008. *Politics, Gender, and Concepts: Theory and Methodology*. Cambridge, UK; New York: Cambridge University Press.

Gorman-Keith, Tanya. 2004. "Sihasin—Meaning of Graduation to Navajo College Students at Northern Arizona University: An Interpretive Case Study." Educational Leadership, Northern Arizona University, Flagstaff.

Griffin, L. 1993. "Narrative, Event-Structure Analysis, and Causal Interpretation in Historical Sociology." *American Journal of Sociology* 98:1094–1133.

Griffin-Pierce, Trudy. 1992. *Earth Is My Mother, Sky Is My Father: Space, Time, and Astronomy in Navajo Sandpainting*. Albuquerque: University of New Mexico Press.

Heizer, Robert F. 1993. *The Destruction of California Indians: A Collection of Documents from the Period 1847 to 1865 in Which Are Described Some of the Things That Happened to Some of the Indians of California*. Lincoln: University of Nebraska Press.

Henson, Eric C. 2008. *The State of the Native Nations: Conditions under U.S. Policies of Self-Determination*. Harvard Project on American Indian Economic Development. New York: Oxford University Press.

Holm, Tom. 1989. "Mechanistic versus Organic Human Land Relationships: The Navajo Hopi Joint Use Area Dispute as a Case Study." In *Native Views of Indian-White Historical Relations*, edited by Donald Fixico, Occasional Papers in Curriculum (7). Chicago: Newberry Library.

Holm, Tom, J. Diane Pearson, and Ben Chavis. 2003. "Peoplehood: A Model for the Extension of Sovereignty in American Indian Studies." *Wicazo Sa Review* 18 (1):7–24.

Hopf, Ted. 1998. "The Promise of Constructivism in International Relations." *International Security* 23 (1):171–200.

Hopf, Ted. 2002. *Social Construction of International Politics: Identities & Foreign Policies, Moscow, 1955 and 1999*. Ithaca, NY: Cornell University Press.

Jenkins, Myra Ellen, Albert H. Schroeder, New Mexico Cultural Properties Review Committee, and New Mexico State Planning Office. 1974. *A Brief History of New Mexico*. Albuquerque: University of New Mexico Press.

Jorgensen, Miriam, ed. 2007. *Rebuilding Native Nations: Strategies for Governance and Development*. Tucson: University of Arizona Press.

King, Gary, Robert O. Keohane, and Sidney Verba. 1994. *Designing Social Inquiry: Scientific Inference in Qualitative Research*. Princeton, NJ: Princeton University Press.

King, Jeff, Maud Oakes, Joseph Campbell, and Bollingen Foundation Collection (Library of Congress). 1943. *Where the Two Came to Their Father, a Navaho War Ceremonial.* Bollingen Series. New York: Pantheon Books.

Kracker, Daniel. 2010. "Navajo Nation Could Elect First Female President." Flagstaff: National Public Radio. http://www.npr.org/templates/story/story.php?storyId=17452654.

Kraker, Daniel. 2008. "Navajo Seeks Support for Tribal Constitution." Flagstaff: National Public Radio. http://www.npr.org/templates/story/story.php?storyId=130913322

Landry, Alysa. 2007. "Navajos Speak Out About Hawaii Trip." *Farmington Daily Times,* Farmington, NM, November 28.

Laylin, T. 2015. "Gold King Mine Spill: Navajo Nation Farmers Prohibit Animas River Access." *Guardian,* August 16. https://www.theguardian.com/environment/2015/aug/26/gold-king-mine-spill-navajo-nation-farmers-animas-river-water.

Lee, Lloyd L. 2006. "Navajo Cultural Identity: What Can the Navajo Nation Bring to the American Indian Identity Discussion Table?" *Wicazo Sa Review* 21 (2):79–103.

Lee, Lloyd L. 2007. "The Future of Navajo Nationalism." *Wicazo Sa Review* 22 (1):53–68.

Lee, Lloyd L. 2008. "Reclaiming Indigenous Intellectual, Political, and Geographic Space: A Path for Navajo Nationhood." *American Indian Quarterly* 32 (1):96–110.

Lemont, Eric D. 2006. *American Indian Constitutional Reform and the Rebuilding of Native Nations.* Austin: University of Texas Press.

Lerma, Michael. 2008. "Concepts of Indigenousness." *Red Ink Magazine* 14 (1).

Lerma, Michael. 2012. "Indigeneity and Homeland: Land, History, Ceremony, and Language." *American Indian Culture and Research Journal* 36 (3): 75–98.

Lerma, Michael. 2014a. *Indigenous Sovereignty in the 21st Century: Knowledge for the Indigenous Spring.* Gainsville: Florida Academic Press.

Lerma, Michael. 2014b. "Shocks to the Navajo (Diné) Political System: Resiliency of Traditional Diné institutions in the Face of Colonial Interaction (Contact to 1923)." *Indigenous Policy Journal* 25 (1).

Levy, Jerrold E. 1998. *In the Beginning: The Navajo Genesis.* Berkeley: University of California Press.

Little, Maybelle. 2010. "Traditional Navajo Governance." Lecture, Flagstaff, AZ.

Lukes, Steven. 2005. *Power: A Radical View.* 2nd ed. New York: Palgrave Macmillan.

Mahoney, J. 2003. "Long-Run Development and the Legacy of Colonialism in Spanish America." *American Journal of Sociology* 109:50–106.

Mahoney, James. 2010. *Colonialism and Postcolonial Development: Spanish America in Comparative Perspective.* Cambridge: Cambridge University Press.

McPherson, R. S. 1991. *Sacred Land. Sacred View: Navajo Perceptions of the Four Corners Region.* Provo: Brigham Young University, Charles Redd Center for Western Studies, 29.

Meriam, Lewis, and Hubert Work. 1928. *The Problem of Indian Administration: Report of a Survey Made at the Request of Honorable Hubert Work, Secretary of the Interior, and Submitted to Him, February 21, no. 17.* Baltimore, MD: Johns Hopkins Press.

Mitchell, F., C. J. Frisbie, and D. P. McAllester. 2003. *Navajo Blessingway Singer: The Autobiography of Frank Mitchell, 1881–1967.* Albuquerque: University of New Mexico Press.

Moreton-Robinson, Aileen. 2006. "Towards a New Research Agenda? Foucalt, Whiteness, and Indigenous Sovereignty." *Journal of Sociology* 42 (4):383–395.

Moreton-Robinson, Aileen. 2007. *Sovereign Subjects: Indigenous Sovereignty Matters, Cultural Studies*. Crows Nest, N.S.W.: Allen & Unwin.

Morgenthau, Hans Joachim. 1948. *Politics among Nations: The Struggle for Power and Peace*. New York: A. A. Knopf.

Navajo Nation. 2013. "Navajo President Shelly Signs Legislation For Energy Policy and Another for NTEC Funding." Last modified October 24, 2013. http://www.navajonsn.gov/News%20Releases/OPVP/2013/oct/102413%20PR%20Shelly%20Energy%20Policy.pdf.

Navajo Nation Council. 2002. *Amending Title 1 of the NNC to Recognize the Fundamental Laws of the Diné*. Navajo Nation Council.

Navajo Nation Government. 2008. "Navajo President Joe Shirley, Jr., Launches Government Reform Initiative, Submits Language to Reduce Council to 24 Members, Obtain Line Item Veto." Last modified April 29, 2008. http://www.navajonsn.gov/News%20Releases/George%20Hardeen/Apr08/Navajo%20President%20sets%20council%20reduction%20line%20item%20veto%20plans%20into%20motion%20for%20April%2029%20%282%29.pdf.

Navajo Nation Supreme Court. 2010. No. SC-CY-03-10 NAVAJO NATION SUPREME COURT Timothy Nelson, Petitioner-Appellant, v. Initiative Committee to Reduce Navajo Nation Council, Office of the President, Joe Shirley, Jr., Respondents-Appellees.

Needham, Andrew. 2014. *Power Lines: Phoenix and the Making of the Modern Southwest*. Politics and Society in Twentieth-Century America. Princeton, NJ: Princeton University Press.

Nielsen, Marianne O., and James W. Zion. 2005. *Navajo Nation Peacemaking: Living Traditional Justice*. Tucson: University of Arizona Press.

Olson, Joel. 2004. *The Abolition of White Democracy*. Minneapolis: University of Minnesota Press.

Parsons-Yazzie, Evangeline, Margaret Speas, Jessie Ruffenach, and Berlyn Yazzie. 2007. *Diné bizaad bináhoo'aah = Rediscovering the Navajo Language: An Introduction to the Navajo Language*. Flagstaff, AZ: Salina Bookshelf.

Pavlik, Steve. 2014. *The Navajo and the Animal People*. Golden, CO: Fulcrum Press.

Pierson, Paul. 2004. *Politics in Time: History, Institutions, and Social Analysis*. Princeton, NJ: Princeton University Press.

Ragin, Charles C. 1987. *The Comparative Method: Moving beyond Qualitative and Quantitative Strategies*. Berkeley: University of California Press.

Ragin, Charles C. 2000. *Fuzzy-Set Social Science*. Chicago: University of Chicago Press.

Ragin, Charles C. 2008. *Redesigning Social Inquiry: Fuzzy Sets and Beyond*. Chicago: University of Chicago Press.

Ragin, Charles C., and Howard Saul Becker. 1992. *What Is a Case? Exploring the Foundations of Social Inquiry*. Cambridge, UK; New York: Cambridge University Press.

Ragin, Charles C., Kriss A. Drass, and Sean Davey. 2006. *Fuzzy-Set/Qualitative Comparative Analysis 2.0*. Tucson: Department of Sociology, University of Arizona.

Roese, N. J., and J. M. Olson. 2014. *What Might Have Been: The Social Psychology of Counterfactual Thinking*. New York: Psychology Press.

Roessel, R., and B. H. Johnson. 1974. *Navajo Livestock Reduction: A National Disgrace*. Tsaile, AZ: Diné College Press.

Said, Edward W. 1978. *Orientalism*. New York: Pantheon Books.

Sartori, Giovanni. 1970. "Concept Misformation in Comparative Politics." *American Political Science Review* 64 (4):1033–1053.

Schwarz, M. T. 1997. *Molded in the Image of Changing Woman: Navajo Views on the Human Body and Personhood.* Tucson: University of Arizona Press.

Singer, James, Moroni Benally, Andrew Curley, Nikke Alex, and Wendy Greyeyes. 2007. Navajo Nation Government Reform Project. Early draft. Tsaile, AZ: Diné Policy Institute.

Smith, Linda Tuhiwai. 1999. *Decolonizing Methodologies: Research and Indigenous Peoples.* London; New York; Dunedin, N.Z.: Zed Books, University of Otago Press; St. Martin's Press.

Tetlock, P., and A. Belkin. 1996. *Counterfactual Thought Experiments in World Politics: Logical, Methodological, and Psychological Perspectives.* Princeton, NJ: Princeton University Press.

Trafzer, Clifford E., and Joel R. Hyer. 1999. *Exterminate Them: Written Accounts of the Murder, Rape, and Slavery of Native Americans during the California Gold Rush, 1848–1868.* East Lansing: Michigan State University Press.

United States and Charles Joseph Kappler. 1972. *Indian Treaties, 1778–1883.* New York: Interland Pub.

United States, Charles Joseph Kappler, and United States. 1971. *Indian Affairs. Laws and Treaties.* New York: AMS Press.

United States, United States, and Charles Joseph Kappler. 1903. *Indian Affairs. Laws and Treaties.* Washington, D.C.: G.P.O.

United States, United States, and Charles Joseph Kappler. 1904. *Indian Affairs: Laws and Treaties.* 2nd ed., 2 vols. Washington, D.C.: G.P.O.

Voyageur, Cora Jane, Brian Calliou, and Laura Brearley. 2014. *Restoring Indigenous Leadership: Wise Practices in Community Development.* Banff, Alberta: Banff Centre Press.

Waltz, Kenneth Neal. 1979. *Theory of International Politics.* Reading, MA: Addison-Wesley.

Wilkins, David. 1987. *Diné bibeehaz'áanii: A Handbook of Navajo Government.* Tsaile, AZ: Navajo Community College Press.

Wilkins, David. 2002a. "Governance within the Navajo Nation: Have Democratic Traditions Taken Hold?" *Wicazo Sa Review* 17:91–129.

Wilkins, David E. 2002b. *American Indian Politics and the American Political System.* Lanham, MD; Oxford: Rowman & Littlefield.

Wilkins, David E. 2003. *The Navajo Political Experience.* Rev. ed. Lanham, MD: Rowman & Littefield.

Wilkins, David E. 2013. *The Navajo Political Experience.* Rev. ed. Lanham, MD: Rowman & Littlefield.

Wilson, Shawn. 2008. *Research Is Ceremony: Indigenous Research Methods.* Halifax, NS: Fernwood.

Yazzie, Herb, Eleanor Shirley, and Louise Grant. 2010. "Timothy Nelson, Petitioner-Appellant, v. Initiative Committee to Reduce Navajo Nation Council, Office of the President, Joe Shirley, Jr., Respondents-Appellees." Navajo Nation Supreme Court, Window Rock.

Yazzie, Robert. 2009. Discussion of Navajo Philosophy with the author. Tsaile, AZ, Summer 2009.

Yazzie, Robert, Moroni Benally, Andrew Curley, Nikke Alex, James Singer, and Amber Crotty. 2008. *Navajo Nation Constitutional Feasibility and Government Reform Project,* edited by Robert Yazzie. Tsaile, AZ: Diné Policy Institute.

Yazzie, Robert, Avery Denny, Amber Crotty, Dana Eldridge, Moroni Benally, Michael Lerma, and Andrew Curley. 2011. *Recommendations for Restructuring the Navajo Nation Council*. Tsaile, AZ: Diné Policy Institute.

Zolbrod, Paul G. 1987. *Diné Bahane: The Navajo Creation Story*. Albuquerque: University of New Mexico Press.

INDEX

Tables, figures, and boxes are indicated by an italic *t*, *f*, and *b* following the page/ paragraph number.

CPSIA information can be obtained
at www.ICGtesting.com
Printed in the USA
BVHW040553220623
666080BV00001B/1